Nicols
Chicag
le printe

D0945017

$19.95

Diplomacy

Diplomacy

THE DIALOGUE BETWEEN STATES

ADAM WATSON

NEW PRESS

McGraw-Hill Book Company

New York   St. Louis   San Francisco
Hamburg   Mexico   Toronto

1 2 3 4 5 6 7 8 9 9 D O D O 8 7 6 5 4 3

ISBN 0-07-068461-8

LIBRARY OF CONGRESS CATALOGING IN PUBLICATION DATA

Watson, Adam, 1914–
Diplomacy: the dialogue between states.
1. Diplomacy.   I. Title.
JX1662.W34 1983   327.2   82-12753
ISBN 0-07-068461-8

To my wife

Contents

Preface

This book reflects my long preoccupation with the behaviour of independent states involved with one another in an interlocking system. What – without giving up their independence, their adherence to their principles and the pursuit of their interests – can such states achieve together by means of a constructive dialogue to establish rules and codes of conduct and institutions, and within this framework to evolve by negotiation and persuasion ways of solving or at least managing the problems of their conflicting interests and of a rapidly changing world?

I grew up in a Europe which had suffered crippling damage to its civilization by the cataclysm of the First World War. This unforeseen trauma not only ended European dominance of the world but left all the larger states in the system spiritually exhausted and rigid, preoccupied with their own domestic social upheavals and, in the case of the European powers, gravely damaged materially and genetically. The flood of literature about the causes and origins of the war, which I read eagerly till the second war broke out, did not seem to me to explain why the diplomatic dialogue, the Concert of European States, which had worked very adequately for a century, should then have failed to see the real problems, let alone solve them. The miserable inadequacy of the post-war settlement, the legalism and power-blindness of the League, the absence from serious participation in the dialogue of the four most dynamic major powers of the century – the United States, Russia, Germany and Japan – and the grisly sides of the new totalitarianism left the way open for a slide into a second world war within twenty years. Two outstanding thinkers about statecraft and diplomacy whom I saw much of during and after the second war, Herbert Butterfield and George Kennan, both saw World War One as the fatal disaster from which the world did not recover in time. 'The more you go into it,' Butterfield wrote to me at the beginning of the cold war, 'the more the first war stands out as the decisive thing.' Kennan, in the introduction to his *Decline of Bismarck's European Order*, which is concerned with why the diplomatic dialogue failed to prevent that war, says more explicitly: 'It was borne in on me to what overwhelming extent the determining phenomena of the inter-war period ... and indeed then the Second World War itself, were the products of that first great holocaust. .... Thus I came to see the First World War as I think many reasonably thoughtful people have learned to see it, as *the* great seminal catastrophe of this century, the event which more than any others, excepting only perhaps the discovery of nuclear weaponry and the development of the population-environmental crisis, lay at the heart of the failure and decline of this Western civilization.' That is how I also saw the tragic scene.

Thirty years of professional diplomacy in the British service kept my mind focused on two major questions which might help to provide an answer to the statesman's dilemma about how to manage international society while preserving the independence of its member states. The first theoretical and indispensable question is: what is the nature of the diplomatic dialogue; what are the conditions necessary for it to reach its full potential; and what can it achieve at its most imaginative and most constructive? The second is a more practical one: what has in fact been achieved in the management of our radically different and rapidly changing global society since World War Two? Compared with the disastrous forty years before 1945, the forty or so years after that point of exhaustion have not been so bad. There have been only minor wars, and the two superpowers, for all their ideological opposition, have so far shown more than enough restraint to avoid a nuclear holocaust. Under the leadership of a more responsible America, the diplomatic dialogue has devised and operated tolerably satisfactory rules and institutions for ordering the international economic life of the non-communist world. The major task of decolonization has been carried out with little bloodshed – in most cases none – and the new states have begun to be incorporated into a new international society. But much remains unachieved, particularly between the superpowers.

This book is concerned especially with the first question; the nature and potential of diplomacy, now and in the past. I have tried to describe the main diplomatic aspects of the second, the present achievement, though it is hard to see the forest from the inside, and almost every book about current international affairs is rapidly overtaken by events as new trees come into view in what Dante called a 'selva oscura' where every way is 'smarrita'.

I have indicated the broad sense in which the term diplomacy is used in this book in the subtitle: by diplomacy I mean the dialogue between independent states. A complex activity of this kind is difficult to comprehend in a single phrase. *The Oxford Dictionary* defines it as 'the management of international relations by negotiation'. The management of international society, and negotiation, are certainly at the heart of it; but there is more to the dialogue than this rather limiting definition suggests. *Webster's Dictionary* has 'the conducting of relations between nations', which, though less immediately informative, is more comprehensive and therefore covers better the range of this book, except that the term 'nations' is not a synonym for states.

I think it is a mistake to tie the concept of diplomacy too closely to resident embassies and professional diplomatic services, as is often done. These institutions make up only one way of conducting the dialogue, though it is the one in which I have spent much of my working life. Diplomacy flourished before these useful institutions existed; they themselves have changed their character many times since their beginnings in Renaissance Italy; and states will continue to negotiate with one another and work out imaginative solutions to their difficulties if, for instance, resident embassies lose their importance or are completely transformed in character. I also think it preferable not to use the word diplomacy as a synonym for the foreign policy of a state, although this usage is also frequent and is perhaps now sanctioned by custom. The distinction between *foreign policy* as the substance of a state's relations with other powers and agencies and the purposes it hopes to achieve by these relations, and *diplomacy* as the process of dialogue and negotiation by which states in a system conduct their relations and pursue their purposes by means short of war, is worth preserving, especially as an aid to clear thinking. I have written about the foreign policies of individual states in this book only to illustrate issues which arise in international politics and with which diplomacy seeks to deal.

I have described the diplomatic practices of other systems of states, and dealt at more length with European diplomacy, in order to indicate the elements of continuity and change in the conduct of the dialogue between states over the centuries, and in order to provide an adequate account of the general nature and practices of diplomacy and of the particular ways in which it functions in the present worldwide diplomatic society of states. It is a fact of some relevance that the principal heritage which has given shape and character to modern diplomacy is the European experience. For the details of diplomatic history I must refer the reader to the many excellent accounts, especially of the international affairs of the European system.

Nor is this book another manual of diplomatic procedure, in the tradition of the guides that made their appearance early in the European system and are described in Chapter VIII; a tradition which continues in the successive editions of Ernest Satow's invaluable handbook, the *Guide to Diplomatic Practice*, and the corresponding works in other languages. For the same reason I have not described again the internal organization of foreign ministries and diplomatic missions, or multilateral agencies. Nor have I tried to enumerate the personal qualities of honesty, perceptiveness, tact, a sense of timing, a flair for entertaining, a flair for poker and so on which a long line of distinguished statesmen and ambassadors have compiled as desirable for diplomats.

In recent years attention has been given, especially in the United States, to the researches and models of those who take the natural sciences, particularly physics, as a framework and try to fit past and present international practice into it. I have not discussed these interesting enterprises in this book, because they have so far seemed to me, with certain distinguished exceptions, to be disappointingly unproductive of understanding of the nature of diplomatic activity and of the management of international society, which is a complex human and social activity that eludes numerate calculation. They also tend to put more stress on conflict and less on co-operation than does diplomatic reality taken as a whole. But they do produce a number of insights and aphorisms, whose validity varies with the perceptiveness of the writer. Nor are those young disciplines, sociology and social psychology, yet able to offer an understanding of diplomacy which is more useful than statesmen of the second rank acquire by practical experience.

The immediate origin of this book was a paper I wrote for the British Committee on the Theory of International Politics. This committee consisted of a group of academics and practitioners interested in international theory, which met first under the chairmanship of Herbert Butterfield, then of Martin Wight, later of myself, and now under that of Hedley Bull. Maurice Keens-Soper, a member of the committee, suggested that the paper ought to be expanded into a book. No good book on the wider aspects of diplomacy, as distinct from foreign policies of individual states and the details of diplomatic practice, had been written since Harold Nicolson's classic *Diplomacy*, which was first published in 1939. We agreed to write such a book together, for the interested general public and also for students of international affairs. Some of the original writing was contributed by Maurice Keens-Soper. However, after this joint start, he became heavily involved in other activities and wrote to me that 'the writing is on the wall, not in the book', and suggested that I should make the project entirely mine. This I reluctantly did, and this book sets out my own ideas and approach. I am grateful for the help afforded me by the University of Virginia in completing it. In particular my research assistant, Kimberly Andrews, made a large number of suggestions for improving the manuscript, most of which I have incorporated in the text. Frances Lackey of the Center for Advanced Studies gave me invaluable help in editing the final version. I also acknowledge with thanks the typing assistance given me by others in the Center for Advanced Studies. Of course I must accept the sole responsibility for the book and its contents.

The practical conclusion which emerges for the reader from this book is that diplomacy is a major and ubiquitous activity of governments in our time, and therefore of importance to us all. But it is an activity which can only be properly understood in its particular context of a number of independent states closely enough involved with one another to form an institutionalized international society or at least a system of states. The need for states to communicate with one another first gives rise to the diplomatic dialogue; but only a developed society of states provides diplomacy with its full possibilities and sets its limitations. States systems are the product of history, in the sense that they develop over a period of time. To analyse the influence of diplomacy on the closely knit relations of the independent states which constitute the international society of today, or any other states system, requires both an awareness of the nature of politics and an historian's responsiveness to the dilemmas of order and change in the progress of events. I ask the reader, both as a student of affairs and as a citizen with his or her part to play, to consider diplomacy with me in this light, and in the process, I hope, to acquire a clearer understanding of what it can and cannot do.

Adam Watson
Center for Advanced Studies
University of Virginia
January 1982

CHAPTER I

The Nature of Diplomacy

States are committed to diplomacy by the nature of the world in which they exist. In times and places where there are several separate states and their actions affect one another, they cannot function in a vacuum of isolation, with each community considering only how to manage its internal affairs. Each state is obliged, by the very desire to control its own destiny as far as possible, to take account of the neighbours who impinge on its interests and those of its citizens, whatever it considers those interests to be. In more formal terms, members of a group of independent states are obliged to manage the consequences of the fact that they enjoy their independences not absolutely and in isolation but in a setting of interdependence. When a group of states forms a closely knit system, the involvement of many self-willed political actors imposes upon each state a continuous awareness that the others have interests and purposes distinct from its own, and that the things other states do or may do limit and partly determine its own policies. Jean-Jacques Rousseau expressed this succinctly in the late eighteenth century when the states system he knew was a European affair. 'The body politic,' as he called the state, 'is forced to look outside itself in order to know itself; it depends on its whole environment and has to take an interest in everything that happens.' So today every state in our global system depends not merely on itself but on its whole worldwide environment.

States which are aware that their domestic policies are affected by 'everything that happens' outside, are not content merely to observe one another at a distance. They feel the need to enter into a dialogue with one another. This dialogue between independent states – the machinery by which their governments conduct it, and the networks of promises, contracts, institutions and codes of conduct which develop out of it – is the substance of diplomacy.

The essential condition of diplomacy is thus plurality. It arises out of the coexistence of a multitude of independent states in an inter-dependent world. Like household arrangements, diplomacy is a response to the recognition by several decision-making beings that the performance of each one is a matter of permanent consequence to some or all the others. Initially diplomacy appears as a sporadic communication between very separate states, such as the Kingdom of the Pharaohs in ancient Egypt and the Kingdom of the Hittites, which found themselves in contact with one another through the trade conducted by their merchants and through disputes over border territories. To put it more formally, the purpose of diplomacy was initially, and still is, to reconcile the assertion of political will by independent entities with what Edmund Burke called 'the empire of circumstances' around them. And we should notice at the outset that much of this empire of circumstances has always been military, and much of it economic.

Many thinkers about the nature of statehood have claimed that this ability to deal with the outside world is an essential aspect of that nature, and that what constitutes a state is not simply the machinery for ordering the domestic life of a community. They hold that if a community does not have a collective authority which is in a position to determine for itself the extent and the force of its dealings with other states then it lacks in a crucial respect the very powers which gave substance to its claims to statehood. Some thinkers see the ability to deal with other states, and therefore to conduct a dialogue with them, as the very heart of 'sovereignty'. While the ability to conduct a diplomatic dialogue with other states is a hallmark of statehood, the importance which external contacts have varies in practice from one state to another. Sometimes the interests of a number of states are so closely intertwined, and the activities and indeed the existence of every state are sometimes so largely determined by what its neighbours do, that there is a 'primacy of foreign policy' in every such state's decisions. This concept, attributed to the German historian Ranke, refers not only to political and strategic relations in the narrow sense, but to the whole range of external contacts from military conflict to the goods and ideas which states with entwined communities habitually import from one another.

Where a group of states are so involved with each other that without their losing their independence what one state does directly or indirectly affects all the others, it is useful to talk of a states system, in the sense that we talk about the solar system for instance. The term has been in general use since it was put forward by Pufendorf, a seventeenth-century professional diplomat who worked for various countries and published *De Systematibus Civitatum* while in the service of the king of Sweden. There is room for discussion as to whether there have been a number of states systems in the past, or whether the only fully developed states system, conscious of itself as such, was the European one which grew up after the Renaissance and has now developed into the contemporary worldwide system. These distinctions, in so far as they affect diplomacy, are covered in Chapters VII and VIII.

Moreover, where there is a shared cultural heritage, or at any rate common values, and where the communities which compose the states in a system are engaged in active exchanges of goods and ideas so that there is a high degree of interdependence, those states may as a result 'conceive themselves to be bound by a common set of rules in their relations with one another, and share in the working of common institutions', as Professor Hedley Bull puts it. In such cases it is possible to go further and to regard the system as a single international or inter-state society, whose member states, though politically independent, are not absolutely separate entities but parts of a whole. In such cases each sovereign and individual state has not achieved its civilization and its standard of living, and the needs and aspirations of its people, in isolation, but has only been able to do so within the wider society. It takes, says Professor Charles Taylor, 'a long development of certain institutions and practices, of the rule of law, of rules of equal respect, of habits of common deliberation, of common association' and, one may add, of cultural cross-fertilization and an equipoise or balance of forces and interests, to produce the modern individual state in an international society. The preservation and the effective functioning of that society as a whole is therefore a real interest of the states which form its parts, to be weighed along with their more particular and individual interests and aspirations in the same general way as the individual human beings in a civilized community have an interest in the functioning of the community as a whole. We are used to regarding individual human beings as having not merely interests but certain moral responsibilities towards the community in which they live; and some of their responsibilities are formulated as legal obligations. But the prudential and moral responsibilities of states towards international society are much less clear cut. This imperative question, and the role of diplomacy in this context, are discussed in Chapter XIII.

Historically, an effective multilateral diplomatic dialogue within a states system has required more than the chance coexistence of a plurality of independent states with entangled interests. In the past, sustained dialogues developed and flourished between groups of states in a circumscribed geographical area and with a history of close contacts. Such groups of states formed, so to speak, a single magnetic field of political forces. Their identity was determined by membership of, or close contact with, a common civilization. Their diplomatic dialogue was conducted, and the pursuit of their separate interests was mediated, in terms of the concepts of law, honour, morality and prudence which prevailed in that civilization. Even war between them was not indiscriminate violence: it was regulated by the rules of the system. In war, such groups of states recognized not only 'laws of war' which regulated the right of a state to resort to force and how war might be waged, but beyond that certain codes of conduct towards enemies and neutrals, and the right of other member states, including enemies, to some degree of independence. If these groups of states expanded outside their original geographical area, they inevitably took their assumptions, their laws and codes of conduct with them.

For example, in the European society of states, diplomacy emerged as an organizing institution, bearing its distinctive styles and manners and its own networks of procedures, rules, treaties and other commitments. The European system, so organized, was able to exercise influence and restraint over the assertiveness of its members because they were bound from the beginning by much more than a mere political arrangement. The states of Europe had in common the strong traditions of medieval Latin Christendom, and the inherited elements of unity were never entirely subordinated to the newer movements of fragmentation and diversity. Other systems of states, such as the Hellenic, early Chinese and Indian, also developed highly sophisticated diplomacy. But all of these were after many centuries finally absorbed into a conquering empire like Rome or China without expanding to encompass other comparable states which remained outside their civilization. Western Europe was an exception. And it is generally recognized that the sophisticated techniques and heightened awareness of how the states system operated, which European diplomacy required from its independent member states, contributed not a little to the remarkable phenomenon, contrary to the experience of other states systems, that no single state proved to be so powerful that it could for any length of time absorb or even dominate all the others. If there was not always a strict multiple balance of power between the states of Europe, for most of the period between about 1500 when the system began to operate and the middle of the present century when it became effectively worldwide, there was a consciously maintained balance or equipoise between the great powers sufficient to prevent the consolidation of power in the hands of a single hegemonic authority. These are the circumstances in which diplomacy is most necessary and in which it flourishes best. European diplomacy could therefore develop to the point where it could expand to organise a worldwide system.

Only in this century has a states system become for the first time truly global, encompassing a variety of civilizations and beliefs. What are the consequences of this expansion for the rules and practices of diplomacy? The European diplomacy which our global system inherited developed as a dialogue between members of a system which (as always in the past) had a cultural and historical identity strong enough to ensure that its members recognized certain rules. It is necessary to look at the historical origins and the cultural context of any given diplomatic practice in order to understand it. Therefore we must keep in mind the European origins of present-day diplomacy if we are to see where it has become inadequate and how it can successfully be adapted and in some respects wholly transformed to meet the requirements of its global expansion and of radical change. For in spite of optimistic talk about a global international society, the common assumptions and codes of conduct which derive from a shared European cultural heritage hardly receive general recognition outside the West. This major challenge to an effective dialogue and other problems of adaptation required to enable modern diplomatic practice to deal with unprecedented and rapidly changing conditions constitute an important aspect of this book.

That there are advantages in the diplomatic dialogue is obvious. But is it necessary for all states? And if not, in what conditions can some states, or at least special classes of states, dispense with diplomacy? It is difficult to find examples of an important state in a system which tries to manage without a regular diplomatic dialogue. Nevertheless it is historically true that there have been both powerful and miniscule states which have remained isolated or aloof from the pell-mell of international relations for long periods of time. These states have been on the political or geographical margins of integrated systems of states, or outside them altogether. Remote states, separated from an active states system by natural obstacles such as an ocean or desert, can afford to be marginal members of it and to maintain fitful and selective relations with the states more closely involved in the system. George Washington warned his countrymen against entangling alliances, by which he meant that degree of involvement in the European states system which made alliances necessary. Since then, however, the United States has become increasingly entangled, and isolation has become an ever less realizable ideal. States too small to carry weight in the diplomatic dialogue can sometimes also, by historical accident, become excluded from it. Andorra, Lichtenstein and Sikkim are examples.

However, what was possible at certain periods for the United States or Tibet or Andorra is not an option open as a general rule. The most striking case is that of China. For many centuries the Chinese Empire, more a civilization with a suzerain structure than a state, maintained no regular dialogue with other states: there was, so to speak, isolation behind a wall, with nomads from Central Asia occasionally able to gain control of the apex of imperial government. The 'central kingdom', once established, forgot the indigenous traditions of diplomacy which had developed to a high degree by the time of Confucius, because the unified empire which replaced the Chinese states system was powerful enough to command its immediate neighbours and to remain indifferent to matters further afield. China first consented to a regular diplomatic dialogue and exchanges of envoys with Western states in the middle of the nineteenth century, when the fortunes of the last ruling dynasty were diminished and when the powers of the West could no longer be ignored. China was obliged to have dealings with other states when European powers, with superior military and maritime technology and a determination to trade with her on their terms, progressively involved her in international politics: that is, when she found herself up against independent and uncoercible fellow states. The consequences for China were profound and exceptionally unfortunate.

To grasp the evolving pattern of modern diplomacy, it is equally important to notice the effects on a states system itself of the incorporation of more distant states into the relentless and inescapable mesh of international affairs that makes the system. Where it has been a matter of bringing single states into a ready-made system, the acceptance of a diplomatic dialogue carried with it the need for important adjustments by the incoming state. For instance in Western Europe, where diplomacy in its recognizably modern forms had its origins, one of the principal conditions making for the elaboration of permanent contacts between the independent parts was precisely the rough and ready moral and legal equality of the society's constituent states, large and small. This condition of the European dialogue appeared almost unacceptably alien to the Chinese Empire. For somewhat different reasons the Moslem Ottoman Khalifate for a long period, and the Soviet revolutionary government for a much shorter one, were also reluctant to concede this equality to other states. But these three major powers agreed to conform to the outward rules and conventions of European diplomacy because as the European powers impinged ever more insistently on their interests and purposes, all three found the diplomatic dialogue with those powers indispensable. How far these three states remained alien to the cultural and historical assumptions which engendered the rules and conventions of European diplomacy is another question.

The position is different when a large number of outside states come into a system in a short time, so that in effect the system itself is extended far beyond its cultural cradle. Then the adjustments are not so one-sided, and many concessions have to be made by the original members to the newcomers. Today the contemporary global system is gradually evolving new rules and conventions to replace those of its more purely European predecessor.

Because states talk to each other privately and confidentially, and this aspect of their dialogue naturally excites curiosity, diplomacy is sometimes thought of as essentially bilateral. But the ties which bind states in systems are by definition multilateral. Consequently the calculations which shape the policy of each member state towards the others are multilateral; and the dialogue between them also becomes more multilateral as the system develops. Only the most primitive diplomatic contacts have ever been purely bilateral. Leagues and alliances, and indeed also all occasions on which representatives of three or more powers are gathered together, are examples of multilateral diplomacy. But these dialogues only include some players in the game. Comprehensive multilateral or 'omnilateral' diplomacy, that is to say the attempt to include all or at least all significant members of a system in a simultaneous negotiation, is characteristic of a more advanced stage. It usually first appears as a negotiation for a general peace after prolonged warfare, and is later organized into permanent institutions like the League of Nations and the United Nations. So far, multilateral diplomacy has complemented the bilateral dialogue: it shows no sign of replacing bilateral contacts between sovereign states.

Independent states deal bilaterally with each other and meet together in multilateral organizations not only because they have interests in common, but also because they have interests which conflict. Moreover, the fact of independence fosters suspicion and doubts. Another power may be insincere in what it says and promises; or if sincere it may change its mind. History is full of examples of conflict, duplicity and reversals of policy, and the news brings fresh examples every day. Diplomacy is intimately concerned with these problems. It is an organized pattern of communication and negotiation, nowadays continuous, which enables each independent government to learn what other governments want and what they object to. In a developed international society it becomes more than an instrument of communication and bargaining. It also affects its practitioners. It is an activity which even if often abused has a bias towards the resolution of conflicts. It is a function of the diplomatic dialogue to mitigate and civilize the differences between states, and if possible to reconcile them, without suppressing or ignoring them. Conflicts of interest are a major subject of diplomacy, which can function effectively only when the necessary level of understanding exists between the parties to the dialogue about the maintenance of the system as a whole and about the rules for the promotion of their separate interests within the system. The diplomatic dialogue is thus the instrument of international society: a civilized process based on awareness and respect for other people's points of view; and a civilizing one also, because the continuous exchange of ideas, and the attempts to find mutually acceptable solutions to conflicts of interest, increase that awareness and respect. This civilizing tendency visibly does not prevent diplomacy from being perverted and misused – its methods lend themselves to duplicity. But the bias towards understanding other points of view and other needs, towards a search for common ground and a resolution of differences, is unmistakably there.

CHAPTER II

Alternatives to Diplomacy

What are the alternatives to diplomacy? In order to dispense with diplomacy, that is with the methods used by independent governments to work out their own relations with one another, mankind would either have to let independent governments exist without the diplomatic dialogue, or else dispense with independence and 'sovereign states' altogether.

I consider the first alternative purely fanciful. It would mean a world which would have to resign itself to a condition of anarchy and isolation, of chronic insecurity and war: something like what Hobbes called a state of nature. States would have to live by and for themselves. They would not be able to conclude peace settlements or treaties with their neighbours, for such settlements are the essence of diplomacy. Each would have to stand alone against a more powerful and aggressive neighbour. They would not be able to get into touch with one another, to band together or form leagues and alliances for mutual protection. For these activities too are works of diplomacy, and, incidentally, ones which are particularly criticized by those who argue that a diplomatic network of alliances helps to spread wars and conflicts beyond the limits which they would otherwise have, by involving other states which are not directly concerned. Nor could there be nuclear or other arms limitation agreements which require sustained diplomatic negotiation both to bring them into being and to maintain them as circumstances change. In the absence of dialogue or agreement, each state would have to concentrate on its own defence. In an age of primitive weapons and communications this was possible – at a price – especially for those whose territory lay away from the mainstream of world affairs. But in a nuclear age such an arrangement, or lack of arrangement, is hardly practicable at all. Apart from the problem of defence, the citizens of a state in isolation, without diplomatic contacts, would have difficulty in organizing either trade or those exchanges of men and ideas which develop civilization.

Altogether, the idea of armed sovereign states existing in a highly developed technical world without diplomacy is quite impractical. For this reason, people who distrust diplomacy have preferred to look to the abolition of independent states.

What then about the abolition of independent states? Can we, and should we, work towards a world government or a world federation? Is the world of states as we know them destined to wither away, in spite of present appearances? Here the prospects seem rather more realistic. There are viable alternatives to international society as it now exists and as it has existed at various periods in the past. Such alternatives have functioned at other periods in history; and it is not difficult to imagine how they might work again. A world of many independent states is not the only practical world.

The most obvious alternative is what is often called world government. This is the fullest opposite to the plurality of independences in a states system. World government can, broadly speaking, be of two kinds. It can be government from one centre, by a single ruling authority, established and maintained by superior and unchallengeable force; or it can be a system formed by a voluntary union of all the important states in the world who surrender some of their independent authority to a central decision-making body that represents and governs them all. The more voluntary the formation of such a union is, the more federal it is likely to be, with a greater degree of autonomy for the constituent parts.

Government of the world by a single authority, and maintained by the ultimate sanction of unchallengeable force, has worked fairly well at times in the past. Such, within the limits of their worlds, were the Roman and Chinese Empires. They were not democracies, nor was there any right of secession. The Emperor governed through a bureaucracy, backed by armed force that could be effectively challenged only by a rival military commander. The role of the subject peoples was not to choose their rulers, but to obey them. Nevertheless, under wise government people were contented. There was not freedom. But there were peace and order, which are major blessings in themselves, and arguably the conditions in which individual liberties are most likely to develop. Gibbon concluded that the Roman Empire under the enlightened Antonines was the happiest period mankind has known; and others have believed this about the best periods of the Chinese Empire too. In the anarchy of the Middle Ages, Dante in his *De Monarchia* extolled a single empire for all Christendom which could ensure the blessings of peace and the rule of law. Could, but not necessarily always did. When the Government was oppressive in such empires, everyone suffered help-lessly.

A world government of this kind is certainly imaginable today. To take one example, it could come by the extension of Soviet authority beyond the Soviet Union and the present 'Socialist Commonwealth' to the whole world. A global supremacy of this kind need not go so far as formal annexation: it could leave its subject states the shadow of independence and a considerable degree of local autonomy within the limits laid down by the paramount power. Such a world government could bring the blessings of peace and order at the price of freedom. And it is arguable that when the new world government settled down, individuals would not necessarily be less free under world government than they now are in many existing states, for the independence of a state tells us little about the liberties of its individual subjects. A single world government would have to maintain its dominion by authoritarian means. In a world of many languages, races, cultures and beliefs, national and other communities tend to assert their separate political identity if they can. Although recorded history and the news of the day are full of examples of this tendency, some thinkers and even some historians have denied that it is innate and have pointed to the willingness of men to accept a 'universal' empire once it has been established by force. But there is a decisive body of evidence that without continuing force to hold any empire together there is soon secession. One sobering example is provided by the communist world. Lenin and other communists believed that the quarrels and disagreements between states were the result of previous social systems, and assumed that communist parties in power would collaborate; but poly-centrism and the Sino-Soviet quarrel have shown the unreality of this assumption. If the world authority used force to restrain various national and other groups from re-asserting their independence, many of them would still try to do so. If the world authority allowed this to happen, we should be back to the patchwork quilt of independent states, and diplomacy between them would become necessary again.

What most people in the West who want world government have in mind is not the establishment of one authoritarian government over the whole planet, maintained by the sanction of force, but a voluntary merging of sovereignty by the governments and peoples of the world (or more specifi-cally by the states in the system) so as to form a world federation. There would be a union established and held together by universal consent. Historically, independent communities which come together to 'pool their sovereignty', that is to hand over essential parts of their decision-making process to a central government, have three characteristics. They already have a great deal in common. In most known cases they have emerged as uncomfortably small fragments from the break-up of a previous empire and come together to form 'a more perfect union'. And thirdly, they are constrained to do so by outside pressures, 'to hang together in order not to hang separately'. This was the case with the thirteen ex-colonies of North America who formed the United States (from whose history these familiar quotations are taken): and it will be the case with the Western European countries if they form a single confederal European government.

What are the chances of a world government of this voluntary kind in the absence of these three characteristics? The fact that something has not yet happened in the past does not mean it cannot happen in the future. Those who look forward to world federation point out that all mankind is now much more one interdependent society than its various communities, with their fierce love of independence, have realized; that we are all living on one 'spaceship earth'. Moreover, in the 'nuclear and famine age', independent and absolute sovereignties are alleged to be as out of date as the sailing ship and the crossbow. For mankind as a whole, it is said, is now beset by common dangers and common problems, which if not tackled by all of us together, might actually lead to the destruction of our species. A nuclear holocaust, pollution, the population explosion, the growing shortage and cost of energy and raw materials, are dangers quite as formidable as any which once menaced the American colonies. Even those who consider that the world federationists exaggerate both the degree to which mankind in its variety has become one society and the dangers which threaten us, have to admit that the world is moving that way – that the different communities into which mankind is divided are becoming more interdependent and that the dangers which threaten all of us are becoming worse. Since the first step in politics is recognition, it is already significant to be able to point to a measure of consensus about which of the perils that confront mankind are to be treated as problems requiring international political effort for their resolution. In so far as there is agreement about the problems to be tackled (either already or for the near future), two basic issues arise about world federation as a solution. Is such a radical step necessary to solve these problems? And would such a step create more serious problems than it resolved?

Given that we want to solve these pressing problems by consent, and not by compulsion in a new Roman or Chinese Empire, the issue of necessity is this. Can we get all, or a decisive majority, of states to act together to solve these problems 'inter-nationally', while leaving the decisions about how to go about it, and of course the residual sovereignty too, to the individual member states of our international society? Or must the states agree first of all to 'pool their sovereignty', at any rate for these purposes, in a world government, and then let the world government decide on the measures required to deal with these world problems, and enforce its decisions?

If we look at what is actually happening in international affairs, we see that the first alternative is the one being tried. There is an intensifying search by independent states for areas of consent in which they can act together (that is, agree to adopt parallel policies) to solve common problems. Indeed the whole of the twentieth century has been marked by this search, in spite of great setbacks. As interdependence grows and the possibility of going it alone diminishes, the larger and more established states of the world are becoming more acutely aware of the need to collaborate. They are therefore increasingly willing to delegate decision-making responsibilities to international bodies composed of delegates appointed by them and answerable to them, and designed as an integral part of the diplomatic dialogue between them. Provided these criteria are observed, states will often bind themselves in advance to accept the decisions which such international bodies reach. In this way they agree to add to the rules and codes of conduct which determine how the members of an international society of states will behave, or in other words to add to the body of regulatory international law.

The need for maritime conventions has, of course, been recognized for centuries, and postal and civil aviation conventions are now taken for granted. International economic life is regulated by monetary and tariff agreements: these are hammered out first by the major non-communist industrial states, and the communist states then work out their own relation to the agreements. From time to time the agreements themselves break down. But the net of these agreements, both those which are regarded as part of international law and those which are more in the nature of legally binding contracts, gradually and steadily restricts the freedom of action of all states. On matters like pollution and conservation, independent governments agree to accept the collective decisions of a majority of their fellows, even if they dislike certain individual decisions, because on balance it pays them to do so.

In the more sensitive technical fields like the control of oil or armaments, which have great political implications, international agreements are also gradually being negotiated. More purely political issues, such as territorial boundaries between states, the right of would-be states to international recognition, and in general all those issues that seem seriously liable to lead to war, are inevitably more difficult to resolve (partly because they do not appear as problems which mankind faces in common). They come into a category of their own which requires separate examination.

The issues raised by men's increasing interdependence and what has been called the 'generation of a world society' are bringing about an increasing awareness that mankind has a common identity in the face of them, and must take common political action to solve them. On a great and increasing range of questions which are both technical and political, many of them vital for the future of man on earth, international agreements are being reached by a process of free collective bargaining between states. These agreements commit the signatories to surrender certain specific and precisely defined aspects of their future freedom of action in order to combat a threat by acting together. This is the way forward which the leading states of the world have chosen to try.

The point for us to note is that *this way forward is the way of diplomacy.* It is an evolution of great interest, both because of the enlargement of the content of diplomatic negotiation and because the direction in which international affairs are moving is towards a more collectively organized society of states. Previous concepts in international politics (and the vocabulary used to describe them) are being increasingly stretched by the wealth of new collective experience. Each agreement of the kind described above involves some delegation of an individual state's power of decision to a technically qualified international authority or to a group of states in which it may often be in a minority. But it is important to remember that these delegations of authority are themselves decisions of independent states. A state can revoke its delegation of authority and resume its right to decide. In sensitive areas like nuclear testing, certain powerful states such as France or China may refuse to accept the convention at all (just as in smaller groupings like the European Community an individual state refuses to accept majority decisions against it on an issue that it considers vital). Moreover, the experts who make the decisions at international bodies of this kind may be technical experts and not members of foreign offices, but they act as diplomatic agents. They take their decisions and cast their votes as representatives of their states, and act according to the instructions they receive from their government, whose envoys they are and who can recall them at any time. Their deliberations and decisions, and their governments' acceptance of them, are therefore a branch of modern collective diplomacy. Governmental envoys who help to conduct the continuous dialogue and negotiation between governments in this way are in an entirely different position from, for instance, elected members of a parliament, who are not agents receiving instructions from a government, but principals voting according to their own judgement or, more usually nowadays, that of their political party. Put simply, we may say that the supervising function of a legislature is to restrain an executive authority, while the function of an international conference is to establish consensus between a number of executive authorities.

As governments increasingly commit themselves to collective diplomacy through international bodies, instead of regarding these bodies as supplements to the decisive procedure of bilateral negotiation, the operation of diplomacy changes, as it has in the past. But it is still as much diplomacy as before. All these collective negotiations are in practice multilateral dialogues between states; and they are supplemented by bilateral diplomacy directly between the individual governments. The role of bilateral diplomacy in this field is largely to make the reasons for a state's hesitation understood in other capitals, and to look for ways of persuasion and adjustment which will bring the hesitant states in. (How these parallel processes affect the working pattern of modern diplomacy is described in Chapter VII.)

As these discussions move from technical problems to more political ones, voluntary cooperation between independent states becomes more difficult, and willingness to 'pool sovereignty' rarer. In highly political issues, and especially those connected with peace and war, modern diplomacy uses two main approaches. One is through many-sided bilateral diplomacy with a number of states consulting each other privately, usually through their resident ambassadors, to prepare the way for multilateral negotiations on specific topics at *ad hoc* conferences. The other is through the United Nations and its associated bodies. The first need not be considered in this context of alternatives to the present system, except to note that on especially difficult issues the major states, particularly the communist ones, consider *ad hoc* conferences more effective and more likely to produce results than omni-lateral public debates at the United Nations, even when these are sup-plemented and given some coherence by parallel private consultations. Recent examples are the negotiations for the disengagement from Indochina and the two major conferences on peace and security and on balanced force reductions in Europe. It is recognized that the United Nations as now constituted has a 'ceiling of usefulness' above which it pays in terms of effectiveness to use the more traditional forms of negotiation between states.

Nevertheless, the United Nations is a highly significant innovation in the ordering of relations between states. It is the most important international body, because it is not specialized but a general and universal association of states, and specifically authorized in its charter to deal with political issues. It and its predecessor, the League of Nations, represent the first tentative steps towards an international authority on a worldwide scale, designed to be more than a regulatory and security agency. The various general and specialized bodies of these omnilateral organizations have made it possible to formulate and explore global objectives and to gain wider acceptance for them by states and peoples than would be possible by bilateral exchanges alone, and are at times able to act as a conscience of mankind formally expressed. But in spite of certain quasi-parliamentary procedures, such an organization is not a world legislature, let alone a world government. It is, formally and in fact, a permanent gathering of diplomatic envoys, representing almost all the independent states of international society. A great deal of confusion, disappointed wishful thinking and unjustified criticism about both the League and the United Nations has resulted from expecting them to be what they are not. Andrew Young, a former United States Ambassador to the United Nations, put it succinctly: 'The United Nations was not designed to be, nor is it adequate to serve as, either a law-making body for the world or a court to judge the nations of the world. It is a forum for diplomacy, and true diplomacy is the art of dialogue in pursuit of common goals and the avoidance of war.' There is no executive authority capable of issuing or enforcing orders: it is for the states concerned to decide how far they will implement the recommendations of the General Assembly and the rarer but theoretically mandatory decisions of the Security Council. But the United Nations is also a world forum, where states, even very small states that might not otherwise be heard, can instruct their envoys to make their views and decisions on certain subjects publicly known.

The General Assembly is designed to ensure universality rather than effectiveness. It provides equal representation for every member. Most states are now so small in population and in influence that a majority in the Assembly can easily be, and inevitably therefore often is, quite unrepresentative of either world opinion or world power. Unlike a legislature, and unlike the United Nations Security Council, the Assembly can only make recommendations to states; and it controls no taxation or purse strings except the sums that governments may give it. And yet, relatively ineffective and relatively powerless as it is, it does already exercise a certain control over the actions of governments – some governments more than others – in the same sort of way as an advisory chamber can do inside a state. This omni-lateral influence of the collectivity of states on its individual members through public debate and voting is something new, or at least the germ of something new. But it is an innovation in diplomacy – in the art of dialogue between states – not a move away from it. One of the principal constructive functions of the Assembly, and to a lesser extent of the United Nations generally, is to provide a permanent, continuous and automatic meeting-place for pro-fessional diplomats, who can privately take account of each other's real strength and influence outside the formal equality of the public debating chamber which gives the large number of weak states a say disproportionate to their power. The occasional attendance of foreign ministers and even heads of government reinforces this opportunity for discreet dialogue on neutral ground.

The growth of collective diplomacy, and of commitments by states which limit their freedom of action in practice, make it impossible for us to regard independent states and world order by consent as two mutually exclusive concepts. On the contrary, there is a wide spectrum of transition between a fully 'anarchic' international system, with bilateral diplomacy and states grouped in alliances but with no collective institutions, and federal or hegemonic world government with no independent states. In this theoretical range of international societies the sovereignty and independence of states is always present, but diminishing and subject to greater restrictions as we look across it from 'anarchy' to world government. In *The Anarchical Society*, Hedley Bull describes the present situation, where states are still independent but subject to many restraints and limitations. The limitations are to some extent the result of collective diplomacy. But the real restraint, on which the general independence of the member states depends, is still what it was in the days before collective diplomacy: namely the balance between the stronger ones which prevents the hegemony of any one of them. Only a breakdown of the present structure of international society – not a Vietnam or an energy crisis but mass destruction – could make statesmen consent to a genuinely federal, as opposed to hegemonic, world government, especially one which would tend to take decisions against them. If something radically upset the balance of power and left one superpower in a position to exercise a world hegemony, that power might dress up its domination in a federal garb, or be content to have the United Nations ratify and consolidate its control so as to endow the new hegemonic reality with collective legitimacy. In either event real independence would disappear, and with it real diplomacy. But between such developments and the present system there is a wide stretch of our theoretical zone in which freedom of action of states is increasingly limited by diplomatic negotiation.

By and large statesmen, and especially statesmen of the larger powers, consider that the problems which arise from the growing interdependence of mankind and from the dangers which threaten us are being tolerably managed by diplomacy: that is, by sovereign states negotiating agreements for common action to solve them. So long as governments hold this opinion, or at least consider that the dangers and evils of the states system are less than those which would result from their pooling their sovereignty in a world government, they will continue to operate on the present basis. But it seems likely that as interdependence grows and the dangers of nuclear war become more terrifying, the larger powers will collaborate or respect each other's wishes more effectively than they have in the past. The prospects of our international society moving further in this direction are discussed in Chapter XII on the growth of state power and interdependence.

So the answer to the question as to whether a world federation is necessary to solve the problems arising out of our growing interdependence, in the sense that nothing short of such a federation will serve, is that so far this has not been proved. But we may see the General Assembly of the United Nations and other international bodies, full of grave shortcomings as they are, as reflecting the beginnings of a new way of thinking about international affairs which may well in time transform relations between states and thus the nature of the diplomatic dialogue.

The question of whether a world federation is a practical way of ordering human affairs, or whether it would give rise to even graver problems than those it is designed to solve, belongs to the study of government – how authorities work and are controlled – rather than to the study of diplomacy. Intense diplomatic negotiations would certainly be necessary for the states of the world to agree to merge in a federation: but the diplomatic dialogue would end once independent states ceased to exist.

The best hope for orderly and peaceful adjustment to the change in international practice made necessary by the pressures of rapidly developing technology and changing concepts of justice seems to lie in extending the scope of the diplomatic dialogue between states and modifying its institutions and techniques (which is already happening) rather than in seeking to abolish both it and independent states in favour of some wholly different world political system. When we have examined the past and present workings of diplomatic institutions, it will be possible to look at improvements, and ways to modify both the demands of states on the states system and the methods by which states work to attain them.

Before we leave the question of alternatives to diplomacy altogether, we should consider the idea that the organization of the world may change radically, in ways which we cannot now foresee, so that there might no longer be either a society of basically independent states or a world dominion or federation. This is of course possible. The Middle Ages were entirely different, both in the whole structure of society and in the relations of one ruler to another, from what went before and what came after. Those thinkers about international affairs who want to allow for this possibility sometimes speak of a 'new medievalism', meaning not a reversion to the Middle Ages themselves but a new and utterly different system. A few have suggested that perhaps transnational corporations like the big oil companies and other international bodies like the Communist Parties and the Catholic Church may so cut across the state system as to produce radical change. So far these influences do not seem to have proved successful in condemning or replacing the authority of independent states or the voluntary order of the states system into which they have been absorbed. In fact a recognizable alternative is not yet over the horizon of political consciousness. Most thinkers who use the term 'new medievalism' mean by it something that we cannot imagine today any more than the Romans could have imagined the feudal system. Since they cannot imagine it they do not discuss it as an alternative, but simply allow for the fact that the future cannot be foreseen.

.

CHAPTER III

Aims and Policies of States

We established in the last chapter that states or political entities which wish to retain their independence, whether within their existing boundaries or by forming a community or union with some of their neighbours, are fated to communicate with other states and unions outside their own. *This negotiation between political entities which acknowledge each other's independence is called diplomacy.*

What then do states (including communities and unions of states) want of one another? What, as economists say, are their demands on each other and on the system? Each independent political entity has certain goals or objectives which it – or more specifically its government – wishes to achieve, certain things which the government and perhaps the people also wish to say and do. These goals, which reflect the values of the people, may be publicly proclaimed, or they may be unspoken and perhaps only half consciously held. Sometimes a government proclaims goals which are quite different from those it actually pursues. Because this is the language of politics, much is written about the policies of leaders and political parties and governments in terms of long-term goals. But a goal is something outside you, something fixed and immovable, at the end of the road or the other side of the field. Goals certainly come into the diplomatic dialogue between states, and especially into that part of it which is conducted in public. But what almost all states ask of one another in their day-to-day relations, what they discuss and negotiate with one another about most of the time, are their more immediate needs and requirements, and their responses to pressures and circumstances. Indeed, a government's responses to pressures, its manner of coping with problems not of its own choosing, usually go far in determining its external policy. Of course the policies of a government are modified by its long-term goals and objectives, and its responses determined by its values: though often much less than governments like to proclaim.

A large number of the problems which confront a government, and most of the political goals of a ruler or a party, are inward-looking and domestic. Similarly, the day-to-day policies of a government are mainly concerned with the internal affairs of the state which it governs. The reason why governments value independence so highly is because they want to be able to take these internal decisions themselves. In the modern world the government is the ultimate and decisive authority inside a state; and as the power of the state (that is, the government) over all activities within it increases, so it becomes more absolute in the sense that its decisions determine what shall happen in matters that are within its control. More particularly, inside its own domain a government can make laws and issue edicts, in the expectation that they will be generally obeyed, even if sometimes grudgingly; and it has means of law enforcement to compel those who disobey. But in so far as the problems which face a government are due to causes outside its boundaries, in so far as what other states do affects its problems, and indeed its policies and its goals, and in so far as its policies affect other states, we say a government has a foreign policy. *Aussenpolitik* (outward policy) is the useful German term. In the field of outward policy the position of a government is entirely different from its position at home. A state is not normally strong enough, or for a number of reasons is unable or unwilling to use its strength, to coerce other states to behave as it wishes. And since if it did, the other states concerned would not be meaningfully independent, we may broadly say that by definition an independent state is compelled to negotiate and bargain with other states on all matters where the policies of other states affect its own. Sometimes negotiation fails, of course, and states resort to force. But not all the time, and not with all other states. Most of the time states further their interests, and make their demands on the system and respond to its pressures, by negotiation.

There have been periods of history when the political entities in a certain area had so little contact with one another that they hardly had need of outward policies. But the more closely knitted together a system or society of states is, and the more interdependent the individual states in that society are, the more each will be affected by the outward policies of the others, and the more obliged it will be to take account of them and to enter into a dialogue with them, whether it wants to or not. The world as a whole has never been so closely knit, so interdependent, as it is today. Consequently there is today more diplomacy, and it is more complex, than ever before.

It is a matter of common observation that the interests and principles, and the goals, of states differ: that each state has a distinct outward policy. Only in imaginary models designed by political scientists for the purposes of study do all the states in a system have the same policy towards each other. The main reason for these differences is that the outward policy of each state is largely determined for it by the needs of the area concerned and of the people who live there. Thus, for instance, every government of Mauritius will be concerned to sell its sugar at a good price; every government of Russia will want to ensure safe passage through the straits out of the Black Sea; every government of Britain has to ensure imports of huge quantities of food and raw materials. But there is also an area in the outward policy of any state which is not determined in this way but open to choice. This area of choice varies according to the circumstances of each state, and is usually much more limited than is often supposed; but it receives a great deal of attention precisely because it is a matter of choice, and therefore of controversy. Choices are possible about some long-term goals, but more usually they involve decisions about reactions to external events and pressures, and methods of responding to them, including ultimately involvement in war.

　　Every state, whether comparatively insulated from others or highly interdependent, is above all concerned to preserve the right and ability to take its own decisions, that is its independence. This is not to say, of course, that every state or political entity wishes to stay exactly as it is, in composition and territorial extent. Certain small states, and especially their populations, are willing to merge into a larger, equally independent state. Sometimes quite large countries want to do this, especially where the populations feel that they belong to the same nation or group. The German and Italian states pooled their independence and their sovereignty in the nineteenth century to form two large nation-states. Perhaps the Arab states, or those of Western Europe, may do the same tomorrow, and agree to share in the decision-making processes of a larger state. Indeed from ancient times many groups of similar states have merged or formed unions in order to defend their collective independence more effectively. Similarly, groups or nations which are incorporated in existing states like the United Kingdom or India, may have the will and the opportunity to secede and to form smaller states on their own. In all these cases, new states emerge, and the desire to preserve independence from other states which people consider to be outside their own entity remains as before.

　　The desire of every political entity to look after its own interests and take its own decisions arises from the fact that the interests of different states and groups differ. It is wholly false to suppose that the interests of different groups of people do not, or need not, ever conflict. If states were replaced by other structures, these conflicts of interest would remain. However, this does not mean that interests are irreconcilable. Interests can be harmonized, or reconciled, or fairly divided by consent, as well as maintained in the teeth of opposition. What this means is that, to take our first example, the people of Mauritius, who live mainly by producing sugar, want to get as many other goods as possible in exchange for their sugar. In Western economic terms they want as high a sugar price as they can get; whereas the foreigners who consume the sugar and export manufactured goods in return want to pay no more than they have to. Sugar may be an easier issue to settle than oil, but it is the principal export of many countries today, and a great deal of negotiation and bargaining, a great deal of diplomacy, goes into determining sugar prices and quotas. In this as in all the other issues of modern diplomacy, each state concerned wishes to take its own decisions and defend its own interests. For instance, the major practical justification of the independence of small, underdeveloped countries from colonial and neo-colonial rule is that their interests are not as well served by leaving their vital decisions in the hands of others.

The principal concern of each state, then, is to preserve its own independence. In a system of states where the policy of each affects the others, many states recognize that they have a joint interest in maintaining their independence; and they come to see in the independence of their fellow members the means to preserve their own. It is not necessary that every state should attach importance to preserving the independence of every other state, nor that it should formally recognize all other states as having the same moral right to a separate existence as it claims for itself. For example, governments committed to national unification are apt to consider certain existing states to be entities which are destined to disappear, either by absorption or by partition. But even in the case of revolutionary régimes, and especially those on the defensive, the maintenance of one's own independence is soon seen to involve some recognition of that of others (though not necessarily all others). It is clearly shortsighted of a state to concern itself with the preservation of its own independence only, while a more powerful neighbour establishes its domination over other states, for sooner or later its turn is likely to come, and it may not be strong enough to withstand alone that increasingly powerful neighbour. From this practical and vital involvement in the independence of other states, the concept develops that states have a general right to be independent, and that those which want to exercise this right have an interest in supporting each other in asserting it. So states in systems come to recognize that the mutual acceptance of the principle of independence, even with exceptions, is a necessary condition of a society of states, and that diplomatic intercourse between them must therefore be based on this acceptance. Recognition of independence, where it exists, both in practice and of right, is a prerequisite of diplomacy. For a state must recognise that other states are able and entitled to take their own decisions if it is to communicate and negotiate with them effectively about how they will act.

The independence of all the states in a system is *compatible*, just as within a state the rights of political parties are compatible with one another. This concept of compatibility is important for all collective diplomacy, and it applies to other aspects of international life which most states regard as highly desirable, though they are not prerequisites of a diplomatic dialogue, as independence is. For instance, peace and security are not essential preconditions of diplomacy. Diplomacy can be very active even in wartime: within an alliance, and with neutrals, and between the warring states in order to bring the war to an end. Peace and security are not the same; and though they are bracketed together in the Covenant of the League of Nations and in the U.N. Charter, even there concepts like 'enforcing the peace' and 'military sanctions' clearly illustrate that the maintenance of security may require the capacity and the perceived will to use military force. But peace and security are like independence in that they are also compatible. Every state can work for them without denying them to other states; and diplomacy can aim to establish and maintain them on a universal and collective basis.

Therefore when we say that in an international society or system of states independence, and peace, and security are compatible, we mean that broadly speaking the states which desire these conditions can all attain them at once. Similarly we may say by extension that there is a wide range of issues where the interests of states differ and indeed conflict, but where solutions can be found which both parties find it in their interest to accept. For instance, if we take again the issue of sugar, there is a price at which it is in the interest of the seller to sell and the buyer to buy. Since trade is mutually beneficial, the interests of the buyer and seller are opposed but not incompatible. If all the states in a system, all the political entities in an international society, had only compatible purposes, diplomacy would involve a great deal of hard bargaining, and perhaps some ill feeling between competitors, but there would be no serious threat to peace and order in the international community.

However, in the real world not every state, and certainly not every active political entity, has peaceful and compatible aims and policies. There are at present and always have been a number of states, and of political entities that do not quite have the international position of recognized states, which consider that the world is wrongly ordered and is unjust either in general or in some particular. They do so for a number of reasons. They may have revolutionary governments, or at least governments who consider it their duty to change the way in which other states are governed (e.g., to spread communism, or democracy, or a religion like Islam). Or another state may occupy territory which they consider ought rightfully to be theirs. Or they may demand equal opportunities for trade and expansion which other states monopolize (this was the complaint of Japan between the two world wars). Or they may be rebel movements that wish to set up new and independent states or gain control of existing ones. All these aims and demands, and other similar ones, have been considered legitimate, and indeed heroic and praiseworthy, by different peoples at different times. So far as diplomacy is concerned, what matters is that all of them are *incompatible* with the interests and demands of some other state or states.

There are two great difficulties about incompatible demands. The first is the 'subjectivity' of controversial values. Independence, and peace, and the price of sugar, are for practical purposes objectively definable. Diplomats talking about such matters have no great difficulty in agreeing what is meant, even though concepts like independence and peace are not absolutes but mean rather different things in different contexts. Some incompatible demands are equally definable, especially concrete ones like claims to territory. But a demand for justice, a plea for a wrong to be righted, are based on subjective judgements, on which there is normally no agreement. The state against which the demand is made will probably regard it as unjust, using other criteria which are also controversial. For instance, if we take the dispute between the United Kingdom and Spain about Gibraltar, both sides have criteria of their own, according to which they are in the right. A decision by the International Court that Gibraltar is legally British would not convince the Spaniards; and votes by the General Assembly of the U.N. in favour of Spain have not convinced the British. The second and even greater difficulty about incompatible demands derives from the fact that where a state or political entity feels very strongly about what it considers to be an injustice, it or at least certain of its members tend to resort to violence in order to correct the wrong. This is especially true when the criteria or values on which one state or group bases its claim are not universally accepted. The history of Palestine over the last sixty years is a good illustration of this difficulty.

If peace were to be the supreme goal of all states, and there were to be no recourse to war or other forms of violence in order to right wrongs or to change the world, then only those wrongs could be righted and only those adjustments made which a state could be induced to accept without the use of force. It is true that the values of states change; and that a state may sometimes be persuaded to yield by argument, because its government and people acknowledge the justice of the case brought against it. For instance, imperial states may freely, and without the use of force, grant independence to colonies – as Britain, France, Spain and other countries have done. Or a state may be induced to give way by other member states of the international system applying pressure short of force, such as economic sanctions. But in practice such changes are limited. The renunciation in advance of the use of force in order to right a proclaimed 'injustice' is recognized in practice as a diplomatic formula weighted heavily in favour of the status quo. So peace, the exclusion of violence by one political entity against another, is essentially the policy of satisfied states, weak states and states which consider that the changes they really care about can be achieved by diplomacy and the help of their friends without recourse to violence.

Peace, then, does not mean a condition in which there are no conflicts between the needs, demands and goals of states, for these are always present. It means – in the United Nations Charter, for instance, and in common usage – a condition where states and political entities do not use violence against one another in pursuit of their incompatible goals. War is a highly concentrated and specialized form of violence between states. It is usually on a much larger and deadlier scale than other forms of violence, and is also usually subject to certain rules and conventions, like the treatment of prisoners, which other forms of international violence do not respect. But like other forms of planned and organized violence it is a means to an end. Political entities do not resort to force for pleasure, though some individuals may enjoy the thrill and excitement of violence and war. They resort to force in order to attain a political goal: for instance, in order to correct what they consider an unjust or unfair situation, or to defend what they consider just and right against violence by others.

In order to understand this crucially important aspect of international affairs, and the role which diplomacy can play in it, we must therefore next examine in more detail, first, subjective ideas of justice, and the conflicts to which incompatible ideas of justice give rise; and then the general relation of diplomacy to force.

CHAPTER IV

Diplomacy, Law and Justice

Law is associated in our minds with justice. The blindfolded figure of Justice holding a pair of scales symbolizes the law's intent and its impartiality, and we call a judge a justice. In this sense international law is linked to the quest for international justice, between states and between other organized groups and individuals on the international scene. The quest for institutionalized international justice also involves the attempt to give a legal status to any new and in the eyes of its advocates more just arrangement which may be realized, and to revise the rules of international law accordingly for the future. But international law must be distinguished from the quest for justice, and so must the parts which both play in the diplomatic dialogue.

International law is a vast and subtle subject, about which large numbers of books have been written. We here are concerned with its relation to diplomacy. International law is that body of rules which the states in an international society agree at a given time to observe in their relations with each other, and in the main do observe, and which they thus recognize as having the status of laws. Since there is no supranational executive, these rules are unenforced, except by the power of other states acting individually or collectively. They depend for their executive effectiveness not on consent, as is sometimes claimed, but on their active observance by the member states, particularly the more influential ones. On what corresponds to the legislative side, the conventions and rules of an international society are established, and continually elaborated and modified, by the member states, by means of negotiations between executives in a multilateral dialogue. This body of international rules obviously differs from domestic law, which is enforceable by a sovereign executive and which can be enacted and modified by a sovereign legislature. There are resemblances, of course. International law, like domestic law, is the formulation of the rules, customs and traditions of a society: it sets out what most members of a society consider right and reasonable. Both types of law are formulated in similar language. But much of the mistaken thinking about the role of law in the relations between states comes from transposing ideas, derived from law inside a single state under the authority of a government, to the quite different context of a society of states which recognize no common government.

There are two principal aspects of international law: the regulatory, or the quest for order; and the ethical or normative, involving concepts of justice. The regulatory function is easy to understand. The rules and codes of conduct which international societies observe are in this sense like traffic regulations, designed to maintain order. Because they are in the main observed, they give a pattern of conformity and thus a sense of predictability to the way in which states – and other organizations such as private corporations – behave on the international scene. This in itself is an immense achievement. The alternative to order by consent which these rules make possible would be international chaos. Confusion and unpredictability may be possible where states have little contact, but the members of a society of states require a high degree of order and predictability in their relations if they are to agree to depend on one another to anything like the extent which we now take for granted. Many authorities on international law, as well as many statesmen, have considered that this indispensable regulatory function is a sufficient task for international law, and that a society of states is not nearly closely integrated enough to go beyond this achievement. But as a matter of historical fact, international rules and codes of conduct have contained some elements of the other aspect, the quest for justice and the desire to establish ethical rules and standards at which states should aim. International law, and its equivalent in other such societies, has always been concerned with both mutual advantage and moral scruple.

The spirit of international law as we now know it goes back to Hugo Grotius, the Dutch jurist and diplomat who in the seventeenth century first formulated it for the European society of states in his *De Jure Belli ac Pacis* (the laws of war and peace). He began by establishing the patterns of conformity which regulated the international society of his day – the ways in which European states actually behaved to one another. He then examined the relation of these international practices to tradition, to natural law, to Judeo-Christian revelation and to the many treaties and conventions made by various states which established particular rules. He then suggested where these practices might be modified to make them more rational and more conducive to peace. He related the regulatory to the ethical, looked for principles which would be acceptable both to God and to princes. He aimed to combine material advantages with moral values, and theory with experience. For Grotius as for other jurists of his time, international law was to be 'the harmony of the world'.

From Grotius's day to this, one of the major tasks of diplomacy has been to establish and revise the rules of international society. Usually the practice came first and the law was a formulation of it. But the rules of a developing society of states require constant change. Law in the modern world cannot be an immutable canon like the Ten Commandments, but is rather an ongoing process.

The complex business of modifying international law is not really like the enactment of new legislation inside a state, though many lawyers are anxious to give it that appearance. Trained jurists are needed to formulate the general practices that states agree to observe, as well as to draw up the individual contracts which they enter into in conformity with the general rules. But since there is no government over an international society, the member states themselves must negotiate the formulation of the general rules which order that society, and thereafter the continuous adaptation of those rules to cope with changing circumstances. Each state must also negotiate the individual treaties, agreements and contracts to which it commits itself. There are now enormous numbers of such agreements in force between states, bilateral and multilateral. The United Kingdom and the United States are parties to about 10,000 each; and the treaties registered with the United Nations now fill some thousand volumes. This ongoing process of *the negotiation of the rules of international society between its member states* is one of the great constructive achievements of diplomacy. The number and complexity of these rules, and the continuous need to update them if they are to be effectively observed, ensure that discussion of them occupies a major place in the dialogue between states. The diplomatic dialogue must not only determine the regulatory mechanisms of the society, from the law of the sea and the rights of neutrals to the reporting of cholera; it must also undertake the modification of the principles and the standards which underlie the specific rules.

The rules which Grotius and his European successors formulated into a body of law, and which European statesmen and juridical draftsmen developed and extended, derived their regulatory and practical aspects from enlightened self-interest in the light of experience, and their ethical assumptions and aspirations mainly from Latin Christianity and Roman jurisprudence. They were rooted in the culture and religion of Western Europe. They were an integral part of its diplomatic society (described in Chapter

VIII) in the same way as the rules which we call the international law of the Hellenistic world, for example, were rooted in the culture and experience of Ancient Greece. However, the European society of states expanded far beyond its original West European matrix to encompass the whole world. In the heyday of white dominance, the majority of international lawyers and statesmen ignored the problem of cultural diversity, and simply asserted that international law was applicable only between civilized and Christian peoples of European stock. It was these peoples who made the writ of their international law run globally, and the few non-European states like the Ottoman Empire and Japan who were accepted into European international society in the second half of the nineteenth century agreed to conform to its rules. Similarly, the Hellenistic states after the death of Alexander were governed by men who accepted Greek culture and values and ignored the other cultural traditions of their subject peoples.

Our contemporary global society of states is not culturally homogeneous. It now has a majority of states whose peoples have other cultural traditions than those in which modern international law developed. The diplomatic dialogue is therefore faced with a major new problem: how to adapt international law to a multicultural world, so that states with different traditions and aspirations consent to it and observe it. The regulatory side, which is concerned with self-interest, has not proved unduly difficult. Many international regulations are matters of administrative convenience or general practical advantage; and regulatory rules, even when they involve serious conflicts of interest, are well within the scope of the traditional diplomatic dialogue. The specific issues which line up states on one side or another in negotiations about the revision of the rules of international society, like the law of the sea or military security, are not usually cultural but economic or strategic. Most international jurists who in recent years have discussed the process of the revision of international law have concentrated on these aspects of the negotiations. Thus Professor R. P. Anand characteristically writes: 'In fact, the attitudes of the Western countries, as well as those of the Asian and African nations, whether toward the traditional principles of customary law, international organizations or newly developing areas of international law, are determined as always by their views of their interests. It is this conflict of interests of the newly independent states and the Western Powers, rather than their differences in their cultures and religions, which has affected the course of international law at the present juncture.'

So long as states are concerned with revising the regulatory side of international law, they approach the task in the same way, and diplomacy is well suited to the task. But when states move from problems of order to problems of justice, the issues become harder to resolve. On the one hand there are deep cultural differences about what societies traditionally have considered just, which are likely to come increasingly to the fore as Western influence on the rest of the world diminishes. These differences have to be accommodated alongside the changes in men's opinions everywhere about what is just. There is also the basic difficulty that conflicting concepts of justice are incompatible, in the sense explained in Chapter III, and moreover are much less susceptible to compromise and bargaining than conflicting interests. It is not surprising that the results of international negotiation about justice have been much less satisfactory than those about order.

Most member states of an international society want certain conditions to prevail like independence, peace and order, and the diplomatic dialogue has no difficulty in establishing whether these conditions prevail or not in a given case. But states, and individuals who think about international affairs, also make value judgements about what is right and just; these opinions differ sharply from one another on many issues, and there is a large contentious area where there is no general international agreement about what can be labelled right or wrong. The attempt to enforce these differing standards internationally is often called the quest for justice. We may accept the term. But before we look at the relevance of diplomacy to justice, and how far justice can be obtained by diplomatic negotiation, we need to see more clearly what the concept means.

Men hold differing opinions about what is just, even at the same time and in the same community, and certainly in different communities and at different times. Not only do ideas of justice vary: they are continually changing. Among the most powerful forces making for change within every society or state, and also within every system or society of states, is the continual mutation of men's opinions about what is just. The subject covers such a great range that the theoretical understanding of justice, the attempt to put the criteria or yardsticks of what is just into categories, is very complex. The first comprehensive attempt was made by Aristotle. He produced a formula which is useful in international affairs as it is in the relations between citizens in a community: that 'injustice arises when equals are treated unequally and when unequals are treated equally'. Of course this does not tell us what is meant by equals: but equality is a more mathematical concept than justice and therefore an easier thing to measure and for diplomats to agree about.

If we turn to the more concrete aspects of the problem, we may say that justice requires some authority to enforce it. If in any community there are no rules, no means of deciding and enforcing what is fair, if there is anarchy in its literal sense, then might will prevail, whether it seems to most people right or not; and that is not justice. An authority here means some person or

group of persons, some body or organization which is generally accepted in
the community as having the right to say what is just and whose judgements
will normally be implemented without the need to enforce them; but which is
in a position to order its judgements to be enforced if they are not carried out
voluntarily. In a civilized community, which is not a mere tyranny, the
power to judge and the power to enforce judgements must rest mainly on
consent. This is true of a society of individual states, as it is of a society of
individual men.

In the days of the Vikings and other wild peoples, when the king was little
more than the leader of a band of warriors and did not have the authority to
dispense justice according to his judgement, two other ways of tackling the
problem were evolved. The first was trial by combat, or by ordeal; and the
second was the judgement of a man by his peers. Both are still highly
relevant to an international society of independent states where by definition
there is no overall authority.

Trial by combat seems to most of us nowadays utterly different from
justice between citizens of a state. Whatever the rights and wrongs of a
quarrel, surely in personal combat – whether a formal duel or a clash between
two groups – it was the better fighter who won, not the juster cause? In the
main, so it doubtless was. But in the ages of faith there was a belief that God
would be on the side of the just cause; and so a man's strength was greater if
he knew he was in the right. (Biological research shows that the same is true
of animals. A squirrel defending the nuts he himself has buried will perform
miracles of bravery; but when the same squirrel goes raiding, he does not
fight nearly so well.) Certainly when we move outside the state with its
duly constituted authority into the international area, we find many people
who regard combat, the use of force, as the only way to right wrongs, or at
least to advertise wrongs and touch the conscience of mankind. The idea that
there are just wars as well as unjust ones has played a cardinal role in the
European states system. This propensity to resort to force in order to obtain
justice raises several issues for diplomacy which need careful consideration.

The idea of touching the conscience of mankind derives from the other
method of trying to secure justice without any authority to pronounce a
verdict and enforce it: judgement by a man's peers. It was held that if you
took twelve good yeomen and true to judge a yeoman, or twelve barons to
judge a quarrel between two barons, their judgement would be in line with
what such people consider fair and just. It was the community speaking,
less likely to be biased than a single voice, even that of the king. This is the
important idea of diffusing authority rather than concentrating it. In relations
between communities where there is no kind of supernational authority, can

authority be diffused in a similar way? Can wrongs be righted, justice obtained, by appeal to some international and impartial tribunal? Many people, perhaps not those most passionately concerned with a particular issue, believe that this is possible.

We should note two separate ways of obtaining such an international judgement. On one hand it is possible to set up a committee of jurists to establish what international law, or a treaty if there was one, actually says or implies. On the other it is possible to constitute a group of states or of eminent individuals who will decide not only what international law, such as it is, may say, but also such questions as equity and new ideas of justice; and of course also expediency, politics being the art of the possible. One way leads to bodies like the Court of International Justice of the Hague; the other to bodies like the Security Council of the United Nations.

Diplomacy is closely involved with both procedures. The preparation and presentation by a state of its case before an international court or tribunal is a diplomatic proceeding. The principal experts involved will be professional lawyers, but are none the less envoys of and spokesmen for their governments. Moreover, foreign offices have legal advisers, and many other professional diplomats have legal training. Further, where there is a court case, the litigants will try to settle out of court rather than go through its formal procedures if they think they can strike as good a bargain; and the business of settling issues out of court is precisely the job of diplomacy. And since an international court has no enforcement procedure, the question of implementing the verdict is also a matter for diplomacy. With the Security Council the case is much clearer. Made up of diplomatic envoys from five permanent large states and a rotating number of smaller ones, it is itself the most developed example of formal and continuous world diplomacy now in existence.

Both these procedures might work better than they do if there was any general agreement about what constitutes justice between states, or between a state and groups opposed to it. But at present this is simply not the case. Not only do the subjective ideas of individuals and communities differ very fundamentally, but they also continually change in several ways.

First there is the category of external activities. Men's attitudes towards an individual state can alter because it includes certain territories, or behaves in certain ways towards other states, that were previously thought legitimate but with the passage of time come to seem unjust or no longer acceptable. For instance, a state may include ethnic minorities who want to secede, or colonies; or it may sell goods below the cost of production or refuse to sell them for political reasons. Colonialism and dumping were not always considered unjust. Questions of secession and colonies may conveniently be included in the category of external relations, because they affect the question of where other states, or international society collectively, consider that boundaries of a state should run, and what territories should be outside it.

The second category concerns the domestic or internal activities of states. Changing views of what constitutes justice also mean that a state within its own boundaries which are not in dispute, may begin to practise, or merely continue, policies which have become so out of tune with the times that the 'injustice' shocks and outrages opinion elsewhere to the point where other states take sanctions against that state, or perhaps intervene in its internal affairs. The classic example in the European society of states was the suppression of the slave trade (which led to frequent British naval interventions to achieve it) and then of domestic slavery, which had not seemed very shocking in the eighteenth century but came to seem so in the nineteenth. Human rights in communist and other dictatorships, and apartheid in Southern Africa, are modern examples. Since the Soviet government began there have been groups of individuals who have demanded international sanctions against its internal behaviour; and arguments at the United Nations in favour of sanctions against, or the exclusion, of South Africa or (formerly) Communist China have mostly been based on the unacceptability of the *domestic* policies of these governments.

A third and more radical change in attitudes towards other states in an international society comes when men question what categories of political entity should be accepted as members of that society.

New criteria of justice call for the formation of new states by the splitting up or amalgamation of old ones, and sometimes for a fundamental rearrangement of the whole structure of power. It is worth noting that over half the present members of the United Nations are states that had no independent existence at the end of World War Two when the United Nations was first set up. Such new states are weaker than the old empires, and some are tiny; but there are many more of them, and the midwife of these new members of the family of states has been a change in what is considered internationally just and legitimate. However, fusion occurs as well as fission. The demands in the nineteenth century for the creation of German and Italian national states, the demands today for the formation of a single federal Western Europe and a United Arab Republic, all challenge the moral authority of certain existing states to continue as they are, and aim to create new and much stronger powers within the society of states. This challenge to the moral authority of existing states in the name of a principle such as nationalism corresponds to similar challenges in the names of other crusading ideologies.

The wider effects of ideology on diplomacy require a chapter to themselves, and are discussed in Chapter VI. Here we need to note that prevailing standards or criteria in an international society about what is just and legitimate sometimes alter so radically that certain kinds of state gradually become ostracized from the diplomatic dialogue and in extreme cases may be overthrown by organized international pressure, including force if necessary, in favour of states organized on a more acceptable basis.

Thus changing ideas of justice affect and gradually modify *international legitimacy*. This is a key concept in the relations between independent states and international bodies. If these relations and the diplomatic dialogue by which they are conducted are to function smoothly, it is necessary to establish which government has the right to administer a certain territory and what obligations that government accepts; and also what are the rights and duties of international organizations like the United Nations. As ideas of right and justice change, what was regarded as legitimate and proper comes to seem illegitimate: that is, unacceptable and unjust. Examples from the European states system are given in Chapter VIII.

Earlier this century, self-determination became established as the principal criterion of legitimacy; and with many exceptions in practice, it was held that in disputed territories a plebiscite or election was needed to indicate the will of the majority. Today new ideas about what constitutes legitimacy are beginning to oust self-determination, in Eastern Europe and elsewhere. Movements of Popular Liberation demand recognition as 'the only legitimate government' of a territory they do not control and where there is no convincing evidence that they would be the people's free choice. Tomorrow it may be considered illegitimate for a state to permit pollution of the environment or an increase of its population to the point where these internal activities impose a burden on other members of international society. Already the criteria of international legitimacy enshrined in the United Nations Charter in 1945 have in some cases become obsolete, or their application has become more limited. Article 2(7) states that the United Nations shall not have jurisdiction in any matters which are wholly or mainly the internal affair of a member state: but that limitation is now regularly set aside in cases where newer criteria such as human rights or racial non-discrimination have acquired a greater legitimacy in the eyes of the majority of member states.

Advocates of a new legitimacy or a new standard of international justice have not usually been prepared to wait until the passage of time converts the 'unjust' to their way of thinking. Means of coercion short of war, at the disposal of international society, like boycotts and economic sanctions, are regularly demanded; and the just war is soon advocated by the more convinced. The conviction that neither peace nor independence is as important as justice has a long and respectable pedigree. The trouble is that there are honest and deeply held differences of opinion about what constitutes justice, as we have seen, and a change in men's opinion can call any international legitimacy or recognized right in question. Moreover, it is obvious that if any state or group is to be allowed to resort to violence merely because it declares that the aims for which it is fighting seem to it just, extreme disorder will result. Therefore those powers who want to preserve international order have turned, and are today increasingly turning, to the diplomatic method of trying to establish agreed criteria for legitimacy and for measuring what is just, in place of unilateral declarations.

When men's ideas of what is just are rapidly changing, what objective yardstick can diplomacy set up about justice in the international field? How can this emotional and subjective issue be turned to practical use? Here the United Nations Charter is not much help. If priority is given to peace, and if also each state recognized as an established member of international society is to have its independence preserved, that is if it is to be allowed to decide for itself what is just – which are the two basic ideas of the United Nations Charter – then new ideas about justice will only prevail when they are accepted by those states which stand to lose by them. The governments concerned are unlikely to welcome such changes, especially if it means the disintegration of their state, though they are usually able to accept them if they are merely injurious to the interest of the state and do not portend its disintegration. Major changes such as decolonization can take place by mutual consent without resort to violence. But if there are to be revisions of international law by 'consensus' without the consent of certain states who stand to lose, followed by sanctions and even violence to suppress what were legitimate and established rights, the desire to establish new standards of justice can become the enemy of peace, as it was in the past. A great deal of diplomatic activity, both collectively at the United Nations and directly between governments, has been directed towards extending the ideas in the Charter establishing certain basic human rights which the states that want to belong to international society must observe, even though they are matters of domestic jurisdiction. These legalistic definitions are important, but they are inadequate for the resolution of international conflict, and also dangerous because they are charged with emotion. Diplomatic activity has therefore concentrated in practice on the alternative to trial by combat mentioned above, namely judgement by a man's peers.

Most states value membership of international society. They do not want to be, and usually cannot afford to be, ostracized; and so they have what the American Declaration of Independence calls a decent respect for the opinions of mankind, even though they may not share them. A state can in fact be judged not only by a court of international law, which usually has little effect and in any case may not be able to deal with internal matters: a state can also be judged by its peers. The government of South Africa is in no doubt about the opinion of mankind about apartheid, or the Soviet Union about emigration. These are particularly difficult cases, both deeply rooted in the philosophy and practice of the régimes. How useful, in such cases, is the diffused authority of judgement by a state's peers, whether expressed in a United Nations resolution or through the direct contacts of bilateral diplomacy? The answer is that over a period this moral authority of international society does have some effect, even though it cannot be enforced like law inside a state. Even the greatest powers want certain advantages, especially in the economic field, which may be denied them if they do not conform. On the whole there is today probably enough movement towards conformity with the changed opinions of mankind to prevent the quest for justice becoming the enemy of peace. There are exceptions, but they are manageable.

Thus diplomatic activity does not merely operate in favour of securing the observance of new standards of justice. States are also usually concerned with peace, and always with independence. Therefore the diplomatic dialogue continues to indicate the limits beyond which the quest for justice endangers other important values: that is, what exceptions to a new legitimacy are necessary. Diplomacy also tends to sift out ideas of justice which, however noisily proclaimed by a minority, do not in fact reflect the opinion of mankind, or at least not of a majority of states including the more powerful. In this way diplomacy through its omnilateral debates and its bilateral exchanges, helps to determine what is the opinion of mankind, as well as to bring the influence of that opinion to bear on the conduct of member states in an international society.

So in the field of law and justice we see diplomacy, as so often, indicating the limits of the possible. Diplomacy is interested in achieving and making do with the adjustments that can be obtained by bargaining and compromise without resort to force or the disruption of international society. Adjustment is a valuable concept: related on the one hand to what is just, and on the other to the concept of a balance, aiming at solutions which are not absolute but shifting, relying on persuasion, and like all diplomacy accommodating international society to the winds of change. Those who champion this or that demand for justice chafe at the restraint imposed by the diplomatic approach, as they do at the similar restraints imposed by democratic methods within a state. When we remember that there is no authority in international affairs capable of enforcing decisions, like the power of a state within its domestic jurisdiction, it is remarkable how much has been achieved internationally by diplomatic methods. These adjustments by persuasion are sometimes aptly called the brokerage of the system. Brokerage of this kind is more conducive to generally accepted norms of justice than the ever-present alternative of a resort to force.

CHAPTER V

Power and Persuasion

In this chapter I wish to examine the relation between diplomacy and the power of the states which conduct the dialogue. Inside a state, as we saw in the last chapters, there are laws and governmental instructions; there is a general disposition of the subjects or citizens to obey these; and machinery for their enforcement where they are disobeyed. In the international arena, where there is no common government to speak or act with this generally recognized authority, states speak with such authority as their ability and willingness to act may give them. Such ability and willingness derive ultimately from their power. This is the case both when they speak individually and when they speak in association with other states in the system. The extent to which one state can persuade another to act or refrain from acting in a certain way depends on the power which each of them commands, including the will to use it, and the extent to which other states support them – that is, lend their power to one side or the other. In the last resort an individual state, or a group of states acting together, or perhaps the collectivity of states acting in the name of international society itself, may use economic pressure and finally military force to make another state behave in a certain way. That is why in the earlier period of the European states system, war was called the ultimate argument, the ultimate reasoning, of kings. But force is only the ultimate resort. Until that extreme point is reached, or at least until a state resorts to economic sanctions, its ability to persuade others will depend not on its power in any absolute and quantified sense, but on how other states perceive its power and its will to use it. Diplomatic persuasion is therefore not a matter of mathematical calculation; it is not an exact science; it remains a matter of human skills and judgements.

The power of a state is made up of a number of elements, some of which cannot be exactly measured. What a state's neighbours perceive to be its power takes into account such things as the numbers and skills of its population, the extent, resources and strategic location of its territory, its wealth and productive capacity including the sources from which it derives its wealth and how far it controls them, its internal organization, public attitudes and the competence of its government, its existing and potential military capacity, and other more intangible but essential factors like its international aims and the degree of its determination to achieve them. These perceptions may vary. A state's neighbours are likely to perceive its power somewhat differently, and the reality may change faster than their perceptions. But states in a system must exercise constant vigilance; so even when information was much more haphazardly gathered and slowly transmitted than today, statesmen kept themselves reasonably well informed on such vital matters. They were aware that their ability to persuade, their need to yield to persuasion, depended on their power relative to that of other states, as perceived by themselves and by the other actors in the system.

We now need to look at: 1) different views about the relation between power and diplomacy; 2) the relation between diplomacy and the ability to constrain states, including the ultimate argument of war; 3) the role of alliances, and the development from alliances between individual states in a system into a more general compact or league, which exercises the collective authority of most of the states in an international society by their acting together in that society's name; 4) the connection between the diplomatic dialogue and deceit, which is also a form of pressure; and 5) the part which diplomacy can play in restoring more cooperative and less dangerous relations between states when these have slipped or seem likely to slip towards the ultimate arguments of constraint and war.

Frederick the Great once declared that diplomacy without power was like an orchestra without a score. The issue to which this saying of his refers is one of great significance for the understanding of bargaining and negotiation in international politics. Frederick's view of this crucial relationship deserves close attention partly because it was the considered thought of the statesman who successfully asserted Prussia's claims to be one of Europe's great powers and who was perhaps the most discerning practitioner of war and diplomacy in the eighteenth century. The view he expressed is, however, also of continuing relevance because it still commands wide acceptance as an accurate account of what calls the tune in international politics, if tune there is to be.

What Frederick had in mind was that the diplomatic dialogue of his day was concerned with negotiating adjustments to the continual changes in the power of the independent but closely involved states of Europe. These states

saw themselves as preserving their independence by means of a just balance
of power. As some states grew stronger and others weaker, corresponding
adjustments needed to be made in order to maintain the equilibrium. These
adjustments might involve transfers of territory, but were also concerned
with the stationing of troops, the rearrangement of alliances, political
guarantees and economic privileges. It was usually possible to effect by
diplomatic negotiation those adjustments which power could, and did, compel by military means if negotiation failed. But other policy aims, which were
beyond the power of a state to insist on, could not be achieved in this way.
In other words, when diplomacy addressed itself to the changing reality of
power it could produce concerted music; otherwise, when it dealt with the
demands of states unrelated to their power, it produced a babel of incoherent
sound.

Circumstances have changed since Frederick made his dictum. The
closely knit European states system has become worldwide, and the borders
of states more fixed than in the eighteenth century. Furthermore, in
Frederick's day war was not considered morally wrong or unduly damaging to
civilization. Pitched battles fought by trained soldiers and sailors were much
less destructive than the embittered wars of religion of the preceding age or
the appalling destructiveness of war in the twentieth century. Today 'hot
war' has become less acceptable, at least in more developed states, and even
economic sanctions begin to seem unduly costly to them. The diplomatic
dialogue between non-communist states is largely about economic and
financial problems, and especially about how to organize a continuous and
orderly modification of existing international arrangements to reflect changes
in economic strength. Between communist and non-communist powers the
dialogue is mainly concerned with how far the economic and technological
power of developed states shall be translated into actual military capacity,
including strategic facilities outside those states' borders; and to what
extent it is possible by mutual agreement to devote a larger proportion of that
power to more constructive uses. But today, as in the eighteenth century,
if the orchestra is to produce concerted music it must address itself to the
changing reality of power and to the adjustments which this requires.

There is a wide range of alternative assertions to Frederick's about where
diplomacy, as the voice of persuasion, fits into the political operations of a
states system. Frederick's observation is of course not the same thing as the
more cynical claim that the capacity and the will to use force is what 'really'
influences the relations of states, while diplomacy serves as its instrument,
registering and clothing its verdicts. Another such assertion is the familiar
argument that because diplomacy is persuasive talk taking place in situations
whose outcomes are said to be determined by the balance of armed force, it

is therefore always a deceitful activity. According to this view, diplomacy is not the instrument by which shifts in the balance of power are adjusted by non-combatant professionals, but a mannered device used by wily persuaders to obtain unjustified concessions by camouflaging the facts, and one which therefore seeks to distort and alter rather than register 'the realities of the situation'. There is also a well-established body of support for the quite opposite view, which denies that diplomacy is either the mere handmaiden of force or a deliberate blurring of its dictates, but sees it as a fully developed alternative to the domination of power in shaping international politics. Here the argument hinges on the belief that diplomatic negotiation is, or could become, an attractive alternative for states to the politics of force, because the compromise adjustments obtainable through negotiation, though often less than the fruits of military victory, are more economical and more certain than can be had by resorting to such a costly, risky and arbitrary adventure as war. The distinction between 'is' and 'could be', though crucial, is seldom clearly stated, especially by those opposed to the sanction of force, and the elision between actuality and possibility is perhaps typical of this point of view. It draws strength from the awareness of statesmen that diplomacy can be a creative thing, which is able to summon up resources of ingenuity engendered by the dialogue itself to resolve what began as a simple confrontation. It does not contradict Frederick's dictum, but is incompatible with the views that diplomacy is merely the register of force or a figleaf of minor concessions over it.

No one of these formulations is sufficient by itself. The real world of international affairs, the actual operations of a society of states, are visibly too complex for such simplistic concepts. As generally phrased, such formulations suffer from being too neat and tidy; and more fundamentally from being too exclusive, and each too inclined to notice only the evidence which confirms its own viewpoint. Most damaging of all, these rival conceptions are flawed by a common fault: their authors start from some purpose of their own, such as the desire to exclude power from the political relations between states, and ignore the requirement to keep their arguments and their hopes within the field of political realities which determines the scope of diplomacy.

To approach the issue of power and persuasion, not abstractly or within a state but in the context of a states system, we must extend some of the arguments used in earlier chapters. We saw that the primary demand which states make on the international world of their day is the recognition of their independence, which is the basis on which the diplomatic dialogue between them by its very nature rests. Every state looks first to its own internal capacities for the political and other resources necessary to safeguard this most vital of all vital interests. Once this first requirement is reasonably met, states also wish to rely on their own power as far as possible to look after their other interests; and these grow or – more slowly and painfully – shrink as the power of a state increases or declines. At the same time, however, states usually look to their relations with other states and to the states system itself and its institutions, including international law, alliances, aid and the rest, as the means by which their demands and claims can be recognized and fulfilled. In the present state of international society, and in the states systems of the past, states do not expect that the international community will secure for them all that they wish for (since they wish for incompatible things, this would by definition be impossible). They know that they themselves must go out after what they want. In practice they find the system useful because it legitimizes many of the actions governments consider necessary to defend and further their interests – including in certain circumstances the use of force – and provides a sufficiently flexible setting for the pursuit of these interests. In this sense the balance of power, international law, diplomacy (especially collective diplomacy) and the rules of war can be seen as among the arrangements or mechanisms of the setting which member states of a system accept and operate together.

The price of a system comprised of a number of independences, a situation where no hegemonic power can lay down the law to the rest, is a world where no power is strong enough to enjoy absolute security: a world where insecurity is therefore endemic and in varying degrees universal, and not merely accidental or caused by the actions of evil, aggressive and disgruntled men. This permanent and structural insecurity, the constantly shifting balance which is characteristic of all states systems including our own, combined with that diversity of political and economic interests which seems to be an inescapable consequence of many simultaneous independences, produces the expectation that the meeting of these divergent interests will produce clashes as well as harmonies of wills. The mere coexistence of numbers of states does not hold out even the promise, let alone the guarantee, of universal concord.

Open divergence as well as convergence of interests and wills is also the price of freedom within the framework of a single state. Free individuals inside a state will agree about some things, but are not expected to agree about everything all the time. The attempt to influence others is the very stuff of political bargaining and indeed of all political activity. The significant difference which gives such a unique identity to the arena of foreign policy lies in the fact that, unlike the setting within a state which is synonymous with law, the clash of interests in a states system is unmediated by a common government and to a much lesser extent by law or custom. To grasp this cardinal fact is already to move far in the direction of understanding why the dialectic of wills among independent states is so intimately linked with the power at their disposal, including the use of armed force. In circumstances where there is no authority above the sovereignty of states to govern the clash of rival demands and few generally accepted rules by which disputes are to be settled according to law or equity, then power restrained by prudence and used within the limits of self-interest is the *ultima ratio regum*, the final argument of those governments capable of compelling the ones which cannot otherwise be persuaded.

That the use of violence to force a decision can sometimes be highly effective – in spite of the risks, the costs in life and expenditure of resources, material damage and so forth – is confirmed by the history of war. However, it is incorrect to conceive of war as the only example of the deployment of force. The British military historian Liddell-Hart stressed that the most successful use of armed strength is where its mere existence and deployment in the right place is sufficient to bring about the looked-for changes in an opponent's or enemy's conduct. This is an instance of the general proposition that the most economical and thus the most successful use of power occurs when the least violence takes place. In an ideally sensitive international system, superior armed force would not have to be deployed beyond its peacetime dispositions at all: its existence would be enough to bring about the adjustments which are 'justified' by the changing power of the states in the system. But of course no system, no balance of power, is as sensitive and adjustable as that. The rules of every known system provide for the 'deployment in the right place' and indeed the actual use of armed force. Let us leave aside for the moment the important cases of governments which disregard the premise of a society of states that force will be used only when negotiation has failed to procure an adjustment – governments which turn to a foreign war to deal with intractable domestic problems, or decide that successful military operations will enable them to confront their opponents with a *fait accompli*, and so extract from the states system a grudging acceptance of what could not be negotiated by diplomacy or awarded by the collective machinery of the system. War has a recognized place within the logic of an international system, as the ultimate means of effecting the adjustments required by the changing balance of power when other methods of persuasion have failed. So war, within limits, has been established as an instrument of policy available to independent states, and in spite of its obvious disadvantages is tolerated though not approved by international society today. And each individual state has normally honoured as heroic and glorious those of its citizens who voluntarily accept the risks and perils of war on its behalf. But war is at best a dangerous and destructive business. All international societies have therefore sought to control and regulate it, and to limit as far as possible the damage which it causes both to the fabric of international society and to the combatant states. And in fact the 'profession of arms', rooted in force though it is, has shown itself capable of great refinement. The emergence of war as a controlled conflict between states is in all known systems a story of progressive disengagement from mere barbarian bloodletting towards a commitment to use force only in certain ways. In the European system which we have inherited, the *jus ad bellum* regulated the right to go to war, and prescribed the circumstances in which recourse to compulsion was and was not legitimate. The *jus in bello* formulated the rules for the actual conduct of warfare, some of which had developed out of the traditions of medieval chivalry. In Europe as in other societies of states discipline, restraint towards the wounded and prisoners, observance of truces, the rights of non-combatants and other similar limitations have been recognized by warring states; until finally war comes to be governed by elaborate rules negotiated through the diplomatic dialogue and covering everything from the wearing of identifying uniforms to the immunity of those not engaged in the fighting including neutral states. The laws of war have played an important part in the overall development of international law.

These attempts to control the resort by states to force, and to make it a manageable part of the system, have been partially successful, but no more. The passions unleashed by war have often swept away many – though rarely all – of the regulations designed to limit it. In periods of high civilization – periods, some would say, more civilized than our own – the more limited the objective of a state in a war, the more likely it would be to observe the rules and conventions of warfare, and the more open it would remain to the mitigating effects of diplomacy. But the more ideological the war, and the more high-minded the principles for which the combatants claimed they were fighting, the more cruel and ruthless it became.

The most impressive attempt to think through the function of the resort to force as an instrument of state policy within a diplomatic system based on an equilibrium of power is that of the German military theorist Clausewitz, whose ideas grew out of his experience of the Napoleonic Wars. 'War is an act of violence,' he observed, 'intended to compel our opponent to fulfill our will.' But the violence was the handmaiden of a foreign policy objective which to be rational must be commensurate with the state's power. War, he claimed, 'is not merely a political act, but a political instrument, a continuation of political negotiation, an implementation of it by other means'. In other words, force is an additional ingredient which you could inject into your diplomatic argument if you thought that doing so would gain you your objective, and which you could withdraw from the argument once it ceased to serve your purpose. Clausewitz sought to establish the full meaning of war as a device created by states to settle non-negotiable issues between them, as a corrective to the view that the use of force, at least on the scale and with the objectives adopted by Napoleon, indicated the breakdown not only of 'normal' peaceful relations between the states involved but the dislocation of the entire states system. By arguing that, in the circumstances of life between states, war, however brutal and brutalizing, fulfilled none the less an important political function which provided it with a *raison d'être*, he underlined the continuity and overarching reality of the European states system.

With the 'reason' or at least the 'rationale' of war thus identified, it becomes impossible to maintain the simple and misleading image which portrays war on the one hand as mere violence and as the rupture of political relations, standing in polar opposition to diplomacy on the other hand which is seen as bargaining free from the pressures of compulsion. Given the framework of the states system, war and diplomacy, though in a sense alternative methods of adjusting to reality, are linked to such an extent and in so many ways that one cannot give a full account of the meaning of either without dwelling at length on its relations with an acute awareness of the other. War and diplomacy are inseparably joined under the common heading of means by which states, in pursuit of their interests, bring their power to bear on one another as actual or prospective allies and enemies, and indeed as partners or rivals in trade and commerce. Just as war, the concentrated and disciplined use of armed force to achieve political ends, has been and still is one instrument by which states seek to persuade one another, so that in such cases compulsion is the means of persuasion, so diplomacy also is a general means of persuasion, which takes account of and reflects the pressures of all the relevant influences including the existence of armed forces and the willingness and capacity of governments to use them.

But important as it is to recognize the unbroken line which links the persuasiveness of force in war to the influence of threats and actual use of force in the business of negotiation, one should guard against the temptation to overlook what are after all differences of enormous moral and practical significance. To say that war has its 'reason' or 'logic' in the patiently evolved structure of a never-ending dialogue between the actors of a society of states does not mean or imply that war is the same thing as diplomacy, any more than the fact that diplomacy has to take account of the threat and use of force means that it is the same thing as war.

Let us suppose that the states of an international society were one day to negotiate a fully effective agreement to abolish the resort to force by individual members as a means of adjustment between them, in such a way that the collective pressures of the system – that is, the effective power of enough of its members acting together – were manifestly always sufficient to deter any group of states from resorting to force. Or let us say that every state in a system possessed such a nuclear arsenal that involvement in war would mean its own certain and total destruction. Frederick's observation does not mean that in such circumstances diplomacy would lose all coherence and nobody would agree to anything. The diplomatic dialogue has to deal with all forms of agreement or conflict of interests; and war, the use of armed force to realize or defend something of value to a state, to effect or prevent a given adjustment, is only the extreme expression of conflicts of interest between states. If this extreme recourse were eliminated, other forms of pressure would remain. The nature and tasks of diplomacy would still exist, established by the character of the states system in which the relations between members are based on power, and in which as power shifts the elements of insecurity and conflict are inevitable. It cannot be expected of the diplomatic dialogue between independent states that it will transform international relations to the point of abolishing the very divergences of interest which first give rise to the need for continuous negotiation. The most it can achieve is to find acceptable compromises, where necessary by introducing other inducements. Diplomacy is neither the simple casuistry of force, nor is it a guaranteed technique for solving by negotiation the conflicts of states without resort to it.

We must now consider the significance of collaboration and alliances in the relation between power and persuasion in international affairs. A member of a states system does not deal with each member in isolation. On any matter on which certain states agree, it pays them not to act alone, but in association. Even in the simplest and loosest systems, states which have no formal alliance but share a common interest will normally collaborate to attain or protect it, pooling their power and their efforts of persuasion for this purpose. States make limited bargains on different issues with various other states as occasion warrants. For instance, at the time of writing the British and Soviet governments are in fairly detailed agreement on the changes which they wish to see introduced in the law of the sea, and they work together to achieve these, though they disagree on many other subjects. From this collaboration it is a short step for one state to support another friendly state's interest, which it does not share but which does not harm it, in return for reciprocal support by the other state on an issue of importance to itself. The calculation of what is a reasonable *quid pro quo*, given the importance of not upsetting the other states whose collaboration or goodwill is also needed on other issues, and then arranging the bargain, is the common business of diplomacy, as it is of many aspects of political life within a state. A longer and more important step is taken when two or more states find that they have a number of interests in common and particularly when they value each other's well-being and power as helping them to ward off some common threat. They may then agree to support each other on a more permanent basis; and they formulate this agreement in a contract or treaty. Such treaties, especially where they concern military support against an actual or potential common enemy, are known as alliances.

Treaties of alliance, especially those with military clauses and therefore concerned with the use of force, are not by nature permanent. They are designed to deal with a specific situation; as and when that situation changes, so will the interests of the different signatories. But a state must know what other states it can count on, for how long and over what issues, both in negotiation and if necessary in war. More especially, its own military arrangements will partly depend on those of its allies. Therefore treaties of alliance are usually very specific about how long they are to remain valid and just what military obligations each party to the contract assumes. In order to counteract the eroding pressures of constantly changing interests – the pressures of a highly mobile balance of power – all sorts of devices have been used to give alliances greater reliability. These devices have ranged from garrisons of the stronger allies on the territory of the weaker through dynastic marriages between ruling families to solemn oaths, ideological declarations and cultural exchanges. British, and by inheritance American, diplomacy has traditionally been especially sensitive to the danger that alliances may outlive their usefulness, that an alliance designed to restore the balance of power at one stage may disturb it at the next when relative strengths of the states in the system have changed. The tendency to terminate obligations to allies at short notice has earned Britain the epithet '*perfide Albion*'.

Limited and modifiable alliances and counter-alliances no doubt helped to preserve the independence of states in a system, which is the primary interest of states, and to further the individual interests of the parties. But they did not prevent war. In order to preserve peace as well, some statesmen and thinkers have therefore supported a permanent league or alliance of well-intentioned states, who would sign a covenant with each other to stop any state that pursued its interests by resorting to force. Such was the 'King's Peace' in ancient Greece after a succession of wars between changing alliances; such was Kant's draft treaty for perpetual peace; and such was the Covenant of the League of Nations after the nightmare of World War One. This type of permanent multilateral contract or league for peace is a special form of diffused hegemony, based on the expectation that the combination of persuasion and deterrence so organized would make a resort to force too dangerous for a challenger to undertake, and therefore unnecessary for the league. Such leagues have always come as the culmination of long diplomatic experiment in the construction and use of alliances. But though they have taken the form of a quasi-universal alliance, and have usually been the extension of a victorious wartime coalition (e.g., the Holy Alliance of 1815, the League of Nations of 1919, the United Nations of 1945), statesmen like Woodrow Wilson and thinkers like Kant saw their particular leagues as a new kind of diplomatic commitment, not to the individual interests of the signatories but to the common interests of mankind. The most specific commitment was to oppose, by collective force if necessary, the resort by any individual state to the ultimate argument of kings, namely war. The intimate link between power and persuasion remained intact.

There is some justification for the opinion that in spite of the League and the United Nations, twentieth-century diplomacy has been unduly concerned with the negotiation and management of what may be called private alliances and too little concerned with the system as a whole. This criticism is not so much directed at the conviction of many states that they must ensure themselves against the pressures of hostile powers by protective associations with like-minded states, or in other words private alliances, rather than trust to the omnilateral league of the day to protect them. In the actual circumstances that is understandable enough. The complaint of these critics is rather that statesmen, concentrating on their private alliances, did not pay enough attention to managing the relations between the rival blocks and groupings or give diplomacy the scope which it needs to make the international society function adequately. In fact the effective management of an alliance, and the maintenance of a sufficient degree of coherence between the inevitᵤᵤly somewhat divergent interests of its members, entails a vast amount of continuous negotiation and compromise. As a result, the diplomatic dialogue in the cold war after World War Two was dominated by relations within alliances. Before the First World War statesmen were genuinely anxious to maintain an overall balance of power in Europe, but nevertheless devoted more time to managing relations within the opposed groupings of the triple alliance and the triple *entente* than they did to managing relations between the two alliances, which became increasingly inflexible and distant. This was even more strikingly the case in the years of intense Soviet–Western hostility after 1945. Cold war is a useful phrase to describe the climate of relations between the blocs or alliances of that time because it emphasizes the absence of normal diplomatic contacts and their subordination to an intense arms race, ideological rhetoric and mutual incomprehension. The cold war meant that diplomacy at the centre of the states system was 'on ice' and could not sustain a meaningful dialogue because the positions of the two alliances were fixed too far apart. In contrast to this lack of diplomatic dialogue between the strongest powers, relations among the newly allied NATO powers involved great diplomatic activity. Historically, in terms of the sheer amount of effort that has gone into the creation and maintenance of alliances, 'alliance diplomacy' – the dialogue between states within the framework of an alliance – is at least as typical of diplomacy in general as the dialogue between powers with no strong reason to be either allies or enemies, and much more so than the consultations envisaged by the more idealistic proponents of collective security.

In spite of the central position which alliances have always occupied in diplomatic practice in all known states systems, certain observers and indeed statesmen have felt that there is something inimical to the central purposes of diplomacy about alliances. The traditional British concern is that rigid alliances may inhibit the freedom of the diplomatic dialogue and the smoothness of continual adjustment. George Washington echoed these misgivings, and also expressed the dislike which newly emancipated colonies feel for any ties which bind them to a powerful imperial state, and their fear that they may be unduly involved for or against the former colonial power, when he warned his countrymen against entangling alliances. Both these feelings are to be found in the vogue among newly independent states today for 'non-alignment': a vogue which does not inhibit most of them from working together to further their common interests in a 'non-aligned movement' which comes close to being an alliance. Nehru's determination to keep India out of the cold war included a belief that the existence of closely-knit east and west blocs was in itself a source of danger to the peace of the world.

This sense that alliances and the diplomatic effort they attract remain a distraction, a debasement of the coinage of diplomacy, therefore deserves careful examination. It easily passes over into the belief found not only in newly independent states but among those individuals already mentioned who consider *all* diplomacy to be a deceitful sham, especially where its artifices are used to prepare for the use of force. The criticism that alliance diplomacy is either a corruption of diplomacy or proof that diplomacy is merely the handmaiden of war derives much of its impetus from the argument that, whatever the incidental relevance of the distinction between 'offensive' and 'defensive' alliances, the point of all alliances, including such multilateral covenants as the League of Nations, is to make arrangements for the use of force. This is considered antithetical to diplomacy, whose proper function is said to be to enable states to settle their differences peacefully through negotiation, dissociated from power and the alternative of compulsion. Behind this kind of interpretation is the desire to establish an unbridgeable distinction between compulsion and persuasion. Important as this distinction may be to civil law, which assumes that the authority of the state is available when compulsion is needed, it cannot be given the same weight within the states system. The proper reply to the charge that alliances are concerned with the use of force is that indeed most of them are, but that in a world of independent states this does not condemn them out of hand. The use of force is itself an end term in a series of ways in which states bring their power to bear on others so as to persuade them to alter their positions. Alliances are a means by which states add to their capacity to persuade others. At times this will mean a decision among those allied to commit themselves to the use of force in certain, usually carefully formulated, conditions. Such was the case with the members of the League of Nations; and such is the case with the members of NATO who have gone further than any previous alliance in Europe in maintaining an integrated force to defend the whole area covered by the treaty (but note, not to give each other military aid in areas outside the treaty). On other occasions an alliance may be more tentative and may amount to no more than a commitment to consult about possible joint action in certain circumstances. Only when a system of independent states is replaced by a single dominant power, or by an authority capable of enforcing compliance as a government does within a state, in other words only when the diplomatic dialogue between genuinely independent states ceases altogether, is it reasonable to expect that states will not discuss and negotiate with each other about the use of force, or enter into contracts and alliances about it. But having said this, we should recognize that the history of this century in particular illustrates the danger that the diplomacy of alliances can become almost the only form of diplomatic activity and that members of rival alliances can fail to communicate adequately with one another; and emphasizes the need for the leading states in such alliances especially to conduct a meaningful and imaginative dialogue with their opponents in order to find solutions to their differences if a resort to force is to be avoided.

So we may pass from the association of diplomacy with force to the other familiar association of diplomacy, especially secret diplomacy, with deceit. What can be said about the use of diplomacy, either by a single state or by an alliance, to deceive other states about a secret agreement or more seriously about the imminence of invasion? States have certainly often made secret preparations to gain their ends by the advantage of surprise. They have prepared their own striking force while using the diplomatic dialogue to lull the suspicions of those who might oppose them and to keep other countries' forces unprepared and immobilized. A state that acts in this way hopes to present the world with a *fait accompli*, which cannot be undone without a long and bloody struggle. Since states in a system do not usually conduct their foreign policies alone but in association or alliance with other states, alliances have sometimes contained secret or conspiratorial clauses, promising each other support in circumstances which they do not want generally known.

The fear of surprise, and the fear of secret clauses in treaties, heightens the tension between states in a system, and makes others prepare against contingencies which may or may not arise: for instance by keeping larger armed forces than they would otherwise maintain. This fear was very high among all the important powers in the years before World War One. President Wilson's concern with this fear of surprise led him to demand 'open covenants openly arrived at' as the first of his Fourteen Points for a new world order after the war. We shall consider the question of open diplomacy in Chapter X. Here we are concerned with the age-old problem that independent states do use deceit and fraud in the conduct of their policy, and exploit diplomacy to lie to other states. It is fair to say that this fact is not a condemnation of the diplomatic dialogue, any more than the fact that individuals lie to one another is a condemnation of all communications between human beings. The diplomatic dialogue cannot be expected to be more honest than the statesmen who conduct it. Diplomacy has been compared to a knife. The fact that knives can be used malevolently, and can also cut accidentally, means that they are dangerous and should be used with care; but it does not make the case for abolishing knives.

Once a decision to resort to force has been taken, such activities as keeping open the channels of discussion to hoodwink the enemy are in practice an aspect of military strategy, and must be considered in the context of the use of force. If – and this is a big if – it is recognized that the use of force can be compatible with the morality and logic of international political conduct in general, and of a given issue in particular (e.g., the recovery of territory recently taken from a state by force), there is everything to be said for using it to the best effect. And the effective use of force often turns upon not signalling to the enemy the details of one's intention. Surprise attack may not always be decisive but it has usually counted for something in war. Seizing the initiative, and the use of deception in concealing one's intentions so that this can be done, is one of the basic precepts of strategy. Deceit of this kind, not only over imminent use of force but in negotiations generally, is open to justification on the ground that it is the duty of governments to maintain the interests of their state, and that the kinds of dilemmas induced by the workings of the states system may push statesmen to the cynical use of fraud in diplomacy.

In any case, diplomatic deceit has its limits. Diplomacy is a sensitive instrument, designed to register and work on the smallest shifts in the attitudes of states to one another, and is therefore well equipped to detect the attempt to use its mechanisms to intensify rather than mitigate conflicts of interest. It is difficult to prevent the kind of duplicity under discussion from becoming public knowledge, and governments which acquire a reputation for untrustworthiness or for using easy stratagems to obtain striking successes often find that those very successes act as a warning. The frequent resort to deceit is self-defeating because a state which is careless about what credence is placed in the word of its diplomats on individual occasions will soon find that its word is not believed in any context. When that happens and its credibility is debased, a state finds it difficult to make agreements with any but equally fickle partners. There is no substitute for trust in diplomacy. This may go some way to explain the careful attention paid by professional diplomats to good manners and ritual politeness, which the public may be forgiven for believing is sometimes overdone. Where trust is absent, as for example in the aftermath of bloody conflict, it has to begin somewhere, and the most natural place to begin is with the body of men who between them professionally conduct the official relations of their countries. For the same reason, states who enjoy close relations with others cannot afford to squander the ballast of trust thus generated. It is a scarce and fecund commodity. Historically, ambassadors have frequently been used by governments who have decided to go to war to help maintain a belief in the capital of the country about to be attacked that this is not the case. (One of the reasons why it is useful for the country that is about to be attacked to have regular diplomatic contact with the country in question is that it will be in a better position to gauge the truth of such peaceful protestations.) Here it is perhaps of some relevance to suggest the distinction between the personal and professional honour of the envoy and the bearing of behaviour of this kind on the general effectiveness of the diplomatic dialogue. It is certainly not difficult to think of circumstances where for private reasons an ambassador who has invested his own word in cultivating a good opinion in the country of his attachment feels such a tug of duties when called upon to tell barefaced lies that he prefers to resign or call for his own replacement. However, a man who has been charged with representing the interests of his country, and withholding in the process certain information from unfriendly powers, will usually have such a sense of his professional duties that he either comes to terms with the events in question or sees to it that he is removed before the dilemma becomes too morally acute. An envoy's sense of loyalty to a sovereign, a leader or an elected government may work to neutralize any personal distaste for deception.

It is important, if not always easy, to understand that the role of diplomacy in preparing the use of force can be accommodated without doing lasting harm to its credentials as a means of helping to maintain order and manage change in an international society. More obvious are the many-sided contributions of diplomacy in wartime in bringing about the end of hostilities, and after wars in settling terms of peace.

Diplomacy has an important part to play at the onset of a war. When no adjustment can be found which satisfies all the parties, and they are left with the decision to resort to force, the role of diplomacy is to look to the future, to the conditions in which after the clash of arms the effort to compel can once more give way to the dialogue of persuasion. Other states will urge the combatants to accept and declare limited objectives, and to wage their struggle in conformity with the rules of the system and in accordance with its basic aims. Wise statesmen among the belligerents will be mindful of the opinion of other states, whose goodwill they will need during the fighting and whose good offices to bring the conflict to a satisfactory conclusion they may also find useful. They will also bear in mind the future settlement with the enemy, and will see the advantage of making their demands on him as palatable as possible, so that he will be more easily brought to accept them and easier to live with in international society afterwards. During a war, diplomacy generally is obliged to be as relentless and resourceful in seeking to soften the conflict of wills and interests between the belligerents as that conflict is itself relentless. From this point of view appeasement, in the literal sense, is in the true spirit of diplomacy.

All these activities underline the close relationship not only of power but of persuasion to force in a states system. 'Wartime diplomacy' is no more of a misnomer than 'alliance diplomacy', even though in the popular wars of the twentieth century, with their demands for total solutions and unconditional surrenders, wartime diplomacy has been more concentrated on the often uneasy relations between allies with increasingly diverging interests and ambitions than on the exploration through third parties and neutrals of terms for ending the fighting. In general, where war is an instrument of political compulsion in the way suggested by Clausewitz, rather than a way of taking revenge or inflicting punishment, its own political purpose requires that those engaged in using force pay constant attention to relations with the enemy in order to test his willingness to negotiate. Once hostilities cease, peace conferences and the treaties they are designed to bring about are one of the clearest and most familiar illustrations of the connection between diplomacy and war. Wars do not have to be formally concluded soon after the end of fighting, as the aftermath of World War Two illustrates. But the point of war as an instrument of policy, as a means of resolving a conflict of interests, is lost if the use of force does not issue in the establishment of new relations between the belligerents; that is, if the new relationship between them is not legitimized by agreement. No more than the mere decision to use force can guarantee a victorious outcome, can the successful use of force by itself ensure that the political effects of decisions reached in fighting will be long-lasting. To achieve these lasting effects, shifts in the relative positions of states which have been made manifest on the field of battle have to be translated into accepted settlements. This is the work of diplomacy, even where the vanquished (assuming they are not totally annexed) are for the moment militarily helpless in the face of superior force. Prolonged negotiation resulting in agreement between allies, who were often brought together only by a pressing common danger which war has removed, is necessary in any case for a general settlement. Sometimes, as in 1945, that agreement is unobtainable. The amount of negotiation between former enemies will of course depend on the extent to which the war ended in one side defeating the other or in stalemate; but even where one side is crushed there is no guarantee that a settlement will follow. The Israelis found in the aftermath of the successful fighting of 1967 that though they did not have the complication of having to reach an agreement with recalcitrant allies, they needed the political agreement of the Arab states and of the international community generally. For they found that they could not force the Arab states to negotiate, let alone accept the military verdict as politically legitimate.

In general it may be said that until a settlement has been either negotiated or imposed, there can be no peace as distinct from a cessation of hostilities. Where a defeated power can continue to resist an apparently superior force, or where victorious allies disagree, or where other powers in the system refuse to accept a military verdict, diplomacy has the major task of organizing a dialogue between all the significant powers in the area to work out a settlement. Even so it may prove impotent to persuade those who consider the injustice so great that they prefer to bide their time until their power recovers and they can modify, by persuasion or by force, the apparent decisions of the battlefield.

CHAPTER VI

Ideologies and Diplomacy

When we examined the aims and policies of states in a system, we saw that they make compatible and incompatible demands on it. Compatible demands are natural subjects for diplomacy. Although a buyer and a seller, for instance, are 'on opposite sides of a table', the essential common interest of both is in the transaction, and their compatible interests can be fairly met by a process of bargaining and negotiation. Incompatible demands, for instance when states differ about what would be just in a given situation, are less tractable; but they can still be discussed, and perhaps some accommodation or compromise reached. In practice a great deal of the diplomatic dialogue between states today is concerned with incompatible demands. Negotiation in such cases is either the search for a compromise, or else is designed to transcend the dispute and to bring in a new element that makes a wider agreement palatable to both sides. Diplomatic negotiations remain possible so long as the incompatible demands of the states concerned are essentially interests, even though suitably clothed for public presentation in declarations of principle. Public polemics about specific territorial claims or even about the price of oil usually dress up the demands of a state in general principles which are more politically respectable; but stripped of this clothing, the demands are a matter of state interest. Even if a state is prepared to use force to maintain the most important of these interests, persuasion is still possible.

But where we move away from the interests of states into the realm of doctrine and belief, the realm of ideology, then diplomacy is apt to find itself at a loss. Ideology in this sense is not concerned with territory or interests – what is ours and what is somebody else's – nor what is fair between one state and another. It is a belief – often a burning conviction – about what is morally right and what is wrong. Ideology and dogma concern the relations between states, and therefore the diplomatic dialogue, when religious conviction and moral indignation do not stop at state frontiers but lead individuals, and states which are composed of individuals, to use pressure and perhaps military force in order to put a stop to intolerable practices in other countries. This is particularly and notoriously true about Messianic religions, whose adherents believe that the faith should be spread by the sword. It is also true of wars of religion in general, and also of political crusades designed to spread democracy or communism. Ideologies and dogmas may vary. But insofar as the government of a state regards what happens in another state not merely as different or as injurious to its interests, but as morally wrong and unacceptable, this conviction blocks the way to dialogue and to compromise. The ideological barrier to diplomacy, and the ways in which diplomacy, like water, tries to get round or over the barrier, are the subject of this chapter.

We can all agree that some things are indeed morally wrong. Even if we cannot all agree about what comes into that category, it is certainly an observable fact of international life, now as in former times, that the rulers of certain states and the bulk of public opinion consider certain internal practices in other states so unacceptable that they are prepared to apply pressures, at some cost to themselves, on those other states in order to get them to modify their resented practices, and in extreme cases even to go to war to stop them. Two or three centuries ago it was a wrong religion, and especially the persecution of the true faith, that stoked the fires of righteous indignation to the point of war. 'Avenge O Lord thy slaughtered saints,' cried Milton, 'whose bones lie scattered on the Alpine mountains cold!' In our time it may be slavery, or racial discrimination, or the Gulag Archipelago. But the cry is the same today as Peter the Hermit's call to the first crusade.

Ideological fervour is a collective emotion, the study of which would take us into the realm of crowd psychology. It is rooted in the ethical convictions of men as individuals, and also in the sense of loyalty and commitment which men feel towards the society in which they have been brought up, or towards a group within that society. Individuals who are not directly involved in affairs of state, and who are not continually made aware of the conflicting pressures that pull in different directions those who make decisions, are inclined to simplify issues they are unfamiliar with. Indeed it is a useful rule of thumb that the remoter an issue is from a group of people, the less they will know from personal experience of its complexities, and the more they will apply sweeping moral and ethical judgements and sympathies to the situation. The main counterweight or ballast which operates against such ideological sympathies is indifference, and a selfish desire not to lose money or especially life in the pursuit of remote causes. This ballast of selfish indifference operates less in the modern world than it did, because of the much greater impact of the mass media and their use by interested parties to stir up moral and ideological indignation and commitment about distant events of which people do not have a first-hand experience.

Rulers and policy-makers are not, of course, a separate breed of men, immune to moral considerations. As individuals they may share ideological convictions, or they may catch the fervour of ideology from those around them. To the extent that they do, in the field of foreign affairs they will set their faces against dialogue and negotiation with evil, and even more against cooperation with wrongdoing states in order to further this or that interest. Instead, they will accept the need for struggle and perhaps for war. Even if a ruler or statesman does not share the ideological convictions of those around him, because he is more keenly aware of the other considerations which are forced on his attention every day, or because he is more conscious of his responsibility for the peace and the prosperity of the state which has elected him or otherwise acknowledged him as ruler, he may nevertheless find it politically unwise to oppose the current ideology openly. Especially in democracies, but also in other forms of government where the rulers need the support of public opinion, they will usually incline to say what is expected of them, and then find ways of avoiding precipitate or dangerous action which would harm the more specific interests of the state and the people they rule or administer.

So, in spite of the mutual antipathy between dedication to principles and diplomacy, ethical convictions, religious belief and ideology colour the dialogue between states. In every age and in every states system the aims and the actions of statesmen have been shaped to some extent by their convictions and their beliefs. These beliefs may be tempered by expediency, and by the realization that where no state can lay down the law international politics is very much the art of the possible, and the possible is severely limited. But the beliefs are none the less there. It is true that few are what Goldsmith accused Burke of being – 'too fond of the right to pursue the expedient'; but none, perhaps, pursue the expedient so exclusively that they are indifferent to what they consider to be right.

The familiar caution and restraint which even ideologically committed rulers and statesmen show when it comes to action in the international field usually has the tacit support of large sections of the public. Such people welcome the prudent approach, and privately share the doubts of their rulers or at least recognize that there must be other considerations besides ideological ones, but feel ashamed to admit selfish or material reasons for refusing to act against practices in far-off countries that they do not doubt are wrong, like apartheid or the Gulag camps. Moreover, not all the reasons for refusing to act ideologically are greedy, such as the desire to trade and so maintain people in employment, or selfish, as the desire to live out comfortable lives. There is the belief that all war is bad in itself, and that ideological war is the worst form of war. This belief is closely connected with the bias of diplomacy.

The belief that international politics should be the struggle not of interests but of principles thus accords awkwardly with diplomacy. It calls in question a fundamental premise of a states system, the independence of the member states and the right of each to decide for itself how to manage its domestic affairs. This difference of assumption goes with a difference in style. The dogmatic formulation of principles, especially in a political or religious crusade, is doctrinaire and inflexible, unlike the elasticity and preference for give and take of the diplomatic dialogue. The more a man is attached to dogmas, the less responsive he is to calls for agreement through compromise, believing that fundamentals may be negotiated away if they are treated on a level with the mundane balancing of interests familiar in negotiations between states. Diplomatic institutions for their part are designed for the business of adjustment. The abuse of diplomacy within its accustomed connections with power and interests is one thing: the damage is limited and usually reparable. But the misuse of diplomatic institutions as vehicles for propaganda and subversion, or for the championing of political righteousness and ideological warfare, is quite another, and can be more seriously damaging because it is more nearly an inversion than an abuse of diplomatic method and can inhibit real dialogue between certain states altogether. Something of this kind can be seen on occasions in the United Nations and in other gatherings where multilateral public diplomacy brings together the representatives of many states with different ideologies. Postures are struck and attitudes hardened. Cold warriors sling ideological slander past each other designed to reach their own public opinion and the still uncommitted countries. What was intended as a gathering of statesmen and diplomats degenerates from an effort to negotiate an adjustment with the ideological enemy into an attempt to win sympathy in an uncompromising struggle. So much indeed did the polemic tradition become established in public debates at the United Nations during the cold war, that when ideological tensions began to ease, the public polemics continued while tentative feelers towards real diplomatic discussion began to take place in private.

In European civilization there was a fundamental difference between the concept of the just war, to protect one's own legitimate interests, and that of the holy war, designed to bring salvation to others. The horror and destructiveness of the wars of religion which followed the Reformation led men to see that expediency, and indeed the maintenance of civilized life, required curbs on ideological and religious fervour. Such men continued to believe that one form of religion was right and the others wrong, but they came to tolerate wrong religion elsewhere and even in their own country, reluctantly, because the alternative seemed even worse. Herbert Butterfield defines this mood as follows:

> Toleration was not so much an ideal, a positive end, that people wanted to establish for its own sake; but, rather a *pis aller*, a retreat to the next best thing, a last resort for those who still hated one another, but found it impossible to go on fighting any more. It was hardly even an idea for the most part – just a happening – the sort of thing that happens when no choice is left and there is no hope of further struggle being worthwhile.

In this atmosphere diplomacy could flourish again, seeking accommodation and compromise between states with very different religious convictions even while these convictions retained their full force, in order to enable these states to deal with all the pressing range of interests which they could only ignore at their peril. So today diplomacy looks for ways to mitigate the stark intolerance of the cold war. It tries to bring states with radically different social systems to tolerate each other, and to work together to further their interests and regulate international society, while still hating each other's political and economic practices and denouncing them as evil.

In Europe the stalemate of the wars of religion and the determination of the states in the system to preserve their independence led to the acceptance of the principle of *cujus regio ejus religio* – each state should determine its own religion – and so to the reformulation of the doctrine of non-interference by states in each others' internal affairs. During the Age of Reason which followed, the importance of ideology greatly diminished and diplomacy was more concerned with territorial and economic issues. In the European states system it came to be a rule of the game, and in time an accepted part of international law, that states and even international organizations should not concern themselves with matters which were wholly or mainly within the internal jurisdiction of another state. The Charter of the United Nations itself expressly states in Article II: 'Nothing contained in the present Charter shall authorize the United Nations to intervene in matters which are essentially within the domestic jurisdiction of any state or shall require the members to submit such matters to settlement under the present Charter.' Of course this rule was never absolute. Like other rules based on broad, simple principles, it was and is treated by states as a guideline, and interpreted elastically, along with other considerations and reasons of state. It was intended to rule out intervention on ideological grounds, but not in cases where activity within a state is a direct and manifest menace to the interests of other states. This is a most important distinction for diplomacy.

It has never been easy in practice to draw a line between those internal affairs of a state which are not the legitimate concern of other states and the ideology which threatens to spill out beyond a state's borders and to damage the interests of other states. The distinction becomes clearer if we consider the similar case of armed forces. The armed forces which a state maintains are inevitably and naturally the concern of its neighbours and, by extension, of all other states in the system, since armed forces point outwards. So the issue comes into the diplomatic dialogue, and other states will make representations to the state concerned about the level of its armed forces – its allies perhaps urging greater strength, others suggesting that the level of strength is already ominously high. Most international societies have recognised that while other states may make representations, public and private, forcible intervention is not legitimate unless there is evidence of imminent attack. In the eighteenth century the Swiss diplomat Vattel argued that if you met a man in a wood who pointed a pistol in your direction, you would not have to wait till he declared his intention of firing at you to take measures of self-defence. But a preventive war to ensure that another state will not become so strong that it could attack if it so decided, has generally been condemned by international society and in fact has rarely occurred.

On this analogy, what if a state, or important organizations within a state, set themselves to subvert the loyalty of a group in another state – a religious or national minority for instance? Let us say that this agitation and propaganda threaten an upheaval in the other state, but in this case without invading it or using force in any way. This has always been a difficult issue for diplomacy, and remains so today. Of course if the government itself issues any call to disobedience or allows guerrillas and freedom fighters to raid the other state's territory, or supplies the dissident groups with arms and asylum, as has happened often enough in all recorded states systems, then the state which suffers these interferences has a legitimate cause for complaint. In extreme cases it may resort to military measures against the offending state, if it decides that the risks of war are less than those of continued subversion (as was the case when Austria–Hungary invaded Serbia in 1914). But if the accused state replies that it is not itself breaking any rules of international society, but is merely allowing its citizens to disseminate and broadcast their passionately held beliefs and ideologies, diplomatic remonstrations may not have much effect, unless the aggrieved state and its friends are able to bring pressure to bear in other fields and by other means. Here again we see diplomacy widening the issues, and trying to deal with a narrow conflict by introducing other considerations into the dialogue. Diplomacy of this kind is sometimes able to induce states to show restraint about the dissemination of disruptive ideology. In the long run, said Bismarck, every state has to pay for the windows which stone-throwing by its press breaks. In a tightly balanced system like the Europe of his day this is true, not immediately perhaps, but in the long run. It is all too easy to make enemies, and statesmen usually prefer not to do so unless real and material interests are at stake.

Subversion aimed at another state can reasonably be considered a threat to the peace because it is liable to provoke retaliation. But there is something implausible and unreal about the extension of the argument, to claim that a threat to the peace, as defined for instance in the United Nations Charter, can be caused by internal policies of a state which are not in themselves either military or directed against other states, but which are ideologically so objectionable to other states that they drive these states to warlike measures. A number of states have made such charges against South Africa, and others against Israel. Such arguments need not be taken too literally; they are rather in the nature of legal sophistries, designed to make it possible to vent strongly-felt ideological convictions against a state in a form which is technically valid for debate in the United Nations General Assembly. But in noting the spurious form of the argument, we should not doubt the strength of the convictions, or the complication which they present for the diplomatic dialogue and the effective working of the present states system.

The most important of all the interests of states, which are the real business of diplomacy, is independence, the very survival of the state. Where a powerful state threatens its neighbours, however great or small the ideological element in its motives may be, the threatened states will feel impelled to cooperate against the common danger, in spite of their own ideological differences. In the Thirty Years' War, which was in a very real sense a religious war, the coalition against the Catholic Habsburgs was built by the devout Catholic Cardinal Richelieu and Protestant statesmen, and even included the Moslem Sultan of Turkey. During World War Two the ideological differences between the allies were suspended in face of the common peril. Churchill declared that he would speak favourably of the Devil if Hitler invaded Hell. Today the leaders of communist China warn all governments, however ideologically different, of the need to stand together against the threat of Soviet imperialism. It is not the Gulag camps and the persecutions that Chinese diplomacy calls attention to, but the size of the Soviet armed forces and the menace which the Chinese argue these represent. A build-up of armed force may be wholly or mainly an internal matter, but it is the most obvious and generally accepted example of an activity that does affect the legitimate interests of other states. The Chinese leaders are pursuing classical diplomacy of a traditional kind.

But when the threat to a state's vital interests, and especially to its independence, becomes less acute, ideology tends to assume a larger part in shaping its foreign policy and the content of its dialogue with other states. An ideological foreign policy is in this sense a luxury, born of the feeling that it will not prove unduly dangerous. Just as toleration grew out of the exhaustion and the suffering of religious wars, so the revival of dogmatic intolerance feeds on the sense that it will not lead to war. The cold war which followed World War Two could afford such a high ideological content due to the fact that the enemies which had threatened the United States and the Soviet Union and had kept them in the same camp had been destroyed. The limiting factor in that ideological orgy was the fear of the destructive effect of nuclear weapons, which led to a resumption of diplomacy between the governments of the two super-powers, based on the common interest in keeping within manageable limits the nuclear peril which threatened them both alike.

In our own day questions of ideology and principle continue to occupy a prominent position in the diplomatic dialogue. Three of the many and complex reasons for this increase in the role of ideology are important in the present context. First, the ebb tide of the European empires and the end of western dominance over the rest of the world has given or restored independence to a large number of countries with non-western traditions. As a result there has been a renaissance of other cultures and values, which have been influenced in varying degrees by western precepts and practices, and also by the impact of industrial and technological development; but not obliterated. An outstanding example is the revival in various Moslem countries of Islamic values and law modified by legal and ethical concepts derived from the West. The differences of outlook that result from the growing cultural diversity of the world are distinct from clashes of ideology within the same culture; but they can also lead to sharp conflicts of principle, especially in the field of human rights. The position of women in society, the kinds of punishment used, the suppression of criticism of the established government, and many other practices which vary from one cultural tradition to another raise important ethical issues and often considerable moral indignation. This kind of ideological tension is heightened by international proclamations like the Universal Declaration on Human Rights. Such statements of principle are widely endorsed, and though they are interpreted very differently in different states, they encourage the assumption that the countries of the world ought all to be moving towards the same standards in the area of human rights, in spite of the evidence of de-westernization and the restoration of a greater degree of cultural and ethical diversity.

Secondly, the two contemporary super-powers are both more committed than the major European powers of the past to an ideological stance in international affairs, both dedicated to certain general propositions as well as to the defence of their interests. At the same time a large number of new states at the other end of the power scale have attained independence as a result of the ideological belief held by them, and also by the former colonial powers, and by the community generally, that empires were no longer legitimate and that the day of self-determination had come, rather than by successful insurrection or the operations of the balance of power. The furtherance of the ideological principle to which they owe their independence, and of associated principles such as the outlawing of racial discrimination and a right to economic justice, naturally seems important to the rulers of these new states. Thirdly, the discreet and even secret dialogue between the member states of international society has been supplemented by more public discussion of issues than before. The various bodies of the United Nations and other substantially public conferences have provided a large number of forums and occasions for public debate, and the news media have naturally given more attention to these than to the private discussions, where in fact more is settled but where less information is available.

The ideological conflicts of the past often led to wars for righteousness. 'If you wish war, nourish a doctrine,' said William Graham, who concluded that diplomacy must be divested of a crusading spirit if peace and amity between states are to prevail. But today the violence to which ideological passion and polemic can so easily lead does not normally result in wars between states. Instead, ideological violence takes a form familiar in the past, of guerrilla activities within a state or across state frontiers, with varying degrees of support from other states. The quicksilver-like quality of guerrilla violence and reprisal, which cannot be pinned down as acts of a state, removes it still further from the diplomatic dialogue than formal war for ideological reasons, which is at least an activity for which states acknowledge responsibility. The Russian writer Solzhenitsin has perceptively said that the opposite of peace is not merely war but all political violence. Indeed, even where something like formal warfare occurs, one or both sides in a modern ideological conflict usually argue that it is not a war between states, because the other side is not a legitimate government or even a legitimate state, and that therefore the enemy is not an entity with which one should conduct a diplomatic dialogue, even through third parties or international bodies.

In the same way, the criterion of respectability at the United Nations has become more ideological than its founders intended. It has shifted from whether a state is peace-loving, which was the original and relatively objective formula in the Charter, to whether it is justice-loving, which in most cases is an ideological category.

The fact that the way in which a state conducts its internal affairs has today become a major issue between many states is a consequence of the increasingly prevalent ideological element in international relations. Dictatorial régimes which control the mass media, and which are concerned with the manipulation of public opinion, find this particularly easy as well as convenient with regard to news from abroad. The corresponding ideological incitement of public opinion in democracies is not as a rule the activity of the government. Most democratic governments are committed to some degree, and often a very high degree, of international cooperation; and this requires an effective diplomatic dialogue and a minimum of ideological conflict. But all governments are interested in ideological manipulation of public opinion to some extent, whether they want to stir it up or damp it down on any issue. The mass media are less concerned with making the states system work than with communication with their audience in terms which the audience understands. In foreign affairs this involves simplification and dogmatic or ideological assumptions. The views of most television personalities, press correspondents and other commentators are largely ideological and concerned with general rather than specific issues. But there are also, in democracies, pressure groups and special interests concerned with exploiting the ideological propensities of public opinion for a specific purpose. It has always been possible for politicians and orators to excite a popular feeling on a specific 'wrong' somewhere abroad. Now the manufacture of selective indignation has become something of an industry. Genuine anger and hostility can be built up about the internal affairs of one country, while in another, conditions as bad in a different way pass unnoticed.

In the free democracies in the West this manipulation once seemed to be a speciality of the Left, and particularly of communist parties and their sympathizers. If this was ever so, it is not the case today. The waning of sympathy for the Soviet Union among progressives and people of the Left who previously shut their eyes to the greater harshness of Stalin's régime is largely the result of an anti-Soviet campaign on similar lines to that which denounces the injustices in South Africa.

Such ideological indignation, even if it does not lead to acts of violence, embarrasses professional diplomats, because it is contrary to the purpose of the diplomatic dialogue which is concerned with mutually acceptable compromises over matters of interest, and because they are personally ill-equipped to deal with it. Indeed, statesmen and political leaders who champion widely differing ideologies avoid such issues in confidential discussions and negotiations; or if they feel obliged to raise them, do so in as detached a manner as they can.

In this context diplomats find themselves in the same camp as those concerned with trade: both want to arrive at a bargain, and recognise interests which are compatible, though opposed. State corporations and private enterprises alike are interested in marketing and in buying goods, and in order to obtain the best terms they want as many markets available to them as possible. They also want conditions of stability and order so as to be able to plan their trading activities well ahead and so as to reduce interference with trade to a minimum. Traders do not want to deal only with people and with countries whose political views they share. Only in extreme cases do they willingly accept a state embargo on trade with a country on account of its internal conditions. Both traders and diplomats like to point out that since trade is beneficial to both sides, its interruption usually damages the country that imposes the ban as much as the one against which the ban is imposed. More generally, trade is a form of international exchange. Moreover, the growing control of most states over economic life, and the growing regulation of international trade by negotiation between governments and other representatives of states such as central bankers, has restored international trade to its earlier position as one of the main subjects of the diplomatic dialogue. This subject is examined in greater detail in Chapter XII. Here we may note that a prominent theme of diplomatic negotiations between states with differing social systems and ideological loyalties is the question of how best to manage change and recurring crisis in such a way as to minimize the damage to international economic exchange, and at what level to set ideological and political interference with trade.

The tendency of both trade and diplomacy to play down ideological differences for the sake of peace and prosperity does not preclude the use of economic sanctions by the international community or the majority of states, as a means of pressure to induce a recalcitrant state to behave more in accordance with the demands of international society as a whole. Economic sanctions have an obvious justification, on the ground of maintaining international peace and order and therefore the interests of the majority of states regardless of their ideology, when they are applied against a state that invades or uses force against its neighbour, or persistently arms and trains guerrillas operating in another state. But economic sanctions directed against a recognized state in order to induce it to change its internal policies can easily become sanctions for ideology's sake. Such international action not only sets aside the painfully learned experience of European diplomacy. It is liable to make the diplomatic dialogue, and the compromises which diplomacy naturally seeks, difficult if not impossible.

Clearly peoples and their leaders will continue to hold deep convictions, and except in times of great peril their conduct towards other states will be motivated by ideology and doctrine as well as by the protection and further-ance of their national interests. The ideological element undoubtedly complicates the diplomatic dialogue and hampers its constructive tasks of preserving the peace and managing change. But diplomacy must learn to live with ideology, now as in the past, if it is to function in the real world, just as statesmen and peoples find it necessary to adapt their cherished con-victions to leave room for more mundane benefits to flourish. The most satisfactory compromise is to deal with matters of belief and ideology as far as possible in the public side of the international dialogue. We saw that in public debates, and in open diplomacy generally (quite apart from the cold war) there is a tendency to concentrate on issues of principle, and to dress up even quite specific state interests like rates of interest on loans or the annexation of territory in ideological garb.

A public stand on lofty principles may reflect the deeply-held convictions of statesmen. It may gratify public opinion, or the beliefs of a party or a church. It may make a state's policies more respectable and enlist more support for them in other countries. But in a less direct way it may also serve the purposes of diplomacy. It makes clear to other states certain strongly-held attitudes which those states must take into account if they wish to collaborate with the state in question. Also, it enables public figures and professional diplomats to put certain ideological issues and demands on the record, even to get these issues off their chests, so that in the private dialogue, both bilateral and collective, statesmen and diplomats can get down to a practical discussion about interests and courses of action without the embarrassment caused by discussion of ideology and issues of principle. For just as public debate tends towards issues of principle, so private negotia-tion inclines towards compromise and understanding of the other man's point of view, and tends to bring even matters of principle onto the bargain-ing table. This is not hypocrisy. It is a natural division of labour between public and private dialogue, between the clash of incompatible values and the search for compatible ones like peace and independence, between the vision of the desirable and the art – or the craft – of the possible.

It is in this double light of belief and bargaining that we should view the debates and the negotiations in our time about collective security and aggression, about economic justice and about human rights. As the issues which dominated the cold war and decolonization become resolved or over-taken by events, other issues come to the front of the public debate, and other interests are examined and bargained about in private. Ideology and constructive diplomacy do not easily mix. But the according of a due place to issues of principle in the public dialogue between states may actually facilitate private negotiation, and make the results of constructive diplomacy more palatable to the public when they are announced.

CHAPTER VII

Other Diplomatic Systems

Our present global states system, and the European one out of which it developed, are not the only ones we know about. Independent states have existed and have had dealings with one another in the past, both in war and in peace. Inevitably they evolved regular ways of talking to and bargaining with one another. Sometimes we find a number of independent states who had close and continuous dealings, and who thus constituted a regular states system. For instance, the city states of classical Greece, the kingdoms of ancient China and the more diverse states of India developed such international systems.

Each of these groups of states shared a common civilization, and many of their diplomatic practices grew out of the religion and the customs of their common culture. They were international societies in the sense defined by Professor Hedley Bull as existing 'when a group of states, conscious of certain common interests and common values, form a society in the sense that they conceive themselves to be bound by a common set of rules in their relations with one another, and share in the working of common institutions'. But they were also something more, what the historian Heeren described as 'unions of several contiguous states resembling each other in their manners, religion and degree of social improvement and cemented together by a reciprocity of interests'. The world states system of today is an international society by Bull's definition, but does not meet Heeren's more exacting specifications. But the European states system out of which the present world system developed, and from which it has inherited so many of its practices, does meet Heeren's formula, as do the other systems cited in the paragraph above.

The diplomatic arrangements of these different systems all have a family resemblance, because they were designed for the same purpose: the conduct of a dialogue between independent states. Their ways may not have been exactly ours, because they were rooted in the manners and religion, that is the cultural patterns, of their own civilizations; but they were valid forms of the diplomatic dialogue. These diplomatic practices are worth our attention, both for what they have in common with our present machinery and for what they did differently. It is useful for us to see our conduct of the international dialogue in the light of other practices, so that we do not become too attached to the forms and modalities of diplomacy in current use, and do not let ourselves become unduly disturbed as they change and adapt to new circumstances before our eyes. We should be impressed by what seems permanent in diplomacy, by the continuities and recurrences in different systems, rather than by the individualities which were peculiar to each age and culture. The view of different ways of performing the same function will enlarge our perception of diplomacy. Moreover, some of the techniques evolved by other societies could be usefully adopted today.

The origins of diplomacy date back beyond recorded history to the first heralds carrying oral messages from one independent chief or group to another. Numelin described the arrangements that existed among the aborigines of South Australia in the nineteenth century as follows:

> In Southern Australia, according to the recognised form of government, the heads or chiefs with the consent of the tribe make alliances, determine on war, peace and friendship, and send envoys – on very important occasions ambassadresses – to treat with the neighbouring tribes. Such envoys are treated with the utmost courtesy and never molested in any way while on their mission.

In other groups of primitive tribes, as in more advanced civilizations, heralds and envoys were virtually always granted immunity. Partly no doubt this was because a deeply-felt religious taboo prevented men from violating or molesting a herald who came under a flag of truce; but it was also for the very practical reason that the rulers and commanders and governments wanted to send messages to the other side, and also to know what the other side had to say, even if they did not always believe it. Regular communication between independent states, as opposed to occasional messages, began to take a shape of its own as soon as civilizations became developed and complex enough to keep written records, and for kings and governments to correspond with one another in writing. The practice of sending messengers or heralds to transmit and amplify the written correspondence of course continued, until it developed into the permanent embassies and delegations of our own time. Indeed oral communication, face to face, mainly through expert intermediaries but where necessary by personal meetings of heads of government, remains the fundamental method of diplomacy. But what is said orally is lost to posterity unless it is recorded. We can follow the diplomatic negotiations of long ago only from the moment that archives began to be kept in which a summary of exchanges was recorded.

These diplomatic exchanges developed the arts of persuasion. If you were not strong enough to coerce your neighbour by force of arms, or if for other reasons, moral as well as pragmatic, it did not suit you to go to war at a particular time, you were interested in talking to him and if possible persuading him to do at least some of the things you wanted. You looked for those inducements which might mean a lot to him but which would not make so much difference to you. From the beginning, diplomacy was an alternative to mere reliance on force. It developed in a setting characterized by inequalities of force and conflicts of interest. Moreover, when powerful states with complex interests had to deal with one another over a wide range of different areas and subjects, the rulers and their close advisers began to see a certain balance over the whole range of these issues, so that relations between the two governments became a kind of fluctuating package deal, in which one issue could be offset against another. The communications between two such governments, which spelt out the bargaining in extensive and detailed exchanges, became stylised and developed a language and conventions of its own. It was a language to which lawyers brought a sense of legal precision and was at the same time persuasive, and also a language which never left out of sight the alternative to such exchanges and balance, the resort to force. For in these early experiments in inter-state relations, diplomacy might be the normal and most mutually advantageous form of argument between independent sovereigns, the first resort: but the last resort, what was later to be called the '*ultima ratio regum*', the final argument of kings, was war. And it has been ever since.

All these aspects of diplomacy are clearly illustrated in a very early correspondence between two great powers that has fortunately been preserved for us, the correspondence between the Pharaoh and the great king of the Hittites in the fourteenth century B.C. The Tell el Amarna tablets are written in cuneiform Aramaic, which was not the language of either the Hittites or the Egyptians, but the international language of the time. Most of the time the two rulers seem to have perceived that it was in the interest of both of them to preserve their relations with one another, and not to allow irritation at some trickery or default on the other side to damage the lines of communication, the diplomatic relationship itself. Thus when the king of the Hittites received from the Pharaoh a payment of gold bricks which turned out to contain other matter inside, he wrote very tactfully warning his fellow ruler that there was a dishonest steward in the Pharaoh's household who had substituted bricks with a gold outside for the solid gold bricks which of course the Pharaoh must have intended to send, and suggesting that this dishonest steward was cheating them both. Whatever the king of the Hittites may have suspected, the way to get his full payment of gold with the minimum of damage to his relations with Egypt was to assume that the Pharaoh meant to abide honestly by the agreement. So much that is modern in diplomacy can be found in the Tell el Amarna tablets that some writers have even suggested that there were no serious new ideas or practices in diplomacy until the development of resident ambassadors or even until the founding of the League of Nations! While such claims are nonsense, they do illustrate the way in which diplomatic intercourse between two powers, especially great powers with many interests, develops its own techniques and practices. It is these persistent features which give a perspective to the study of modern diplomacy by suggesting what is lasting and what is likely to change.

In the ancient civilizations of the Middle East even imperial rulers who wished to establish their dominion far and wide over other peoples preferred to achieve their ends by persuasion and by a limited and demonstrative use of power. They tried threats and promises before an actual resort to force, which they realized is always expensive and often unexpectedly risky. The ruthless but calculating Assyrians treated the kings they conquered with publicised cruelty in order to put the fear of Asshur into others and make them submit. When the Assyrians encountered resistance, as they did for instance before the walls of Jerusalem, the Book of Kings describes the Assyrian commander resorting to diplomacy, describing to the Israelites the advantages of submission in as favourable terms as possible while warning them that further resistance could only mean death. The Persians, who succeeded to the Assyrian empire, were a more humane and civilized imperial power. Even in the days of their expansion they made considerable efforts to obtain the essence of what they wanted by negotiation, while mobilizing enough force to get their way by war if negotiation failed. From their encounters with the Greeks they learnt that the outcome of war with a Greek city was far from certain, and they began to rely increasingly on diplomacy as their military capacity in the area declined compared with that of the leading Greek cities. During their expansionist period the Persians used a diplomatic method which has an obvious utility in dealing with people of very different traditions, and is sometimes, but more rarely, employed today. They sent prominent Greeks or neighbouring rulers like the king of Macedon to negotiate for them in a Greek city, usually alongside Persians.

The city states of classical Greece were passionately attached to their political independence. The idea that there should be one government for the whole of Greece, when it occurred to the Greeks at all, was abhorrent. But they recognised the imperative need for the independent states, crowded up against each other, to conduct a dialogue. Many Greeks also attached great importance to the diplomatic skills of persuasion and rhetoric; consequently, in their relations with one another and with the very different Persian Empire which exercised a loose suzerainty over some of them, they laid great emphasis on persuasion, and gave rise to one of the most developed periods of diplomacy before our time.

The most advanced Greek city states did not conduct their external relations in isolation but usually banded together in leagues or alliances. There was active and organised diplomatic communication within the various alliances, and also between the leading states in the different groups and with the Persians. The machinery of their diplomacy was different from our own. The practice was for the authorities in a city to send special envoys (an envoy is someone who is *envoyé*, French for 'sent') to other cities. These envoys put their case as persuasively as they could to the ruler where there was one, and to a council or assembly of the citizens where that was the body which took the decision. Thucydides, in his great history of the Peloponnesian War in the fifth century B.C., tells his story almost as much in terms of these representations, which he describes in detail, as in terms of military and naval operations. One aspect of the pattern of diplomacy inside Greek alliances is worth noting because it tends to be equally present today. When a city was in an imperial or expansionist phase, as the Athenians were for instance in the period leading up to the Peloponnesian War, they tended to dominate their allies and to treat them as subordinates, disciplining those who did not accept their decisions; whereas the alliance or coalition opposed to the dominant city had to depend more on voluntary adherents, so that allies of the Spartans at the time of Athenian imperial expansion used to meet separately from the Spartans and to have a much greater say in policy-making than the Athenians allowed to their allies.

Impressive as the relations between the rival leagues – and within them – undoubtedly were, they remained partial and limited. The Greek world of the fifth century B.C. remained one of feuds and rivalries without any general recognition that the leading cities had an obligation or conscious responsibility to make this system of fiercely independent communities function as a whole. The Greeks came together at common gatherings like games and religious festivals; but from the moment when the Athenians and Spartans gave up their idea of dyarchy – what we should call their collusion or joint management of international society – there was for a long period no multilateral diplomacy outside the alliances and no general sense of responsibility for peace and order.

However, in the fourth century B.C. there was a real, prolonged and systematic effort to limit feuding and to get beyond continual bids for dominion and resistance to it. This was largely the work not of any Greek state but of the Persians. They now recognized themselves to be too weak and too committed elsewhere to advance their interests or even defend themselves against any major Greek alliance by force of arms. Since the Persians could not prevail by war they saw that their advantage lay in a general peace in Greece. This they set out to obtain by diplomacy. The implementation of this major diplomatic effort, in which the leading Greek cities also played active parts, was based, as all such attempts must be today as then, on bilateral diplomacy. There was a constant coming and going of envoys between the important Greek states and Sardis, from where Persian diplomacy with the Greek world was mainly conducted.

The new foreign policy objective shared by many of the states called forth an important new diplomatic technique. The principal powers agreed to convene great international political congresses at which the leaders, or men empowered by their city to act, came together from all the politically important states in Greece and from Persia to discuss a general settlement of outstanding issues and to lay down rules for the future. The Persians no longer tried to stay neutral or simply to support the weaker side; they tried to find a formula for the maintenance of peace by cooperation with the dominant Greek power as well. The plan for a general peace in the Greek world, known as the King's Peace, was based on the concept that as many city states on the European side of the Aegean Sea should have their independence as it was politically possible to negotiate, while the Persians should enjoy the nominal suzerainty over the Greek cities on the Asian side which they had possessed in former times. There were eight congresses in all between 392 and 367 B.C. They not only established a territorial stalemate, with guarantees against an aggressor similar to those which later figured in the Covenant of the League of Nations; after much discussion they also agreed on certain general principles, such as the right of all Greek states to be heard, and on detailed practical rules of conduct for regulating international affairs. The great powers found it to their advantage to act as hosts to these congresses (which were usually held at Athens, Sparta or Sardis) and to listen to what the spokesmen for the smaller states had to say, both because the smaller states carried moral weight and because together they did add up to something politically.

It is true that the principal codes of conduct laid down at these congresses were often broken, and that war between the quarrelsome leading city states of the Greek world and their allies continued. But the congresses were nonetheless a very important innovation. Though they did not stop breaches of the rules, they kept these breaches within manageable bounds. The more powerful cities accepted obligations to enforce the peace. This they often did very high-handedly, but nevertheless with more respect for the independence of others and for the rules of the game, and more awareness that there was an 'international system', than existed before the congresses or would have existed without them. The Persians, for their part, had to be fairly honest brokers because they could make their views prevail only by persuasion, usually backed up by subsidies. One of the most seminal features of these congresses, though it did not seem so significant to the more powerful city states at the time, was the idea that, with certain tactful exceptions, even the smallest cities had the right to be independent and the right to come to the congresses and to be given a hearing there. This idea of universal representation has come to be valued again today. Many states, too small and underdeveloped to be accorded an effective voice in the European diplomatic system, are now admitted to the United Nations as a matter of course.

The Greek city states relied, both for their direct contacts with each other and for representation at congresses when this multilateral pattern developed, on envoys sent for the occasion. But distances were long and it was not always easy to know what was going on in other states, or to send an envoy there in time to affect a sudden decision. Greek diplomacy felt the need for some sort of permanent contact or spokesman in other cities. The Greeks did not hit on the idea of resident ambassadors, which proved to be much the most effective diplomatic device when invented in Italy in the Renaissance. Instead a Greek city would be represented in other cities important to it by one or more citizens of those cities. Such a representative was called a proxenos. The function of a proxenos was to promote the interests of the city which he represented with his own fellow citizens, and to find ways of harmonizing the interests and policies of the two city states. He would speak up for the city he represented in debates in his own assembly, lodge the visiting envoys and delegations from that city when they came, and brief them on the political situation in his own city.

Proxeny, as an alternative to sending resident embassies to other capitals, works well if the interests of the two states are not in serious conflict; but when they are, the loyalties of the proxenos are bound to be torn between the interests of his own city and those of the one he represents. Nowadays an ambassador in a democratic country will have close contact with one or two prominent citizens, especially members of the parliament or legislature, who are good friends of his country and will give him advice about how to improve relations between the two and will also speak up for his country in public. But the invention of resident ambassadors, both to other capitals and to international bodies like the United Nations, has prevented the use of proxeny as an important device in our own international system.

The Graeco-Persian world after the collapse of Alexander's brief empire was entirely different. Alexander's generals divided up his empire into a number of independent kingdoms, and the new royal families were closely connected by marriage and belonged to the same Macedonian officers' circle. Some of the Greek city states continued their independent existence and others formed themselves into closely-knit leagues or federations, but even so they remained minor powers. Since the rulers of the large states were all Macedonians with the same background and outlook and the same connections with Greek civilization, they continued some of the earlier Greek practices. There were attempts to establish codes of conduct between states, with quite elaborate arrangements for arbitration and the good offices of neutrals. It would be too much to call these codes of conduct international law in our sense; but there were the beginnings of generally accepted maritime law, developed especially by the great trading city of Rhodes. But the basis of diplomatic life in Macedonian times was a complex web of alliances and treaties between the much intermarried Macedonian ruling families, who never trusted one another and were often divided by bitter family feuds. In such a world, as might be expected, diplomatic intercourse was not at all like the stylized and cautious exchange in a third language between the Pharaoh and the king of the Hittites. It was a much more intimate affair, consisting largely of argument and bargaining between cousins, often conducted by the women members of the family; and therefore, unfortunately for us, all too little of it survives in our written accounts of the time. This diplomacy was a curious foreshadowing of the courtly diplomacy of Europe of the seventeenth and eighteenth centuries, when most of the important ruling families were related to one another; but Macedonian diplomacy did not develop into a conscious institution in the same creative way as the European system.

At about the same time as the Greek and Macedonian systems, two other civilizations of Asia, namely, India and China, also consisted of a number of independent states with closely interwoven interests. They too developed complex patterns of communication and diplomatic practices of their own. Both the Indian and Chinese traditions looked back to an idealized universal empire ruling over all the territories where that civilization prevailed. As a result it seemed more legitimate for one powerful state to try to conquer the rest and to re-establish universal dominion than it seemed to the Greeks, who regarded it as natural and desirable that city states should be independent of one another.

The most striking evidence that has been preserved for us of diplomacy and relations between powers in ancient India is the Arthashastra. The core of this great manual of statecraft is the advice about how to conduct war and diplomacy, and how to establish universal dominion, which was compiled by a Brahmin minister, Kautilya, shortly after Alexander's invasion of India. But it also contains much traditional wisdom and advice as well as aphorisms about the conduct of international relations, some of which are from an earlier period than Kautilya's writing and some added much later. Kautilya's own outlook and advice were strikingly like Machiavelli's: they show the same admiration of ambition and resourcefulness. The Arthashastra as a whole reads rather as if Machiavelli's Prince had been fused with a number of ideas and maxims from the Middle Ages, and also with later theories about neutrality, diplomacy and international law.

The Indian scene included traditional rulers, military adventurers who made themselves kings, and also republican states. Wars were frequent because one state or another was always making a bid for dominion. Every state that wished to survive, as well as those who wished to expand, had to be watchful and well-informed about what was going on in neighbouring states; and a web of alliances and treaties grew up because no state felt strong enough to stand alone and ignore its neighbours. Both regular communications and spying were highly developed. The Indians, like the Greeks, did not have permanent residents: they relied on envoys who delivered messages and negotiators who were authorized to work out or modify agreements on their masters' behalf (who in the European system are called plenipotentiaries). Both categories were normally Brahmins, the high-caste Indians who enjoyed a certain immunity in any case apart from their protection as envoys or heralds. The Arthashastra says that 'envoys are the mouthpieces of kings. They must carry out their instructions, and it would be wrong to put them to death even if they were outcastes. How much less reason is there then for putting a Brahmin to death?' Such Brahmin envoys would of course have contacts among fellow Brahmins and others in the countries to which they were sent; and indeed Indian kings often sent or used Brahmin envoys less to deliver messages than to find out what was going on. Often these envoys went further. The Arthashastra lists among the functions assigned to ambassadors not only those which we today consider proper, such as the negotiation of treaties and insistence on their observance, but also what we consider less legitimate functions, such as intrigue, subsidies to secret and rebellious armies, the use of spies and the bribery of enemy officials. In the atmosphere of constant conflict which prevailed for many centuries in India, these activities seemed particularly important to rulers. It is remarkable evidence of the value which independent states and governments at all times attach to communications with each other that diplomatic immunity remained an established and generally respected practice in spite of clandestine activities of ambassadors and envoys.

While the methods of Indian diplomacy at that time were realistic and apt to disregard current moral and religious values, the forms grew out of Hindu society and religious observance, modified by Macedonian practice (envoys came and went between Indian and Macedonian rulers). The intricate Indian bilateral web of contacts was sometimes extended to multilateral conferences of allies, which the rulers themselves might attend in person. There was also an elaborate system of mediation, which is often hard to distinguish from diplomatic pressure applied by third parties for their own interest. But there was no system of congresses or general meetings between states not in alliance, of the kind developed in the Graeco-Persian and European systems.

Perhaps the most fruitful part of Chinese history was the era when there was no monolithic unified empire, but a number of independent and intellectually vigorous states. This period ran from 720 to 220 B.C., approximately the same time as the Greek and Macedonian systems. The memory of a unified empire was strong in this period. The central Chinese states recognized the Chou king as a nominal emperor, though he had no longer any authority over them: but the states on the fringes of China did not even do that. Most of the time there were two main leagues or alliance systems. The members of the alliances often changed, and relations between the various states were as shifting and complex as in any other known system. The art of diplomatic bargaining became highly skilled, as did that of finding out other people's secrets. Since this was a period of frequent wars and struggles for mastery, watchfulness was almost a condition of survival, and every ruler needed to inform himself about other states and to keep up a dialogue with them.

The Chinese states of this period had a highly formal style of diplomacy. The outward forms were inherited from the Chou court ceremonials, in contrast to the more religious origins of Indian diplomatic forms. The dialogue was conducted by exchanges of envoys; and the nature of the relations between two rulers could be measured exactly by the rank and behaviour of their envoys and the kind of ceremony with which they were received. So frequent were these temporary embassies, especially between allies, that they often overlapped, so that a second envoy arrived at a capital before the first had left. However haughty and aggressive a ruler might be, he recognised that it was to his interest to send and receive envoys. Towards the end of the period of independent states we can observe the decline of the system, not so much in the treatment of the envoys which stood the tests of time and warfare notably well, as in the more frequent violation and disregard of the treaties and contracts which they negotiated. The growing number of breaches of faith led to increasing mistrust and violence. Diplomatic exchanges and agreements lost their credibility, the expectation of war became greater, and the constructive achievement of diplomacy less. Finally one state, Ch'in, on the margin of the society of states, and with greater resources than the others, conquered the rest, in much the same way as Macedon conquered the Greek city states and Rome the Macedonian states system.

The civilizations described in this chapter have sometimes been ruled or dominated from a single centre, as were the Roman or Chinese Empires; but at other times a number of closely involved independent states, members of the same or similar cultural families, have formed what are now known as states systems. The more intimately interwoven the interests of the states in these systems were, the greater was the need for a diplomatic dialogue between them. Diplomatic forms and practices varied from one civilization to another, as might be expected. In classical Greece the forms were largely based on envoys who addressed councils and assemblies, in India they grew partly out of religious tradition, in China mainly out of court etiquette. But there were certain important common features, which we also observe in the diplomacy of our own states system of today. There was the immunity of envoys, which is necessary if they are to come and go, and the dialogue is to flow freely. There was a formalism of behaviour which enables contacts and exchanges to continue when cordiality is absent and relations are strained. The language was legally precise yet tactful and flexible. And there were always those contracts between states, such as leagues and alliances, which occur whenever a number of states find that they share objectives which they can more easily achieve by banding together than by acting alone. The striking thing about the diplomatic activity of these different civilizations is the way in which the same need for dialogue produced similar rules and institutions.

For some time there has been an increasing interest in other civilizations. We are no longer so sure of ourselves as our grandfathers were. We are attracted by history, archaeology and anthropology because they show us, who live in a world of flux and change and who feel the need to question our own values and institutions, how others ordered their public affairs. Not everything is new under the sun; and we find it instructive to see how men at other times and other places have tackled the problems that we also face. We obtain insights into attitudes and institutions that are useful to us in our own predicaments, and sometimes even seem to have worked better than those we have today, though they cannot be transplanted as they stand into our own system. In studying the past, the interest of many contemporary scholars has shifted from the rise and fall of great empires to those periods when there were a number of independent states or communities within a civilization. What concerns us here is that these communities did not just trade and fight, argue and agree: they developed institutions and rules to manage their relations with each other. We can see that diplomacy, as an instituted way of ordering the affairs of a states system, tends to grow into something more than its machinery, and becomes an accumulation of experience and wisdom which transcends the mere mechanics of dialogue. When the design for ordering the affairs of a system which is implicit in a diplomatic dialogue becomes visible to its practitioners, when it breaks surface so to speak, then diplomacy can achieve its full stature. In contrast, when the presuppositions of diplomacy are no longer regarded as necessary for the management of international society, and when diplomacy itself becomes widely denounced as a combination of privilege and deceit, when the purpose of a number of important powers is not to operate the diplomatic system as a whole but to exploit it, then diplomacy recedes into a technique and a political device.

It is important for the understanding of diplomacy to realize that the diplomatic systems of other highly developed civilizations did in fact develop as constructively as they did. We are thereby made aware that organized diplomacy answers an imperative need in any system of independent states; and that the answers we have evolved to manage our own international system are neither so unique nor always so superior as we might suppose. In particular we may note the impressive attempt of the Graeco-Persian system to organize collective order and security in the fourth century B.C. Nevertheless, the states systems which called forth these diplomatic achievements have long since disappeared. They were either forcibly incorporated into conquering empires, or their sense of purpose and coherence was lost. The thread of continuity has been broken. We may learn much that is valuable from the successes and failures of past diplomatic achievements. But they are not models for us to copy, and they are not living traditions for us to build on and adapt for our present world-wide system.

We must now turn to examine the diplomacy evolved by the European states system, in the last four centuries since the Renaissance. It deserves our attention because it was the most developed, the most self-aware and the most imaginative that we know. But more important still, the society of independent states which produced it has not been absorbed into a single empire or disintegrated; on the contrary, European diplomatic institutions and practices have expanded beyond the society which evolved them to become, with some adaptation, the worldwide diplomatic system of to-day.

CHAPTER VIII

The Diplomatic Society of Europe

Diplomacy reached its full flower as an art, a consciously and deliberately creative achievement, in the European states system.

The European world between the Italian Renaissance and the First World War was very different from our contemporary international society. The reader will understand the context and achievement of European diplomacy more clearly if he keeps the differences well in mind, and does not let himself be unduly distracted by the family resemblance between the present global system and the European one out of which it grew. The 'Europe' into which Latin Christendom slowly developed was a much more integrated entity than our diverse world. It shared a common civilization and common values. In the Middle Ages a real spiritual unity existed alongside lay authority that was very diffused in practice. In post-medieval Europe this political fragmentation took another form: the fluid hierarchical system we call feudalism crystallized into a number of states of varying sizes, from the extensive and elective Holy Roman Empire and great kingdoms such as France and Spain to city states such as Venice and Lübeck. These states were still based partly on the hereditary right of the ruler to specific territories or lordships, and partly on what power and skill were able to acquire. Latin Christendom, though divided by the Reformation, continued to think of itself as an entity, now called under humanist influence the *res publica christiana*, the common-wealth of Christendom and increasingly also Europe. By the eighteenth century Burke could refer to Europe as 'a federative society, or in other words a diplomatic republic', and Voltaire could describe it as '*une grande république partagée en plusieurs états*'. And as we saw in the last chapter, during the Napoleonic wars the Hanoverian Heeren looked nostalgically back and hopefully foward to the states system of Europe as a 'union of several contiguous states cemented together by a reciprocity of interests'.

The transition to statehood, the consolidation of the domestic authority of the ruler or government within this common framework, was gradual and uneven; but it was steady. Power and jurisdiction were concentrated in the hands of central authorities, overriding the multitude of unique local rights and privileges. The state rather suddenly developed in an advanced form in Italy, under a number of rulers whose power was wholly or partly arbitrary, without the legitimation of traditional authority. Such men had to be especially watchful against threats to their power, both inside their domains and from neighbours who considered themselves no longer bound by traditional fiefs and allegiances but who would extend their territories whenever opportunity occurred. An Italian ruler, at once both acquisitive and threatened, had to keep himself informed of what was going on around him: he had to ensure a regular and continuous flow of what we call intelligence. And he also had to conduct a more continuous dialogue with neighbouring rulers: a dialogue full of persuasion, veiled threats, open alliances, marriage compacts, subsidies and conspiratorial plots against third parties. He needed this intelligence and this dialogue in order to cope with the new Italian scene in which power had become divorced from the medieval legitimacies and was liable to be used in any direction at any time.

The channels of information and of discussion which Italian renaissance princes and councils used were those which they found at hand. There were the clerics who represented or reported to the Papacy on ecclesiastical matters; the agents outside Florence of the Medici family's banking interests; and perhaps most important, the network of agents across Europe who furnished the commercial and political intelligence that kept the Venetian Signoria economically prosperous and politically ahead of the game.

These agencies were not yet embassies. The term then had another meaning. The traditional missions from one ruler to another continued as before, in Italy as in the rest of Europe. An embassy of this kind was an appointment of honour and dignity, and was headed by a prominent noble or citizen, often a member of the prince's own family, perhaps in connection with a royal marriage or other compact. Such embassies, which combined pomp and ceremonial with a specific piece of business, were apt to last only a few weeks, but were none the less expensive, and were paid for in part by the noble representative of the ruler's person to whom the honour and glory accrued. In contrast to these glittering gestures, the paid agent was not always *salonfähig*, not normally the social equal of the prince with whom he transacted his master's business; but at least he knew that business, so that the discussion was between interlocutors of presumed equal competence for the negotiations in question. And usually he was an honest and honourable man, often more so than the princes he served and dealt with.

This image of the permanent agent, equally competent but socially inferior, an agent whose master gave him orders and who had access to the prince to whom he was accredited in connection with those orders, lasted a long time in the European system. The practice of maintaining resident representatives spread fairly rapidly from its Italian origins through the rest of the 'republic of Europe'. These new permanent envoys were found to be more efficient than the noblemen or high ecclesiastics sent on special missions, both in reporting a regular flow of news and in conducting negotiations. For one thing, a prince or a council could choose obedient and skillful agents from a wide field, instead of finding themselves limited to representational figures of appropriate rank, which often meant sending a prominent member of the prince's own family who might be anything but capable or trustworthy. Secondly, the paid agent stayed on the spot and got to know both the country and its powerful figures far better than a transient visitor of high estate could hope to do. The same process which caused executive and judicial authority within the state to be withdrawn from the nobility which had traditionally administered local affairs, and transferred to reliable royal agents, intendants and judges, likewise led to the conduct of the diplomatic dialogue being substantially transferred from high-born and occasional embassies to agents abroad of the state – which was the king. The increased pressure of states on each other, as they became more organized and generated more power, and filled out the metaphorical spaces between them which had previously existed, made necessary new means of conducting the dialogue between rulers.

The new method of conducting the intensified diplomatic dialogue did not replace the dignified embassies of earlier times. Princes saw their resident agents abroad rather as supplementing the ceremonial exchanges with which they were familiar and which emphasized the importance of the occasions which those exchanges marked. When the new diplomacy spread from Italy to the rest of Western Europe, where the authority of princes was still much more rooted in legitimacy and depended less on the skills portrayed in Machiavelli's Prince, it acquired some of the usages and conventions – one might say some of the legitimacy – of the traditional diplomatic missions. Extra-territorial privileges – the exemption from the jurisdiction of the host prince or government – furnish an important example of this process. Ceremonial delegations were cavalcades headed by great personages, and brought with them something of the prince and the realm which they represented. Their little court, with its equerries, its uniformed men at arms, its cooks and its servants, perhaps its great lady and her retinue, was more than a reflection of the court at home; it was a part of it, detached and set down in another prince's domains but still obeying within itself the laws and observances, the ranks and rules of its own realm, under the delegated authority of the high personage who represented the Ruler. The extra-territorial privileges and jurisdiction granted by custom to these temporary pockets of foreign courts, the protection and immunity given by the receiving prince to their noble leaders, soon began to be extended to a ruler's permanent agents, who were personally much less exalted, but yet equally bore their master's arms and colours and also represented his sovereign person.

In contrast to the medieval concept of legal and feudal rights and obligations, the Italians of the Renaissance accepted a *stato*, by which they meant the reality of *de facto* power. They were very much aware that the influence of a great *stato* would not stop at the boundaries of its administrative jurisdiction; it inevitably extended beyond them, to induce and compel less powerful princes and cities to conform to its wishes, at least in so far as their relations with other powers were concerned. It was easy to imagine that such a *stato*, with its directly governed core and its penumbra of prudent conformity by weaker rulers, might expand by the momentum of its own increasing success to dominate the whole Italian peninsula, or at a later stage the whole commonwealth of Christendom. Renaissance Italians were no longer haunted by the prospect of the revived feudal authority of the Holy Roman Empire, formerly advocated by Ghibellines and opposed by Guelfs: what men now feared was a new kind of hegemony, a *super-stato*, the *de facto* power to 'lay down the law'. This vision of an Italy united behind a single dominant *stato* animated the Borgias and Machiavelli. This is what Sforza had in mind when he complained that if the power of Venice continued to increase, the Venetians would soon be '*signori di tutta Italia*'. Against such a threat, the only defence was an anti-hegemonic coalition of the threatened *stati*. The eyes of most rulers were fixed on the immediate threat from an existing *stato*. They so feared the prospect of domination that they even preferred to invite the great trans-Alpine powers back into the peninsula to prevent it. It took a banker as perceptive as Lorenzo dei Medici to realise that the danger might come from more than one *stato*, that the destruction of the power of Venice, for example, might and indeed almost inevitably would lead to some other *stato* expanding its penumbra of influence to fill the power vacuum.

The diplomatic dialogue of Renaissance Italy was what we should expect in such circumstances. Through the maze of intrigue and the efforts of rulers to cajole, reward, browbeat and hoodwink each other one can discern something more significant, the elaboration of grand constructive strategies to cover not only Italy but much of Europe. These larger strategies included notably the Ottoman Empire, the great infidel power which stood outside Christendom and was the nominal enemy of all Christians, but was in practice a great *stato* indeed, and available as a major trading partner and even as a military ally. The Ottoman Empire was *de jure* alien but *de facto* an active member of the European system that no ruler in Italy could leave out of account.

The new political world across the Alps remained different from Italy in one significant way. Italian rulers either lacked traditional legitimacy, as did the Sforzas in Milan, or used their authority for illegitimate ends, as did the popes. Their concern was to safeguard and expand their *stato*, and above all to legitimize it. The rest of Europe, on the contrary, laid the greatest emphasis on hereditary right as a legitimizing principle. The problem for sixteenth-century kings and lesser sovereigns was to assert that right. Their aim was to increase *de facto* the power which they had inherited *de jure* but which was much less effective, much more hedged in by traditional limitations, than the arbitrary ability to command and to compel that had developed in Italy. The aim of rulers north of the Alps was to make themselves more absolute at home and more able to defend their sovereignty and assert their claims abroad. This they were able to do: for as Herbert Butterfield puts it, in the sixteenth century there was a wind blowing in favour of kings. Already in the fifteenth century Louis XI, legitimate king of France, adopted Italian techniques of force and fraud to strengthen his domestic power and to bring under his control autonomous French states like the duchy of Burgundy. Soon afterwards Ferdinand of Aragon employed the same methods in Spain. These concentrations of power brought the new-style states of Europe's traditional families more continuously and more intensely into conflicts and alliances with each other. So the diplomatic dialogue outside Italy became more continuous and more demanding, and the new methods of conducting it more unavoidable. But the substance, and also the tone, of this dialogue were more concerned with rights and royalty, and less with the acceptance of naked power however acquired, than were the down-to-earth exchanges of the Italians.

Once French intervention had transformed the struggle for position inside Italy into a general diplomatic and military competition of all Western and Southern Europe, one factor began to stand out in the perception of the participants, namely the power of France. The size, wealth and military capacity of that kingdom, its central geographical position and the degree of internal control which its king exercised over it, aroused anti-hegemonic fears among its neighbours which brought them to put aside their differences and form a 'Holy League' to contain and balance it. The complex negotiations which worked out the terms of this multiple alliance, and the many others that followed, were facilitated by the new-style diplomatic agents, whose business it was not only to negotiate on behalf of their masters but to keep them closely informed of everything else that was going on at the court or capital where they were stationed. And in its turn the pressure of what might be called the great European game fostered the development of the network of agents needed to play it effectively.

In order to make the Holy League more binding and durable, the leading princes of the coalition underpinned it with marriage alliances. Marriage contracts played a major part in their own right in the diplomacy of those times. It was necessary for an upstart, a *condottiere* of mercenary troops for instance, who came to control a *stato* in Italy to knit dynastic links with established princely families. For the rulers of trans-Alpine Europe whose legitimacy was not in question, family marriages remained a major preoccupation, both in ensuring or creating rights of succession and increasingly in forging or holding together alliances. As the pressures increased, the hand in marriage of every member of his family became a more significant asset in a ruler's foreign policy. Matters of such royal honour and commitment could not suitably be entrusted to mere agents who had neither the personal rank nor the social standing to conduct them according to the ideas of the age. The dignity of the old-style noble embassy constituted for the purpose was also necessary. The honourable and professional functions had not yet become fused.

As it happened, the marriage alliances of the Holy League had momentous consequences for the course of European history. A series of royal deaths and military victories led to the concentration of the crowns or lordships of Spain, much of Italy, the Netherlands and the elective office of Holy Roman Emperor in the person of the Habsburg Charles V. A single, legitimate preponderant power was created in Europe which threatened to dominate the Christian commonwealth more than the king of France had done. This threat of hegemony by a Habsburg *super-stato* whose penumbra seemed to overshadow all Europe lasted for about a century and a half. When it was finally dissipated at the settlement of Westphalia in the mid-seventeenth century, it was followed by nearly two further centuries of a similar threat from a resurgent France, which Napoleon almost translated into reality, with a Habsburg marriage to seal it. During all this period the diplomacy of Europe was preoccupied with hegemonic pretensions and anti-hegemonic coalitions; and it was in this context that the whole great constructive contribution of diplomacy to the ordering of the European society of independent states was made.

Among the institutions which made this contribution possible, the most characteristic was the resident Mission. It gave us the word diplomacy itself, from the diplomas or letters of credence which envoys presented to the sovereign to which they were accredited, showing their entitlement to act in their own sovereign's name. But the institution took a long time to acquire the respect and indeed prestige enjoyed by dignified temporary embassies. In the fifteenth century, and for some time later, rulers north of the Alps and their advisers regarded foreign agents at their court as useful channels of communication perhaps, but as dangerous men, akin to spies and involved in intrigue with the ruler's domestic enemies. And so no doubt many of them were. They usually communicated with their masters in code; and in the sixteenth century this practice became accepted on a reciprocal basis along with the inviolability of the agent's correspondence with his master generally. But when codes were deciphered or despatches otherwise inter-cepted they often confirmed the suspicions of the host power. The network of resident agents nevertheless became fairly general by the end of the sixteenth century, because of their indispensability to rulers caught up in the pressures of power politics. Once the great sovereigns of Europe accepted resident agents, security and prestige obliged the lesser ones to follow suit. In Maurice Keens-Soper's words, 'One must notice the conditions which made it possible as well as necessary to arrive at this fundamental organizing element and permit its generalized introduction into the bellicose and un-stable affairs of Europe's rulers. These men had no reason to relish the "eyes and ears" of their rivals in settled and protected positions in their own courts and no obvious reason for undertaking the additional burden of being themselves responsible for protecting the activities of other sovereigns' agents whose explicit purpose it was to report on their affairs.'

The immunities accorded to dignified temporary embassies were ex-tended slowly to the households and servants of resident agents. Grotius in his seventeenth-century compilation of international law and custom explains that a resident diplomatic mission is a permanent detached extraterritorial fragment of the represented sovereign's own territory, flying his ensign and subject to his laws and not to those of the host ruler. Certainly practical convenience played a large part in bringing about this extension. Also, as the position of resident envoys approximated more to the honourable status of old-style missions, they became more respectable, more concerned with the dignified and acceptable sides of their work. Men of greater worth tended to be appointed. It became increasingly advisable in practice for resident repre-sentatives of rulers to avoid interference in the internal affairs of the sovereign to which they were accredited. If they did not, or were otherwise indiscreet, the host sovereign had the sanction, frequently used, of declaring the envoy *persona non grata*, which meant that his personal usefulness at that court was at an end and his own master was obliged to recall him if he wished to continue the dialogue with the offended host sovereign on a basis of amity and reciprocity.

The best-known example of the worthier type of resident negotiator and royal representative in the second half of the seventeenth century, when such men were beginning to be aware of themselves as a distinct profession, was François de Callières, envoy and – as we should say – diplomatic representative of the dominant monarch of his day, the Sun King Louis XIV. Callières was a member of the group of able Frenchmen from the *tiers état* or middle class who aspired to rise through royal service to a position at court and with luck to inclusion in the *noblesse de robe* still distinguished from the old nobility of the sword. His manual on his profession, *De la Manière de Négocier avec les Souverains*, was much valued by his colleagues in the French and other services. Callières also wrote guides to behaviour at court and to polite conversation, designed to pass on what he had learnt about how to succeed at court. The negotiator at foreign courts, he says, must above all have a gift for languages (which so often accompanies a flair for understanding how other people think). He must cultivate a sympathetic charm, and do what makes him agreeable, rather than exhibit such pride in his own country that he gives offence. He should learn courtly manners, entertain well and make careful use of flattery and bribery. Different missions required different skills. Based on his experience in the Netherlands, Callières points out that where assemblies are sovereign they may need to be persuaded by oratory, whereas an individual prince does not take kindly to being harangued. But the negotiator should always avoid fraud and trickery, which impair the confidence of sovereigns and their ministers.

All this advice clearly needed to be given, and it is significant that it did. Callières's book is only one, perhaps the best, of a surprising number of such practical manuals. He and other diplomatic envoys saw a new profession emerging, and wanted to distinguish themselves from amateurs drawn from other walks of life who were not qualified to carry out negotiations. These writers of diplomatic handbooks excluded as unsuitable the often dubious resident agents of former times who did not have the necessary social status. They also excluded the high nobility who were too proud to ingratiate themselves or to learn foreign languages, and who insisted on using their own judgement, not only on how to implement their sovereign's policy but on what it should be. Equally unsatisfactory in their eyes were the military commanders and ecclesiastics who were still often entrusted with diplomatic assignments. They also distinguished their new profession from the law. The task was to persuade another sovereign, not to prove him wrong and your master right. The training of a lawyer, says Callières, breeds habits of mind which are not favourable to the practice of diplomacy. (How many professional diplomats, down to our own times, have reached this conclusion, often reluctantly.) Finally and characteristically, Callières stresses the need for tact towards one's own prince, reporting in ways calculated to persuade him. How necessary this last and greatest art was with the Sun King, Callières understood well; and in due course he reaped a satisfactory reward. In this advice one can also discern an indication of awareness that a ruler's envoy abroad may perceive certain aspects of the sovereign's interest more clearly than does the ruler himself.

The negotiators and foreign representatives at each European court or capital naturally gravitated together. There were interminable disputes over precedence, as well as personal rivalries and jealousies and the inevitable competition for the sovereign's ear. But the envoys realised that they had much in common. They needed to protect their status and privileges, for which purpose they often appointed a common spokesman to act on their behalf. And they saw advantage in exchanging information and evaluation, which became especially common among the representatives of allies: for no one observer sees the whole picture by himself, and he is helped by seeing it also through his colleagues' eyes. Moreover, friendly personal relations between envoys, even when their masters quarrelled, helped to provide the oil which the institution needed in order to function smoothly. There thus came to be constituted a permanent *corps diplomatique* in each capital, a sort of envoys' club, though its individual members might come and go. Diplomacy was becoming more collective.

Similarly, after great and general wars in Europe, major diplomatic congresses came to be held, to negotiate not merely the terms of peace between the warring sovereigns but some general ordering of the affairs of the *res publica* that Europe was recognized to be. The two principal congresses of the period, which negotiated the agreements known as the settlements of Westphalia and Utrecht, were lengthy and complex affairs, involving many negotiations often in different places, attended by many princes or their senior ministers in person; but they were largely carried on and indeed made possible by a great *ad hoc corps diplomatique* of professional negotiators who were used to dealing not only with princes but with each other, and who knew the rules and the objectives of their developing institution. These great congresses helped to focus the diplomatic dialogue and to bring negotiations to a decision.

Diplomatic congresses were not regarded in the seventeenth century and subsequently as isolated events. They were climaxes of the dialogue between the independent states of the European *res publica* which went on all the time and which the professional diplomats and their masters, the statesmen of Europe, considered to have a value in itself. Resident envoys and the diplomatic dialogue they conducted were not there to deal only with crises and quarrels and special requests, but to exchange views and negotiate every day as a matter of course. Cardinal Richelieu, the ablest statesman of the first half of the seventeenth century, stated in the political testament attributed to him his belief in the value of negotiation for its own sake. He wondered how he could remain in diplomatic contact with France's enemies even in periods of war, perhaps in neutral capitals and through other channels. For it was diplomacy that was now continuous and all-embracing in the European society of states, while war was intermittent and only between certain states, with at least some neutrals standing aside from any given military operations. The diplomatic dialogue became less ideological and less determined by religion, since it included both Catholic and Protestant states, and increasingly also the Ottoman Empire which was not Christian at all. Of course religion and religious settlements were an important subject of diplomacy, but both the practitioners and the statesmen gradually learnt to stand back from the convictions and passions which religious differences and religious wars aroused, and to look for settlements that could be accepted by at least the most *powerful* states involved.

For the diplomatic dialogue, increasingly dissociated from moral, religious and other considerations, increasingly elastic and neutral, was always centrally concerned with and determined by the power of the participants. Princes and professionals alike understood that the risk of resort to force of arms was inevitably and always present, a consequence of the independence of states, a structural feature of the system. The voice of violence permeated and coloured the voice of negotiation. It showed itself in the form of threats, open or implied, in the language of treaties of alliance and treaties of settlement, in the assignment by every statesman of funds for military expenditure, in the attempts by the *corps diplomatique* in every court and capital to assess the military capacity of the prince or state, in daily discussion of the news. In the last resort superior force is unanswerable. The authority of force was at its most imperative after great wars, when diplomacy could do little more than register and temper the harsh verdict that had already been determined on the battlefield. But even in less decisive circumstances negotiations between princes and indeed the whole diplomatic dialogue sought for solutions in full awareness of the alternative arbitrament of war, agreements which made due allowance for the ultimate right, the ultimate reason of kings.

Power, and particularly military power, was thus the central inescapable problem to which the ingenuity of diplomacy had to find a constructive answer. The long anti-hegemonic struggle for independence against the

Habsburg *super-stato* led to the collapse of Spain and the effective fragmentation of Germany into a number of principalities whose independence *de facto* was recognized at the Westphalian settlement. The opponents of that hegemony heaved a sigh of relief, only to find that France, the animator of the anti-hegemonic coalition, was left as the strongest power in Europe, with a king, Louis XIV, determined to assert at least as great an authority outside his own domains as the Habsburgs had done. Those who opposed Louis's bid for dominance, and even those who made short-term profit for themselves by working with him, came to see that the real threat to the European order and the independence of its members was not Spain or France as such, not the Reformation or Catholicism, but the concentration anywhere in the system of unanswerable power.

The conviction grew among statesmen that power must not be allowed to become unanswerable. It must be kept in check before it reached such proportions, necessarily by a combination of other powers. Not a permanent coalition, for men had learnt that the ally of yesterday might turn out to be the enemy of today; and not a coalition vowing vengeance and destruction, for the enemy of today might be needed as an ally tomorrow; but enough to balance the power in the system. The Dutch King William III, the great anti-hegemonic statesman of the second half of the seventeenth century, as Richelieu had been of the first, was once asked what he would do if the power of France was laid so low by the coalition with the Habsburgs which he had built, that Spain once again became the threat to the liberties of Europe. He replied that he would then become as much a Frenchman as he was now a Spaniard; which was not much. Both the question and the answer well illustrate the flavour of the diplomatic dialogue at that time. Statesmen began to extend to the whole of the commonwealth of Europe Lorenzo dei Medici's imaginative concept that the affairs of all Italy should be maintained in a state of balance. This basic purpose of diplomacy was explicitly formulated in the settlement of Utrecht, which laid it down that even the right of hereditary succession must give way to the preservation of 'a just balance of power'. This was the culmination of seventeenth-century diplomacy.

After the long anti-hegemonic struggles of previous periods, the eighteenth century from the Utrecht settlement to the French Revolution was a period in which the affairs of Europe did in fact hang in a certain balance, and no state was in a position to make a bid for hegemony. Religion and other ideologies, normally of great consequence for the foreign policies of European powers, were at a low ebb. Their place was taken by a belief in reason, including of course *raison d'état*. The diplomatic dialogue was much concerned with the adjustments needed to maintain a just balance. This balance covered the whole European *res publica*, which now included Russia, and extended beyond Europe to the colonial world and non-European states overseas. It was a concept consciously present in the minds of statesmen, who saw it as corresponding to the balance of the solar system propounded at that time by Newton; and some in more constitutional countries also regarded it as equivalent to the checks and balances necessary to preserve equilibrium inside their state. As the power of any state grew in comparison to its neighbours, so adjustments should be made in its favour, but also the other states in the system should move further away from it and closer to each other. It was the business of diplomacy to negotiate these modifications. Ideally the adjustments would be so continuous and acceptable, and correspond so exactly to shifts in the balance of power, that actual resorts to force would not be needed, and would not be effective if they were made. In practice, the efforts of princes and diplomats were not exclusively concentrated on achieving adjustments in the name of equilibrium. They were often directed to avoiding the losses which their state might suffer (which was especially the case with the Habsburgs), and French diplomats felt that the whole concept of the balance of power operated against France as the strongest single power in the system. Therefore there were wars, both in Europe and in the ever-expanding overseas possessions of the leading European powers. But they were limited wars for limited objectives, as the wars between Italian princes had been. Fought between uniformed soldiers, they produced less of the brutality and destruction that accompanies all violence than the fearful wars of religion that had marked the previous period. So the diplomatic dialogue accepted fairly easily that wars had their place in the system when adjustments could not be made by negotiation. The conscious maintenance of the balance of power preserved the independence of states, by and large; but it did not preserve the peace.

The eighteenth century also saw innovations in the methods of diplomacy. There was a change in the sort of people who became permanent envoys. Bitter quarrels over precedence at court between envoys each of whom saw not only his personal influence but the honour of his sovereign at stake, made princes more aware again of the advantage of being represented at other courts by members of the nobility, high-born enough in that pedigree-conscious age to take their place by birth right in the highest court circles. Moreover the nobility, so long jealous of the growing power of kings and anxious to preserve their own rights and privileges against the authority of the central government, were now more ready to serve the prince or the state in 'noble' employments – for instance as loyal officers in professional armies, as ambassadors and envoys, and as colonial governors. So at last the functions of the resident agent and of the ceremonial envoy on special mission became fused. The dignity and social cachet of resident diplomacy increased: ambassadors no longer needed manuals of court etiquette; and well-born families sought to place their sons through personal influence as secretaries and attachés to ambassadors in the same way as they obtained commissions for them in good regiments. The title of ambassador became reserved for representatives of kings; and below these high dignitaries ranked ministers and other representatives, down to lowly consular agents.

Less conspicuous, but in the long run as important for the conduct of diplomacy, was the institution in the eighteenth century of something like regular ministries of foreign affairs. The rulers of states, whether they were hereditary monarchs, powerful ministers or councils, continued to determine the broad lines of national policy and of the diplomatic dialogue. Envoys abroad remained as much as ever the personal representatives of the sovereign. But in that century the dialogue, the reporting and the negotiation, reached a volume which made it necessary to appoint a special minister in the government to conduct day-to-day business and to supervise the implementation of the main lines of the policy laid down from above. Such ministers of foreign affairs wanted to have as their assistants not only clerks but men with some experience of diplomacy, including some who had served as secretaries at posts abroad, knew the countries concerned and had seen the game from the other side. Diplomacy put a premium not only on awareness and perceptiveness in general, but also on the specific ability to sense what moves the other players were likely to make as circumstances changed. As such ministries became organized, the statesmen who had to make the final decisions naturally turned to them for information about the consequences of different options, and so gave them a role in shaping decisions. The institution of ministries of diplomacy, or foreign offices, was in a sense the logical complement of resident envoys. But it became effective some two centuries later and was to prove an innovation at least as important as resident embassies, and perhaps more so, for the conduct of diplomacy today.

In contrast to the very impressive development of thought and theory about the domestic ordering of the state, the functions of its government and its constitutional structure, which distinguished the three centuries we have discussed and which greatly influenced political reality, theory about the states system and the ordering of the commonwealth of Europe, where it existed at all, was content to follow practice. Machiavelli and other Italians pointed the way to a theory they did not seriously attempt to formulate. Thereafter most writers on the nature of the relationship between the members of the *res publica* were concerned with the description or codification of practice, so that even 'international law' was a generalization of the way states behaved, the rules they usually observed and the traditional norms which they still respected. Others made specific recommendations or produced general plans for the ordering of Europe without much serious analysis of how sovereigns acted outside their territorial boundaries and why. As a result, the shape of the diplomatic dialogue, its rules, its institutions, its great architectural purposes, were not subject to heated debate by large numbers of men with committed beliefs on the subject, but improvized and evolved *ambulando* by practical operators, statesmen and envoys who were preoccupied and hard pressed by immediate problems and by the advancement or defence of their own state interests. So the most interesting generalizations on the subject were produced either by major statesmen like Richelieu and Frederick the Great or by professional diplomats like Pufendorf (who gave currency to the term 'systems of states'), Callières and Vattel.

Vattel formulated with Swiss clarity the consensus of his time about European international society. 'Europe,' he wrote, 'forms a political system in which the nations inhabiting this part of the world are bound together by their relations and various interests into a single body. . . . The constant attentions of sovereigns [we should say statesmen] to all that goes on, the custom of resident ministers [embassies], the continual negotiations that take place, make modern Europe a sort of republic whose members, each independent but all bound together by a common interest, unite for the maintenance of order and the preservation of [their] liberty.' But, he went on, Europe was not a state, with a law-making and law-enforcing authority. In a state each citizen or member must 'yield certain of his rights to the general body, and there must be some authority capable of giving commands, prescribing laws and compelling those who refuse to obey them. Such an idea is not to be thought of between nations.' Europe was held together not by law or authority but by common interests and by voluntary agreements and contracts. Identifying these interests and negotiating these agreements was the function of diplomacy. This is what Burke meant when he spoke of a diplomatic republic.

The diplomatic society of eighteenth-century Europe, the Age of Enlightenment, ensured the independence of most of its member states through the balance of power, but it did not preserve the peace. The avoidance of war began to seem increasingly important to thoughtful men. But before diplomacy could come to grips with this intractable problem, rather suddenly at the end of the century the French Revolution released the enormous energy of France, which was still the greatest and most populous state in Europe but which had remained semi-dormant since the defeat of Louis XIV. The genius of Napoleon harnessed this energy to the creation of a personal *super-stato* in Europe in the style of the Italian Renaissance, combined with a new democratic populism and the opening of careers to talent. Here was apparently unanswerable power. It swept away the careful balance of the eighteenth-century diplomatic republic, the old courts and kings, to install not revolutionary democracies but a great Napoleonic Empire and a penumbra of satellite kingdoms ruled by members of the Emperor's family or his generals. Napoleon's propagandists preached the advantages of hegemony. After the carnage was over, France would protect the other states of Europe and maintain peace, and also establish more just societies to make up for the loss of independence. The anti-hegemonic coalitions that formed and broke against Napoleon aimed to restore the eighteenth-century world. But when, after twenty years of war which saw French troops in Moscow and Russian troops in Paris, Napoleon was finally defeated, the sophisticated statesmen of the day welcomed France back to the family of civilized states on an equal footing with the most powerful of the allies. They did so because they understood that France remained a great power whose cooperation was necessary if the international society which they had been fighting for was to function effectively. But they also recognized that the old order could not really be restored. The diplomatic dialogue was now concerned to combat the challenge of revolutionary ideas and the *pax napoleonica* with something more than mere reliance on the balance of power.

The Vienna settlement appears in retrospect as the high point of practical achievement of the European diplomatic system. It established the boundaries and governments of Europe in place of those swept away by Napoleon, and much else besides. More important, it recognized the need for *collective machinery* to maintain and modify the settlement. Out of the original Holy Alliance of victor states there evolved the most impressive phase of European diplomacy, the Concert of Europe. This was in a sense a hegemonic authority based on the five great powers; and it must be held a mark of great statesmanship that it included recently defeated France. The hegemony would not be exercised by a single power, which was unacceptable, but would be diffused among five watchful states with differing interests, thus incorporating the safeguard of the balance. But the statesmen of the post-Napoleonic era also saw the need to cooperate in order to make their restored European society function adequately. On those occasions where the great powers agreed to act together, they could collectively do what none would let another do alone, lay down and amend the law; or, as they saw it, maintain order and religion and orchestrate the Concert of Europe.

The collegiate sense that ran through the Vienna settlement is reflected in the famous protocol determining exactly the hitherto much-disputed functions and orders of precedence of diplomatic missions. This protocol, still largely in force in the worldwide system of today, confirmed the existence of a diplomatic corps in each capital, and established that its doyen or spokesman should be not the ambassador of the most powerful state, but the papal representative where this arrangement was traditional, and elsewhere the ambassador who had been longest accredited, regardless of the importance of his country.

The Vienna settlement had its weaknesses. As usual after long and general wars in a society of states, it inclined too much towards the *status quo* and to repress rather than incorporate the 'revolutionary' demands of popular nationalism and social change. But it succeeded better than other settlements after major post-war settlements, both before and since – perhaps because its framers preferred complex expediency and realism to simplistic principles. The proof of the pudding was a century of near peace in Europe, during which major adjustments were made and great material prosperity developed. The minor European wars of the following hundred years were little more than campaigns, fought by professionals for limited objectives, which did not noticeably interrupt material progress and the development of civilization and the arts, or the expansion of European dominance over the rest of the Old World. No tragedy on the scale of the destructive American Civil War afflicted the competitive but diffused and balanced power structure of the nineteenth-century European society of states. To a considerable extent this must be attributed to the flexible expediency of the concert of great powers set up as a result of the Congress of Vienna.

The great changes that transformed European society in the nineteenth century inevitably had their effect on the diplomatic dialogue between its states. Of these we may single out two: the growth of a wider public interest in foreign affairs and the development of technology.

Informed public interest in foreign policy, and indeed passionate argument about it, had already become familiar enough, especially during the wars of religion. But the foreign policy of the state was nevertheless normally regarded as the prerogative of the sovereign, usually a monarch who depended on a small circle of experienced statesmen to conduct it. The flavour of the diplomatic dialogue between kings, statesmen and envoys in nineteenth-century Europe was aristocratic, cosmopolitan within the limits of Europe and pragmatic. But as the century progressed, in most European countries a wider public opinion came to exert increasing influence, not only over the conduct of government at home of which it had direct experience, but also over foreign policy about which it was much less well informed. Middle-class public opinion tended to be markedly more concerned with principle than pragmatism, with rights and wrongs rather than cooperation and expediency, with partisanship for popular aspirations and causes rather than urbane compromise, with suspicion of foreigners rather than with cosmopolitanism. The intermarried monarchs of Europe thought of each other as cousins and rivals rather than as foreigners. The aristocratic and cynical statesmen whom the kings usually nominated to conduct the diplomatic dialogue, and who arranged the compromises and political deals of the Concert, had family connections or at least friends and colleagues across the state borders – borders which they did not regard as sacred and which had in many cases been redrawn several times by and after Napoleon. But for the middle ranks of society, increasingly used to thinking for themselves, foreigners were strangers. Consequently, as governments became more democratic and political leaders came to depend for their positions more on popular support, and foreign policy came increasingly into the public domain, statesmen reflected an uncompromising nationalism they did not always personally feel, and a commitment to principle that accorded with the religious temper of the age and not necessarily with their own convictions.

Newspapers enhanced the influence of the middle class on the conduct of diplomacy. They often fed the prejudices of their readers and reflected them back as something close to facts. They also demanded from political leaders, and from professional diplomats, an increasing volume of information about the conduct of foreign policy and an increasing commitment to principles which made diplomatic compromise more difficult to attain and to defend. Statesmen and negotiators resented this inquisitiveness and this constraint on their dialogue, and the need for public accountability on issues that could be more satisfactorily (that is, more quickly and with less tension) settled confidentially. Though the same statesmen recognized that these demands by the press and the public were legitimate in a democracy, they tended to regard them as a necessary evil, and the mutual distrust persisted. The exasperated comment on the press of Paris by the Marquess of Dufferin, British Ambassador there in 1893, to the Earl of Roseberry, then Foreign Secretary, is fairly typical of the period:

The press of Paris is the worst press in Europe. The people who contribute to it are very clever, and know exactly how to excite the rancour or inflame the prejudices of their readers. They have a congenital and instinctive disregard of truth, and they lie – not as an Englishman lies when he does lie, of malice prepense – but because they do not feel that a lie matters much one way or the other. They are for the most part absolutely ignorant of the history, the language, the habits, the politics, the modes of thought, and the geography of other countries, and, with a certain number of honourable exceptions, gain is their only motive, unless when it is spite or revenge. Moreover writers of this class, like angry women, find a certain excitement and relief in reviling people they dislike, even at the expense of the obvious interests of their country, and when they can have no practical end in view. On the other hand, the French newspaper-reading public requires highly seasoned and abusive articles to stimulate their attention and to feed their prejudices. Denunciations of England are therefore pretty sure to command a large and lucrative circulation. As a consequence, not a day passes that we are not taken to task for our sordid politics, our overbearing manners, our selfishness, our perfidy and our other inveterate bad qualities. . . . Nor once a myth of the kind is started, can it ever be eradicated. From a lie it grows into a tradition and eventually passes into history.

Those who watched and commented on the operations of European diplomacy were often equally pontifical and equally critical of those who conducted it.

In central and eastern Europe the ideal of nationalism and the increasing power of public opinion also led nations like the Germans and Italians, as well as the Poles, Hungarians and peoples under Turkish rule, to demand the break-up of the great empires in Europe and the creation of nation-states. National self-determination gradually displaced earlier concepts of legitimacy. But the power-conscious diplomatic dialogue made it subject, as dynastic rights had been, to the proviso that the balance of power must not be upset by the creation of nation-states. The most serious threat to the balance would be the creation of a united German state in the heart of Europe, from the Mass to the Memel and from Vienna to the North Sea, a goal to which many and perhaps most Germans aspired. The realistic Prussian statesman Bismarck, who dominated the diplomacy of the second half of the century, saw the danger and formed a smaller Germany which excluded the Austrian lands; but unfortunately for Europe he did not resist the re-acquisition of the former German provinces of Alsace and Lorraine from France when that country had been defeated in an attempt to prevent the formation of even a smaller Germany. Bismarck had a sense of *raison de système* as well as *raison d'état*. He did not seek greater adjustments in Prussia's favour than rising German power could easily compel and which (with the exception of Alsace-Lorraine) the European society of states would accept. The last great congress of the Concert, to decide the fate of the Ottoman Empire in Europe, was held in 1878 under his auspices. After that, European diplomacy became less collegiate and more focussed within rival alliances. The attempt to negotiate an Anglo-German agreement which would manage the necessary adjustments in Europe and the world was abandoned in 1901.

The development of technology, which produced such dramatic changes in man's mastery over nature and the quality of life in the developed countries, caused minor and more subtle changes in nineteenth-century European diplomacy. It was affected by the revolution in communications, which had remained since Roman times limited by how fast a man could travel on horseback. Now the telegraph made the transmission of messages almost instantaneous, and the railroad and the steamboat made travel and the despatch of documents somewhat faster and certainly safer. Sovereigns and statesmen could now conduct a dialogue with each other by proxy through their envoys on something like a day-to-day basis, instead of having to endure the long delays involved in correspondence across Europe by horseback or round it by sailing ship. The new speed of communication made the dialogue between governments and foreign offices somewhat more intense, and reduced the discretion and the authority to negotiate which previously had to be delegated to ambassadors in order to reach agreements in a reasonable time. Even so, throughout the century diplomacy in Europe remained much as the Vienna agreements had established it. Kings and courts continued to dominate the political or at least the diplomatic scene. The French Republic dated effectively only from 1871, and the newly established Balkan states were provided with kings from the interrelated European royal families. Ambassadors and ministers accredited by one monarch to another were courtiers: aristocrats or at least men capable of holding their own in the world in which they had to operate. In most cases they were also impressively professional and responsible. The best of them were well able to weigh the instructions they received from their king or government against their own judgement and the collegiate sense of their diplomatic colleagues. But being the men they were, they responded slowly to the social and technological change burgeoning around them. Their attitude was in marked contrast to the leaders of the armed services who, drawn from the same background and sharing the same social conservatism, were caught up in a keen competition to adapt industrial advances to warfare and to equip their armies and navies with the latest mass-produced inventions and devices. The preoccupations of the soldiers helped to weaken the diplomatic cohesion of Europe. By the end of the century the oppressive awareness of military rivalry between the groups of states helped to concentrate the diplomatic dialogue on maintaining alliances and to weaken the sense of responsibility to European society as a whole.

We have so far looked at the diplomatic society of Europe as something contained within its own culture and its own power-political system. And so in its own eyes it still essentially was. However, a fundamental transformation was beginning to take place as a result of the expansion of Europe out over the world. What had been a society of states in one continent, held together by a shared culture, now became global. The consequences manifested themselves only slowly.

The position at the beginning of the nineteenth century was as follows: the British and the Iberians, the insular and peninsular peoples of the west of Europe, had settled the new world of the Americas and founded new states there. These settler states had by the time of the Vienna settlement wholly or nearly established their independence, and had for practical purposes virtually excluded other European powers from the American continent. Meanwhile several European states had acquired rival trading and strategic stations round the coasts of Asia and Africa, though only the British in India administered sizeable tracts of land. The new republics set up by British and Iberian settlers in the Americas quickly developed policies of dissociation from the European balance of power and from what Washington dubbed entangling alliances. But they cherished their cultural and trade contacts with Europe, and maintained diplomatic relations with European states. Their desire to avoid relationships based on power and to keep their hemisphere free from the competition of the European states led them, with the United States to the fore, to place more emphasis on international law, and on the rule of law in international society, than did European states. They were particularly insistent about the laws and conventions regulating neutrality in time of war. But the impact of American ideas on international society was not significant until the twentieth century. The European states regarded the transatlantic contribution to the diplomatic dialogue as rather marginal, and saw the attitude of the American states and their virtual immunity from European expansion as a luxury made possible by the *pax britannica*, the British naval dominance of the high seas which inhibited other European powers from pursuing their interests in the Americas by force.

Eastward, on the other hand, there were no such inhibitions. The industrial revolution increased the power of the more advanced European states almost to bursting point, and created an insatiable economic demand both for raw materials and for markets. One answer for the most active states was renewed expansion outward into Asia and Africa. In this enterprise the Europeans enjoyed immense advantages: in the goods they produced and which non-Europeans wanted, in the military means of enforcing their authority, and in the conviction of their own moral and intellectual superiority. Asians and Africans were no longer able to put up effective resistance. The only serious challenge which the European states encountered was from each other. Given the long history of colonial wars between Europeans, the number and size of military and naval expeditions operating in the field, and the intensity of the territorial scramble, it is further remarkable evidence of the effectiveness of the Concert of Europe that this immense assertion of competitive European dominance was ordered and demarcated by the rival colonial powers through almost continuous diplomatic negotiation during a whole century, according to the perceived power and capacity of each, without their actually coming to blows with each other except for the minor clash of the Crimean War. Russia alone expanded by land, consolidating and settling a solid block of empire in Asia that stretched to the Pacific and the Himalayas and that has lasted almost intact to the present. The other empires were necessarily seaborne, and therefore far more fragile; and only the British, which was much the largest, had any significant degree of white settlement. The maritime powers established a plethora of new colonial states, administered by Europeans according to their own purposes and values: some vast like the Indian Empire, some tiny clusters of islands. All were destined to become independent members of a greatly enlarged international society in the twentieth century, as the earlier European empires in the Americas had before them.

European diplomatic society, having accepted the new settler states of the Americas, was now prepared to accept on occasion a few non-European states as well. Some non-European states in the eastern hemisphere were able to retain their independence between the expanding empires. Usually this was because their strategic or commercial importance made the dominance of any one European power unacceptable to its rivals. China, Persia and Afghanistan are examples in Asia, and Ethiopia and Morocco in Africa, though Persia and Morocco were divided into spheres of influence at the beginning of the twentieth century. There were also the more significant cases of the Ottoman Empire and Japan.

Though the Turks had played a major part in the strategic and economic life of the European states system for centuries, entering into its diplomatic dialogue and contracting alliances and other treaties, they had refused to consider themselves members of the European family of states. For instance, they declined to send resident envoys to European capitals in return for the European ambassadors which they accepted at Constantinople, and took no part in the major diplomatic settlements like those of Utrecht and Vienna which formulated the rules of European society. But in the period of decline of the Ottoman Empire, the Concert of Europe decided at the Paris Congress in 1856 to co-opt it formally into the society of states, to ensure more European standards of domestic government and to prevent its piecemeal dismemberment. The same arrangement was soon extended for the same reasons to the weak and extensive Chinese Empire and the remaining independent states of the Old World. Various special provisions for the exemption of Europeans from local law and other 'capitulations' which the Ottomans had evolved to accommodate foreign traders were extended to China and elsewhere. The European society thus became worldwide and its rules were applied globally while remaining entirely European in conception and formulation. For in spite of their formal equality, non-European states were not accorded the same standing as white and Christian states.

All the more impressive therefore was the contrasting case of Japan. The Japanese had remained virtually isolated from even the Asian mainland for centuries until they were forced into more open contact with the West by the United States, which was by then also an imperial power in the Pacific. From then on the Japanese enthusiastically and successfully adopted Western technology and political concepts, until by the turn of the century they were able to negotiate an alliance on an equal footing with the already overstretched British and gained a striking victory over Russia. Japan was the first non-white state to be accepted by the Europeans as one of their directory of great powers, who were the architects of the European diplomatic society. This was a portent for the future. But it did not change the nature of the dialogue: on the contrary, the Japanese were meticulous in observing the letter and the spirit of European practice.

European civilization, which for centuries had developed steadily in power and in prosperity, in the sciences and in the arts, was gravely (perhaps mortally) damaged by the catastrophe of World War One. We cannot here go into the causes of this exceptionally destructive explosion except to note that one contributory factor was the gradual disintegration of the diplomatic Concert of Europe and of the sense that the great powers had a joint responsibility to negotiate the management of changes in the power of the states in the system. The immense amount of detailed research into the subject indicates that the statesmen failed to arrange through the diplomatic dialogue the necessary adjustments to the enormous, competitive and uneven growth of power generated by the industrial revolution, or even to see the problem very clearly. Consequently, that power built up to the point where the constraints of the European system could no longer contain it, and exploded with appalling consequences. Could this over-concentration of energy and capacity have been relieved by 'calling in Asia and Africa to redress the balance of Europe', in other words by a cooperative agreement to establish a new worldwide balance corresponding to the new realities of power? The question was not seriously addressed; and in practice the imperial powers went their own ways outside Europe, in rivalry though not in war. The states on the periphery of Europe – Britain and Russia especially – found it relatively easy to expand outwards into Asia and Africa, whereas post-Bismarck Germany, where power developed later but faster than anywhere else, was unable to achieve 'a place in the sun' corresponding to her strength. So the transition from a geographically European to a Eurocentric global system merely contained rather than relieved the pressure building up in Germany. However, even if we conclude that European diplomacy in the years before 1914 left undone the things which it ought to have done, or which we with hindsight can see that it might have done, that failure was only one among many causes of the war.

The horror of World War One shocked both statesmen and public opinion in Europe, and elsewhere too, into a massive reaction against war and against the international anarchy that had prevailed since the decline of the Concert of Europe and had led to Armageddon. International institutions much more collective and much more tightly knit than the defunct Concert were felt to be required. First there must be a just settlement of boundaries and other claims, based on the new legitimacy of self-determination. Then there must be a league of peace-loving nations to keep the peace, strong enough to deal with any aggressor who took the law into his own hands and tried to challenge any aspect of the settlement by force. Under the influence of the United States whose hitherto latent but vast power had ensured victory to the Allied side, and particularly the vision of its lofty President Wilson, these dispositions were framed in terms of the rule of law, an end to the balance of power and secret diplomacy, and a solemn covenant of nations rather than empires: in short, a world safe for democracy. European traditions, born of experience and more cynical than the American vision, led European statesmen to ensure that responsibility for peace and war was entrusted not to all the states in the League but to a Council dominated by five great powers; and that self-determination was not applied to Germans, for fear of the creation of that greater Germany which Bismarck had wisely refrained from forming, and also not yet to non-Europeans, who were held to be still too backward to opt out of European imperial tutelage. The League of Nations was hamstrung by two drawbacks. Firstly, it and the *status quo* it had to defend were linked to the Versailles settlement, a pathetically inadequate and shortsighted dispensation whose political and economic provisions soon proved unworkably at variance with the realities of power, and which, as some of its authors saw, fell lamentably far short of the achievements of Vienna, Utrecht and Westphalia. Secondly, many of the great powers of the twentieth century stayed aloof or were excluded from the operations of the League: the United States by Senatorial decision; Russia on account of the Bolshevik Revolution; Germany as the defeated power; and Japan which discovered that the new collective system did not allow it to develop its capacities either by open access to the world's markets or by establishing an exclusive empire in China. Britain and France, severely damaged by the war, were too weak to manage the problems of the world alone with the faint support of a number of minor states in the League.

All in all, the Versailles settlement displayed a dangerous disregard of the experience and the lessons of the diplomatic society of Europe. In Frederick's metaphor, the musical score which the League was expected to play ignored the realities of power, and instead of a series of adjustments there was much moralizing on all sides and a cacophony of discordant sound.

But rigid and inadequate though the League proved to be, it was the beginning of a major new development in diplomacy. In place of the occasional congresses of interested European powers that supplemented the conventional diplomatic dialogue to settle specific issues, the League instituted a permanent ongoing diplomatic congress, open to membership by all the independent states of the world. Its omnilateral character brought the non-European states as formal equals into the management of international society and accorded a voice to the small and less powerful states, in contrast to the Concert of Europe which had largely ignored them. The League was not a world legislature, the quasi-parliamentary debating arrangements of the Assembly notwithstanding; and even less a government. It was a piece of diplomatic machinery designed to supplement on a permanent basis, rather than to replace, the traditional bilateral dialogue between the individual states; and the formal equality of these states in the League and in the Court of International Justice did no more than redress the secondary status which most of them had suffered in the nineteenth century. The League also established the principle of collective security – the involvement of all its members in the defence of any one of them. Collective security at that stage provided an insurance only against armed attack, and events were soon to show that such insurance did not work. But the idea of a guarantee by international society of the minimum needs of its members was a new and creative one. It involved a significant new extension of the diplomatic dialogue, and in particular an enlargement of *raison de système* and of the responsibilities of states.

World War One was a European war. Its worldwide repercussions and involvement were greater in extent but not in nature than those caused by previous great European struggles. World War Two was a truly global war. It may be taken as marking the end of the European states system, and of an international society devised and dominated by Europeans. It is true that the transition from a European to a global international society took place without a decisive break such as Alexander's 'universal' empire made between the classical Greek and the Macedonian societies of states. The two super-powers of the global system, America and Russia, are states of European origin; most of the new states of Asia and Africa were European colonies or mandates; and in a hundred other ways the practices of the European society have continued in modified and attenuated form into the new order. Nevertheless, European diplomatic society has visibly given place to something else. What can we say in conclusion about the European system?

A society of independent states is by its nature an exceedingly difficult thing to organize and to operate. By this standard, and measured against the achievement of other states systems, the European system performed remarkably well over a considerable period. It achieved the greatest and most constructive development of the diplomatic dialogue that the world has known, which was able to involve all the major powers of the system in a competitive but also constructive diplomatic *res publica*. It accepted as the basis of political action by its members the pursuit of state interests conceived in terms of power but developed beyond that stage into cooperative ventures which were designed to regulate the system itself in the interests of all its members, not least the smaller and weaker. It evolved, in the network of resident embassies and ministries of foreign affairs with interchangeable cadres of professional personnel, the most sensitive and effective instrument for conducting the dialogue and for realizing its potential. It did not master the problem of resort by its members to ever more destructive force against each other; and in the end this resort to force destroyed the system itself in our century. But no international society, including our contemporary one, can be said to have mastered this problem. What European diplomacy did achieve was moderation and control of the resort to force by its member states, to a greater extent and for longer periods than our history books and our folk-memories are apt to suggest. These remarkable achievements were made possible in particular by a common awareness and a shared experience. European diplomatic society had, at the centre if not at all the fringes, that 'union of several contiguous states' resembling each other in their codes of conduct, values and degree of economic and social development, and held together by shared and reciprocal interests which Heeren considered the basic and necessary attributes of a states system. It is sobering to remember that these attributes hardly exist in the global international society of today.

CHAPTER IX

Professional Diplomacy Today

Diplomacy as we know it today is essentially a function of the modern state: its relations with other states, with the institutionalized alliances and groupings which it or other states may form, and with omnilateral or general organizations like the United Nations. Beyond this dialogue between states and their representatives there is a penumbra of diplomacy where one of the interlocutors to the dialogue is not another state, but nevertheless a significant actor on the international scene: for instance, a political movement that aims to set up a new state, such as the Palestine Liberation Organization, or to take over an existing one, or else an international body such as a church (other than the Vatican which is regarded as a state), or a commercial organization like an oil company. The forms and mechanisms of contemporary diplomacy have been inherited largely from the European states system. That system was a much more homogeneous and closely knit international society than the present disparate global one. Also the range of subjects which now regularly come into the diplomatic dialogue has greatly increased since the system expanded geographically. Consequently the inherited European forms, which had been subject to continual evolution and change even in the European system, are today fairly bursting at some of their seams, and visibly in transition. But as often happens with conventions, it matters less what exactly the rules are than that everyone observes them so that behaviour is predictable; and it is impressive how much of the machinery of European diplomacy is still in active use.

Since diplomacy is a state's means of communication with the world outside it, the principals in the dialogue are governments, and in the final analysis heads of government. (It would be convenient to use the term 'heads of state' here, in the American sense of heads of government; but in practice that usage is merely confusing, because a large number of countries have as their heads of state symbolic ceremonial monarchs and presidents, in whose name professional diplomacy is carried on but who are not heads of government and do not exercise the authority under discussion here.) No head of a large and complex modern government can personally direct all the significant diplomatic business of his state, in the way a Renaissance prince found it possible and necessary to do. He is obliged to delegate not only the actual conduct of the dialogue abroad almost entirely to ambassadors, envoys and other members of diplomatic missions, as has always been the case; but also to delegate many of the decisions on policy to political colleagues and trusted advisers.

In the forefront of these colleagues is the minister for external affairs: in British parlance the Foreign Secretary, in American the Secretary of State. This minister is responsible for directing the state's professional diplomatic service and for dealing with foreign ambassadors. In governments where a degree of cabinet or collegial responsibility prevails, he reports to his colleagues on relations with the outside world, and implements their collective decisions (which he and the head of government will have a large share in making) through the diplomatic machinery which he administers. In the U.S. and other presidential governments he deals more directly with the head of government.

Two tendencies should be noted here. First, other departments of government, and therefore other cabinet ministers, find themselves increasingly carried beyond the determination of the general lines of their government's foreign policy, and involved in the details of the diplomatic dialogue which were previously the domain of the minister and the department dealing with external affairs, because the diplomatic dialogue more directly concerns these other areas of authority. This has long been the case with the ministers responsible for defence, finance and foreign trade: now ministers concerned with subjects hitherto regarded as domestic, and once not even the direct concern of governments at all, like agriculture and public health, are becoming steadily more involved. Consequently, the influence of the minister for external affairs in determining foreign policy and the objectives of his state in the diplomatic dialogue, as opposed to implementing decisions on these matters, tends to decline. And as the prestige and weight of the foreign ministry diminishes, the direct involvement of heads of government in the details of foreign policy and diplomacy is increasing once again. This increase in the involvement of heads of government is reinforced by the second tendency, which is for them (and of course their ministers too) to meet each other much more frequently than was physically practicable even in the recent past, and to remain in closer direct contact in the intervals by telephone and other rapid modern means of communication. The ease and rapidity of travel makes the attendance of ministers or other responsible political personages at international meetings and negotiations much more usual than in the past. Cabinet ministers cannot go all the time; but few international meetings of importance to a state are nowadays not attended by junior ministers, that is, politically appointed deputies as opposed to professional diplomats, military officers and civil servants who are employed by the state on a permanent basis. The presence of a political minister has the merit of conveying direct governmental authority; and even a junior minister is more likely to be entrusted by his colleagues and his head of government with powers of decision on politically sensitive matters than even the most high-ranking professional diplomats, whose experience is in the domain of international negotiation rather than domestic politics. However, a minister, who is likely to be a somewhat transient occupant of his office, will be well-advised to listen to his country's experts both on the technical matters at issue and on the conduct of negotiations and what in any given circumstances can be achieved through diplomacy. An elected or politically nominated statesman is, in Henry Kissinger's apt phrase, not hired as a whiz kid on technical answers but to supply a sense of direction to the diplomatic dialogue conducted by the state he represents.

The principal instrument of the minister for external affairs in conducting his state's relations with other states is the diplomatic service. A Diplomatic or Foreign Service, at home and abroad, is the instrument in the first place for ascertaining the capabilities and intentions of other powers in so far as this is possible, and estimating them where it is not; second for collating them in all their complexity; third for determining the options available to the government and submitting them for decision alongside the other considerations which the government must take into account; and fourth, after the decisions are taken, for communicating and explaining them to the corresponding diplomatic instruments of other powers, and to a limited extent to the public, and for persuading others – governments, individuals and public opinion – to accept and if possible assist the implementation of these decisions.

The principal instrument for discharging the first task of a diplomatic service, namely *finding out or guessing intelligently* what one power needs to know about another, is that major invention of European diplomacy, the resident embassy, immune in its personnel and its premises, and with the right to communicate secretly with its government. The advantages of this function of an embassy and the other functions which embassies perform are still considered so valuable by governments, and immunity and secrecy are recognized as so indispensable to these functions, that almost all governments grant each other these immunities, including diplomatic wireless for instant and unhampered communication with the home base, on a reciprocal basis. These facilities are granted by the most totalitarian and revolutionary governments, though they conflict radically with censorship and the other principles of totalitarian control: and this not because of subservience to tradition or a desire for respectability, but because diplomatic immunities are of real value to both sides.

It is important to note the distinction between capabilities and intentions. A government needs to know what other governments could do to help or harm its state particularly in the military field, and also what non-military forms of aid or damage, for instance economic, they *could* bring to bear on its interests. It also needs to know what other governments seem *likely* to do. To be aware of what is possible and what the probabilities are, and to induce other governments to make favourable choices, is the object of foreign policy. This distinction between capabilities and intentions is often blurred in public debate, especially about hostile powers.

The second task, *sifting and collating* the information received from say a hundred embassies, and from other sources, and of producing a coherent picture of the issues and developments abroad on which decisions are needed, falls on the other major innovation of European diplomatic society, the ministry of external affairs (variously called the Foreign Office, the State Department and so on), and therefore on that part of the diplomatic service which at any given moment is stationed at home. Events nowadays tend to move so fast, and communication is so rapid, that there is little time for the systematic and thorough research required by an academic discipline, which also enjoys the inestimable advantages of selectivity and hindsight. The men and women who sift the information pouring in from posts abroad, from foreign embassies in the capital, from public news media and from other sources must be experts, familiar with the issues and used to evaluating each modification. At and near the top they need first-hand experience of what it is like to report from an embassy, they need to know personally the men who are reporting and what weight to give to their judgement, and if possible to have lived in at least some of the countries they are dealing with. Experience shows that regular interchange between the ministry and the field, and a closely knit service whose senior members know each other personally, and so can make allowance for each other's judgement, gives the most operationally useful balance between the need for speed and the need for perceptive judgement in assessing the course, significance and relationship of fast-moving events, and in putting forward to the government a choice of appropriate responses to them.

The third task, of *determining the options* available to a government and submitting them for decision, sounds a comparatively simple one. But it requires a sensitive awareness of the consequences in other spheres of a decision on a given issue. It is also a function which has aroused much controversy in democracies, because it involves influencing the government. A British cabinet or American president has other means of assessing domestic political reactions to a foreign policy decision; but they cannot know and weigh against one another the reactions in a large number of other countries without the reports and assessments of a diplomatic service made up of embassies and a ministry of external affairs. Senior officials in ministries of external affairs are aware of the range of possible decisions within which a government will make its choice, and which recommendations would be rejected; and they will put up a case as persuasively as possible for the decisions that seem to them most likely to further the interests for which they are responsible. The practice varies in different western capitals. The general practice in the European system was for the ministry to brief its own minister, who would then argue or bargain the case with his governmental colleagues. But, in addition to the growing number of administrative issues which vitally affect more than one government department, there is a whole range of internal political factors such as public opinion, party doctrine and commitments, and pressure from lobbies and the media, especially the press, that also affect political decisions in the realm of foreign affairs, and so need to be taken into account by diplomacy. There are obvious dangers in leaving the balance of such important multi-faceted decisions to be tipped by the persuasiveness and political power of rival ministers. The practice is therefore growing of putting such decisions through a national security council or foreign policy committee, especially in countries where the distinction between officials and ministers of the Crown, or the services and the party hierarchy, is not so marked as it is in the U.K. A good deal of informal consultation between government departments and with the political parties in power is now usual even where more old-fashioned habits prevail.

The fourth task of a diplomatic service, *communicating and explaining* a government's decisions to another government, is the most obvious function of an envoy, one which goes back to the immune heralds of ancient civilizations. Here persuasiveness is especially important, and must be combined with a cool judgement of the degree of acceptability to the other government of each aspect of the envoy's instructions from home.

Governments which attach importance to getting their messages to those in authority in other states as accurately and persuasively as possible have found by experience that the most effective way to do this is to instruct their own representative in a foreign capital to state and explain their views at or as close as possible to the effective level of decision-making in the other governments concerned. This does not always, or indeed usually, mean the top, even though the President or Chancellor or Prime Minister has the ultimate right of approval or rejection. For the effective decision is likely to be made lower down, by experts who understand the complexities of the subject, in the light of general guidelines laid down from the top. These effective decisions take the form of recommendations to the foreign minister, which he or the head of the government may reject but which he is unlikely to do if they conform to the government's lines of policy. A particular recommendation at the right level can thus often clinch the business. Unfavourable recommendations by experts in a ministry of foreign affairs, on the other hand, once fed in are much harder for a foreign ambassador to surmount at a higher level. Therefore well-run embassies make sure that they explain their government's views and wishes persuasively to the experts whose formulation of recommendations will go far to determine the decision their government takes. Of course in practice an embassy makes its case at more than one level; and it does so in more general terms as it goes up the hierarchy of the government to which it is accredited. Moreover, in order to explain and reinforce the instructions they have sent to their own embassies abroad, most foreign ministers or their deputies also call in the ambassadors of the countries concerned. Sometimes this is the more effective way to do business, for instance if the ambassador which the foreign minister calls in is particularly skillful and helpful, or particularly close to the foreign minister or head of government of his own country. Moreover a foreign minister can summon an ambassador, but an ambassador cannot insist on an audience. But usually statesmen find that they will make their case better by instructing their own ambassador than by relying on a foreign ambassador to transmit their arguments back home. This is therefore the way the diplomatic dialogue is normally conducted.

Often an ambassador must coordinate his actions, and compare notes on the results, with other ambassadors in the same capital who have received similar instructions from their governments. Sometimes his orders are to act in concert with certain colleagues: usually those of friendly or allied powers, but occasionally with envoys of countries that have little in common with his own, for instance on facilities for the diplomatic corps or shipping.

The task of persuading another government to accept and perhaps actually help to promote the policies which it is the ambassador's function to advocate still falls primarily on the ambassador himself and his senior diplomatic staff, even in these days of the communications revolution. The cordiality of his personal relations with key figures in the government (even, in countries where this is necessary, at the expense of cordial relations with opposition groups) and their confidence in him as a man of goodwill, make a great difference. An experienced ambassador will have learnt to cultivate such relations as best he can, so as to have a fund of confidence to draw on. Outside the government there are likely to be a large number of influential people, in the legislature, in political parties, in key economic or business positions, in the news media, perhaps in religious life, who influence decisions and public opinion. Ideally the ambassador must cultivate and influence all these people as well. In this task the role of the news media and especially the press has become very important in those countries where they have any significant degree of independence (now perhaps half the states in the global system). In those countries the effectiveness of this side of the work depends on the competence of the office of the press attaché. He and his staff need to develop effective working relationships with editors and journalists. This involves providing information and comment of real use to those busy men and women, accurately, honestly and quickly; and also ensuring their access to the ambassador and to distinguished statesmen and other visitors, and effective introductions when editors and journalists visit the country which the embassy represents. However, the activities of the most effective press attaché can only modify and correct the reporting from his country by foreign journalists there, which provides the main sources of news of the media. There is therefore a constant correspondence and discussion between embassies abroad and the foreign ministry at home about the misconceptions and damaging slants purveyed by foreign reporters, and on ways of making the information services of the ministry more capable of ensuring a favourable picture of the country and its government. This question receives constant attention by every government today. It has become a particular worry of many new and small states, whose governments feel that their achievements and intentions are reported to the rest of the world tendentiously, if at all, by the major news agencies and visiting journalists.

In a democratic society some of the most useful spokesmen for another country are prominent personalities who have a connection with that country, understand its aspirations and problems and want to promote better understanding and more cordial relations between it and their own for one reason or another. Politicians, businessmen, scholars, writers and other leaders in the arts, even retired diplomats, go to make up such a group. If we go back to the classical Greek institutions for conducting the diplomatic dialogue we may call them unofficial proxenoi. Like their formally appointed Greek counterparts, they not only speak up in public or in private for the country they are interested in, they also entertain important visitors from that country and enable them to meet those who shape decisions, and they make the relationship a two-way one by offering valuable suggestions about how the country of their interest should present its case, and what issues they hope can be toned down or modified because in their present form they cause more irritation than they are probably worth to the country which they are advising. These unofficial proxenoi (which ambassadors sometimes call their constituency and sometimes their friends at court) are thus both advocates and counsellors. They are, and have been from the beginning of resident diplomacy, a valuable and legitimate extension of an embassy's function and of the diplomatic dialogue between states.

When the ministry of external affairs at home receives its envoy's report on his representations to the government to which he is accredited, and his recommendations about the next round in the dialogue, often only a few hours after the despatch of the instructions, the whole process begins again. In the days of horse and sail it used to take as many weeks as it now takes hours, which gave more time for considered reflection, but meant that an envoy's instructions often arrived out of date.

The function of diplomacy in multilateral international organizations is basically the same. A loose, all-embracing institution like the United Nations, with its various general and specialized bodies, is a gathering of diplomatic envoys of governments, and thus a collective focus for the diplomatic activity of its member states. On politically sensitive issues which are beyond its capacity to resolve, it provides a convenient meeting-place and perhaps a means of moral persuasion, as well as an instrument for ratifying decisions agreed upon elsewhere. On issues where agreement is easier to reach, and especially on non-political ones, the diplomats posted to the various bodies can work out an omnilateral accord, and coordinate its implementation. The envoys to such bodies operate in relation to their ministry and their government in the same way as envoys to individual foreign states. Bilateral and multilateral diplomacy function together as coordinated parts of the same policy.

Some multilateral organizations, less universal and more effective, acquire a more definite corporate personality. NATO amounts to something more than the sum of its member states and their policies taken individually. Its committees regularly arrive at a consensus or recommendation to member governments which none of these governments put forward originally, but which they all accept. This is even more true of the E.E.C.: member governments have delegated many decisions to its organs in advance. But here too the member states still retain the right and the ability to refuse to conform on important issues; and in that fact resides their ultimate sovereignty.

The international secretariats of such multilateral bodies remain secretariats. They are staffed by an internationally recruited service, which like other such services develops a will and objectives of its own. But they are not international executive bodies, even where an assembly can be regarded as a rudimentary legislature. In time the secretariat of the E.E.C. or the U.N. may become something more. It may develop into a genuine executive with some 'sovereign' authority and powers, engaged in negotiations in its own right with states and checked or balanced by a territorially constituted assembly or council of delegates of member states. But this point has not yet been reached, and may not be.

In a very much looser and less formalized way the diplomatic corps in each capital, that is the diplomatic missions taken together, acts as a multilateral network of diplomatic brokerage. We have seen that ambassadors accredited to a capital often need to coordinate their actions and their reports with colleagues. These exchanges extend to most other diplomats in the capital, at various levels of seniority. There is a constant dialogue, and much mutual adjustment of the various embassies' assessments of the host government's policies and intentions. There can be no resident diplomat in an embassy abroad who has not had the experience of having his understanding of some aspect of the host government's policy corrected and amplified by a member of another embassy which happened to be better informed on that issue. These informal exchanges only function well on a basis of personal acquaintance, outside as well as in offices. There is a strict practical utility in the protocol which requires that every newly arrived ambassador shall call on all his colleagues with which his country has diplomatic relations, and receive their calls in return. Diplomatic cocktail parties and dinners, in the same way, may be boring and often over-elaborate, but the amount of useful business transacted at them is surprising to non-professionals.

A modern diplomatic service also has a subsidiary but important extranational function, which it performs for other embassies, other states, within larger organizations and groupings, and in negotiations over issues in which the direct interest of its own state is minimal. These services help to smooth and facilitate the diplomatic dialogue, which most states recognize to be in their own ultimate interest. For example, embassies perform services for one another of a formalized kind. The most important example occurs during interruptions of diplomatic relations between two states. In the diplomatic practice of the European system the value of continuous contact with other states was clearly understood, and the rule was therefore to maintain diplomatic representation in other capitals except in the event of war, whether one state approved of the policy of another or not. The doctrine developed, and was proclaimed by many governments including the British, that recognition and diplomatic relations implied only that a government was in effective control of a state, but carried no moral approval. To break off diplomatic relations with another state in the system was a grave step, often a prelude to an imminent declaration of war. In our contemporary world system, to maintain an embassy in the capital of another state is increasingly held to indicate a degree of acceptance of the policies pursued by the government of that state. The United States notably regards its envoys in this light. As a result, many countries, especially new ex-colonial states, periodically 'break off relations' or recall their embassies for a while to mark their disapproval of a particular act of policy by another government. As such temporary suspensions become more frequent, the diplomatic dialogue needs to continue in spite of them: especially as the suspending state does not want to destroy the web of governmental and private contacts (including trade, educational facilities and aid) linking it to the other state, just for the sake of a gesture of public condemnation. The responsibility of providing for the continuity of the dialogue in such cases is assumed by another embassy in each of the capitals concerned. This is a major extension of the former practice whereby European powers at war with one another, or in a major breach of relations, allowed a neutral embassy or legation in their capital to 'protect the interests' of an enemy power in such limited matters as the safeguarding of enemy diplomatic buildings and the passing on of certain essential messages. Nowadays, before a temporary closure comes into effect an embassy arranges to hand over the management of its interests to another embassy, with the approval of the host government. The embassy of the 'protecting power' opens a 'British (or Indonesian, or Ruritanian) Interests Section' in its embassy or in the embassy now nominally closed down, to transact the necessary diplomatic business. This may amount to more than the business it conducts on its own account. Often the host government will allow staff from the expelled embassy – other than the ambassador, whose person is symbolic – to man or partly man their interests section under the control of the protecting power. The staff who remain in this way may include senior political diplomats who continue a discreet dialogue with officials of the host government and report it through the protecting power to their ministry of foreign affairs. But whether this is so or not, the ambassador of the protecting power under whose responsibility and direction the interests section acts, also communicates and perhaps negotiates on behalf of the government whose interests he 'protects'.

The list of states who have agreed to their ambassador acting for another state in this way is a long one. The country whose services are most in demand is Switzerland. That country and also certain others like Sweden maintain foreign services which in size and especially in calibre are in excess of their strict national requirements. For instance, the Swiss Ambassador in Havana for many years protected the interests of a score of countries, most notably the United States. This made him the most informed non-communist diplomat in Havana and the one most in contact with Castro and the Cuban authorities. After he had helped to negotiate the 'Varadero Airlift' of Cubans who wished to leave, his embassy had to process many hundreds of thousands of applications and to check out those granted exit visas with the Cuban officials. Many Swiss embassies, and those of other states, perform such services on behalf of international society.

A similar service is sometimes rendered by a well-known diplomat acceptable to two states in dispute when he uses his good offices, mediates or acts as a go-between. For this he needs to be accredited to neither power. Count Bernadotte, for instance, was invited to act in this way between Israel and certain Arab states when he was Swedish Ambassador to Moscow. Statesmen who are not professional diplomats also act as intermediaries in this way, as they have for centuries. The Prime Minister of Sweden and the President of Pakistan are recent examples. Universal diplomatic bodies like the United Nations make similar arrangements for good offices by impartial neutrals in a number of circumstances, following the precedent set by the League of Nations. The Covenant of the League provided for a *rapporteur*, who acted as a go-between. The United Nations Charter does not; so the *rapporteurs* of today – such men as Señor Gallo Plaza of Ecuador in Cyprus, or Herr Olaf Palme of Sweden in Iran – have to function as representatives of the Secretary-General. These functions are parallel to some extent to the use of armed forces of neutral member states on behalf of international society rather than in defence of their particular national interests. In the contemporary world this service takes the form of the blue-helmeted 'U.N. peace-keeping forces' supplied by acceptable states such as Sweden, Ireland and Fiji. One difference is that diplomatic brokerage of the kind described is an active and creative operation requiring high professional skill and experience, whereas peace-keeping troops and observers are not normally expected to be militarily involved, and their presence is rather a diplomatic service.

All these activities have one significant element in common. They are contributions by member states of the system to the maintenance of the diplomatic dialogue and the facilitation of diplomatic arrangements, through the lending of their national diplomatic and military personnel and equipment beyond the service and protection of their direct national interests, in order to make international diplomacy as a whole more effective. They reflect a multilateral sense of solidarity among diplomats, and a readiness both in ministries of external affairs who authorize the extra-national services and in embassies to help each other in furthering the diplomatic dialogue, not only in a given capital but throughout the system.

Personal contact between diplomats thus plays an important part in the functioning of the dialogue. The diplomatic service of a developed state with an active foreign policy consists ideally of a single team of officers for the whole range of its interests: men and women who know each other personally, at least in their own age group. Men who have known each other and who have read each other's letters and telegrams (for these are widely copied within a service) for many years, learn to allow for each other's biases and tendencies, as one allows for a friend's judgement of a book or a play. In this way a kind of consensus emerges about men and issues. Personal acquaintance, helped by such practices as diplomats staying with one another when travelling and so on, was found to reinforce the effectiveness of diplomatic services when they were recruited from the same small social class and often already knew each other at school or at home. It is especially necessary now that members of a diplomatic service are recruited by public examination from a wide range of social and personal backgrounds as is the case in most western countries today. A well-run service takes steps to ensure that a reinforcing network of personal acquaintance is built up and maintained.

Moreover, national diplomatic services do not operate alone. They maintain systematic contacts with their diplomatic colleagues, who are like-minded professionals with much the same training who perform the same services for other states. The professional solidarity among diplomats as they sustain the dialogue with their host government and with each other, or serve in international organizations, is much reinforced by the personal contacts made in previous posts. An official in a ministry of foreign affairs is aware that he will soon find himself again in an embassy abroad, perhaps putting the same kinds of questions to the very man who is now putting questions to him. This ensures a certain give and take. This sense that it pays to assist the diplomatic machines of other powers provided they are not actively hostile, and the assumption that there must be elasticity in diplomatic brokerage and that the world's international political business must be carried on, are notably absent among officials and advisers who have not had this experience and who have not therefore developed a sense of diplomatic solidarity.

CHAPTER X

Criticisms of Contemporary Diplomacy

I have at various points in this book discussed a number of basic arguments against diplomacy: that is, doubts about the assumptions which underlie the dialogue between independent states. Some of these arguments shade off into a condemnation of the existence of independent states at all. Where the continued existence of independent states is accepted as probable and desirable, and the need for a diplomatic dialogue and for some management of international society is fully recognized, there are also certain criticisms of the existing mechanisms of diplomacy – of the forms and conventions practised today or at any rate yesterday. The purpose of some of these criticisms is to decry or warn against the dangers of specific diplomatic institutions, such as alliances or the United Nations; other criticisms suggest changes in current diplomatic practice so as to make diplomacy safer, or more realistic, or more accessible to small and new states, or otherwise improve it.

Serious criticisms of the diplomatic methods of the day have been made for centuries, in the same way as criticisms of the internal operations of governments. Some of these comments, especially when their approach was constructive and well-informed, have played an important part in developing the forms and mechanisms of diplomacy, and adjusting them to changing circumstances. The impact of such criticisms on the evolution of European diplomatic practice can be seen in Chapter VIII. However, the objections made in previous centuries had nothing like the same wide vogue, nor the same influence, as the specific criticisms directed against the bilateral diplomacy of the time which became very widespread after the First World War. These criticisms arose from the general desire to establish the real causes of that disaster of unforeseen magnitude which had overwhelmed

European civilization and had left the leading states of European society in a state of shock or collapse. They continue in modified forms today. They have coincided with, and helped to bring about, a decline in the value of diplomacy in public esteem. They have also sharpened the awareness among governments that some nineteenth-century methods and techniques have proved inadequate to cope with twentieth-century problems, and therefore need fairly radical modifications in order to bring them up to date.

In this chapter I wish to examine first some of the principal criticisms of bilateral diplomacy between individual states, and then some criticisms of multilateral and omnilateral or universal diplomacy.

The widespread stock criticisms of what the critics sometimes call traditional diplomacy may be broadly grouped under three headings. First, the diplomatic institutions and methods in use in Europe before 1914, and even those used after, including the League of Nations as it functioned in practice, are *inadequate*: they failed to prevent disastrous world wars and cannot deal with present dangers. Methods of conducting international affairs which have so clearly proved unsuccessful, it is argued, need to be replaced by more effective ones. Second, there is the criticism that *secret* diplomacy, and also all 'private' alliances other than a commitment to a universal body, are dangerous, entangling and immoral. These two groups of arguments are directly connected with concern over the continuing increase in the destructiveness of total war between major powers, a concern which has been much reinforced by the development and spread of nuclear weapons since World War Two. The third criticism is a more general argument arising from technological development: namely that modern technology has made *obsolete* certain institutions of modern diplomacy, and especially professional diplomats and resident embassies. The problems which governments face, it is said, have now become so technical, and at the same time communication so easy, that 'experts' can and should now deal with each other directly. As well as these general criticisms, there are also more specific and recent suggestions for changing present bilateral diplomatic practice, which deserve our consideration.

Before we look at these proposals in detail, we should note that all these general criticisms have much to be said for them when they are put forward on their merits, and not as special pleading for some other cause such as world government. The history of diplomatic institutions and methods shows them to be constantly evolving to cope with changing conditions. Public debate helps to ensure that they are kept up to date, and is the right and duty of the informed citizen. One of the requirements of effective diplomacy is elasticity about means and procedures: uncritical conservatism about diplomatic institutions that have worked well in the past may lead to less effective diplomacy when the setting changes. Many recent critical suggestions have already had a beneficial effect. But not all change is for the better, and criticisms need to be examined in detail.

The criticisms of a diplomatic society based on bilateral diplomacy between individual states, that it is *inadequate* because it failed to prevent disastrous world wars, is less insistently heard now than after World War One. This is partly because the bilateral dialogue no longer has the field so largely to itself. As a result of this criticism, and spurred by the catastrophe of the war, the League of Nations and, after World War Two, the United Nations were set up as collective omnilateral diplomatic institutions to supplement the existing bilateral system. These diplomatic innovations have also proved inadequate, and have belied the hopes of their more optimistic supporters. The disappointments caused by the functioning in practice of these diplomatic experiments, and suggestions for remedying their defects, are discussed below. A very substantial element of bilateral diplomacy continues, and statesmen are perhaps more inclined to rely on it now than when many of them shared the popular misgivings about it and the faith in collective security that were current half a century ago. So the criticisms are still relevant today.

The basis of these contemporary criticisms is the complaint that the bias of direct bilateral diplomacy is away from the regulation of differences and disputes by the binding and somehow enforceable decisions of a world body or a regional and representative gathering – indeed some would say away from justice and the rule of law – towards a system where what counts is power, and in the last instance military force. These critics argue that unless the balance of power is managed with great statesmanship, which cannot be counted on, it resolves itself into two opposing camps, and this ultimately leads to disaster. The international system before 1914 was, in Lowes Dickinson's famous phrase, an international anarchy.

Anarchy may seem to us in retrospect a strange term for a Europe which enjoyed a century of peace broken only by short local minor wars, which was close to being a free trade area, where international conventions multiplied and the citizens could move almost everywhere without a passport – a Europe more united and orderly than it has been since. Nevertheless, the Concert of Europe had declined in effectiveness, and did not prevent the disaster of the world war. Some critics argued that an anarchical society could not function without such catastrophes, and that therefore the hitherto independent 'nations' needed to have superimposed on them a 'supranational' organization capable of keeping the external relations of all the members of the states system in order, while leaving each of them its cherished independence in running its internal affairs.

By now it has become obvious that neither the League of Nations nor the United Nations is a supranational authority in that sense. A world body made up of envoys of individual states, acting on detailed instructions from their governments, will not supersede the desire and indeed the need for these governments to talk directly to each other; and even if the member states gave real decision-making and enforcement powers to the supranational body, they would still pursue a diplomatic dialogue to lobby for the decisions they favoured. Conflicts of interest between states would not suddenly disappear. Indeed the founders and advocates of the League and the United Nations did not think in terms of abolishing the bilateral diplomatic dialogue with its apparatus of embassies, treaties and the like; but they did expect that the bilateral dialogue would come to be conducted increasingly in terms of supranational bodies and their decisions.

In one major way this criticism of the inadequacy of mere bilateralism has achieved its aim. The need for a world body, indeed a number of world bodies for different purposes, is now generally accepted. Nobody seriously proposes to go back to the form of international anarchy which Lowes Dickinson condemned. But it is also true that the League and the United Nations have not worked anything like as well as their proposers hoped. Though some specialized agencies have done useful work, the central bodies do not appear to most observers to have substantially furthered the cause of peace. During most of the brief twenty-year interlude between the two world wars, and for the first twenty years or so after World War Two, the leading powers of the world system were even more divided into two opposing camps or alliances than before 1914: a division made more bitter and less bridgeable by ideology, which did not play a significant part before the first war. The view came to be widely held that a third world war was only prevented by the very frightfulness of the weapons available to the two super-powers – the 'balance of terror'. Diplomacy, both bilateral and omnilateral, seemed almost to have abdicated its role of managing the system as a whole, and confined itself largely to relations within the two blocs and with the less-developed 'third world' that tried to deal with both sides. When at last the leaders of the two super-powers, and of some of their junior partners, began to feel their way tentatively towards a détente and a resumption of serious diplomatic dialogue, it was the old-fashioned, secret, bilateral methods and institutions that they used. Both sides felt that their hesitant explorations would be halted by the glare of publicity, that a public dialogue would keep both sides locked into the positions they wanted to move away from. The subjects of these exchanges were, first the balance of terror and how it could be managed at less expense to both sides (the most imperative and intractable question of all); and then other aspects of the multiple balance of power in various different parts of the world, crisis management, procedures for organizing change, technical and economic collaboration. The dialogue on many of these subjects could broaden out onto a more multilateral basis later and in some cases soon did. Few suggested that it could be otherwise, or that the super-powers could have entrusted the whole business to the United Nations.

However, many people, including responsible statesmen in countries excluded from the talks, did again see one of the dangers that the critics of bilateral diplomacy put forward. They feared that the two super-powers, and also China which had for many years stood outside the general diplomatic dialogue, were engaged in 'collusion' or even conspiracy, that they were advancing their own interests at the expense of others, even that they were weakening traditional alliances and deserting their friends (though this is not a charge that the original critics of international anarchy and alliances would like to make). These charges have force, now as before. There may be no other satisfactory method of resuming a serious diplomatic dialogue between the most powerful states in the system; but that does not mean that we should not look hard and realistically for one. Meanwhile bilateral diplomacy has certainly come to its own, in defence of state interests and military security and also in the cause of peace and of relaxation of tensions.

Several people on both sides of the cold war argue that it is a betrayal of principle to negotiate confidentially with the ideological enemy, and that the ideas which people believe in and to which states are often said to be dedicated should not be sacrificed to expediency. This is a version of the ideological fundamentalism discussed in Chapter VI, which distrusts all diplomatic dealings with doctrinal opponents. It is in a different category from the criticisms of bilateral methods and institutions which we are considering here. It is certainly true that the bias of diplomacy is to blunt ideological controversy and to play down doctrinal differences: to think in terms of the interests of states rather than moral principles, of conditionals rather than absolutes. However, this fundamentalist criticism does render one service to the bilateral diplomatic dialogue between ideological opponents once it is engaged. It ensures that the negotiators are especially cautious, and always have with them that most useful metaphorical diplomatic instrument, a long spoon.

These considerations bring us to the second set of criticisms, those concerned with the *secrecy* of diplomacy, and especially of traditional bilateral diplomacy. This secrecy remains an active target. In almost every free society where public discussion of such matters is permitted, it is condemned genuinely by people who want a safer and juster world, and believe that the secrecy of much of the diplomatic dialogue works in the opposite direction. (It is also denounced by those who in one way or another would stand to gain by the disclosure of a state's diplomatic secrets: but that is another issue.) Secret diplomacy is said to be dangerous in itself; to mask plotting that would be rejected by the people if they knew; to lead either to war or to shameful compromises. It is said to run counter to the principles of democracy: 'the people have a right to know what is being done in their name'. There should only be, as President Wilson said, 'open covenants openly arrived at'. These covenants might still turn out in the long run to be 'entangling alliances', but at least the people would know what they were being committed to. Moreover, diplomacy is apt to lead to alliances, or at least collaboration, with other states which may have parallel interests on certain external issues, but whose internal policies the people dislike.

There are two unspoken premises in these criticisms. One is that the sovereign majority of citizens have the right, like absolute rulers in former times, to pursue whatever foreign policy appeals to them, whether it serves or damages their interests – whether or not, in more traditional language, it is in accordance with reason of state. The second unspoken premise is that 'the people' are more rational, fairer and more moral than governments.

It seems obvious to professional diplomats and negotiators that confidential discussion is necessary if negotiations between states are to lead to any significant results, if what Professor Hans Morgenthau called 'the translation of conflicting or inchoate interests into a common purpose of the conflicting parties' is to take place. They therefore become impatient of the criticisms of secrecy made against the diplomatic dialogue in democratic societies, especially when made by politicians or journalists whose motives they distrust. Indeed the confidential nature of diplomacy is and has been so universal, at all times and in all places, that it is necessary to examine the reasons for this secrecy in order to see how far it is practicable to give effect to the criticisms of it.

Firstly, a considerable amount of diplomacy is not secret. From the polemical debates of the United Nations General Assembly to the complex technicalities of the revision of international law, much of the dialogue is conducted openly, as were the arguments of envoys before the assemblies of ancient Greece. Secondly, the diplomatic dialogue of an international society is an aspect of politics. And all politics, even in the most open democracies, involves public debate and also private discussions, between members of governments and leaders of political parties, and also between executive governments and parliamentarians and between members of legislatures. All politics is concerned with conflicts and alliances of interests and personalities, even in countries where public debate over matters of principle is permitted as well. Thirdly, a large part of diplomacy, as of all politics, is concerned with bargaining. Allies bargain to determine the extent and limits of their commitments to each other. Adversaries also bargain when elements of implied or explicit threat may be among the inducements used. All the economic discussions which bulk so large in the contemporary diplomatic dialogue involve bargaining. Even omnilateral arrangements for the ordering of international society, such as periodic revisions of the law of the sea, contain a large element of bargaining about the effects of each clause on the interests of each state concerned. The essential feature of bargaining is that the other party does not know how far you will go, and it is therefore most effectively done in private discussion; though the final results of a bargain, or a package of limited conditional bargains, can of course be made public. Fourthly, states do not talk to one another only about their own intentions. They also exchange confidential views and guesses about the other states in the system and the intentions of those states – views and guesses which they do not want repeated to the others. Unless a state can keep to itself the confidences it learns in this way – and this involves not passing on these confidences to other states or to journalists or legislators who make it public – it will soon find itself cut off from the confidence of other states, which will involve a serious loss of awareness of what is going on. Fifthly, reporting between a state government and its embassies abroad needs to be confidential, in the same sort of way as between a lawyer and his clients, and is covered by the general recognition of the value of diplomatic immunity.

It is also instructive to note the similarity between diplomatic and military secrecy. There are occasions when a state or a military alliance finds it useful to make its military forces conspicuous, for instance in order to deter a hostile power, or to invite observers from other states as part of an international agreement. But almost everyone readily accepts that in a world of independent states some degree of military secrecy is necessary. The case for diplomatic confidentiality is less obvious to many members of the public; but governments consider that an area of secret exchanges is necessary, and that they must decide what part of their dialogue with other states they will make public and what they will keep confidential.

The issue of secrecy is therefore not an absolute one. Democratic societies, where the right of the public to be informed is widely and increasingly recognized, usually accept the distinction between confidential exchanges and private discussions that do not lead to any agreement, negotiations and bargaining which does result in an agreement or commitment, and the commitment itself which will need to be ratified. Private exchanges between statesmen and their agents are generally accepted, and would in any case be virtually impossible to prevent. Democratic governments accept on the other hand that covenants should be open, and that they should not make secret agreements, or secret clauses to otherwise open agreements. The significant differences of opinion occur over the confidentiality of negotiation: whether open covenants must or in practice can be openly arrived at, or whether, as many statesmen and diplomats argue, you cannot play serious poker if you have to keep your cards exposed on the table while some of the other players hold theirs close to their chests. If those who demand open negotiation are too insistent, then parallel informal unwritten negotiations are apt to take place alongside the open formal ones, so that the most sensitive points can be discussed in private.

Since nobody realistically supposes that states will not communicate privately with one another, the practical issue is: how large should the area of open diplomacy be? In general those who want to extend this area are those who believe in democracy and open government domestically, and who also believe that international society can and should be made more like the kind of domestic society which they favour, with a greater degree of world authority, more 'rule of law', and a more fully informed public opinion in all countries. Events do not appear to be moving in that direction. The proportion of independent states with more or less democratic governments is less now than it was at the end of World War One, and certainly less than many liberal thinkers hoped would be the case when the great movement of European decolonization began following World War Two. Moreover, a reduction in the area of secret diplomacy has to be fairly universal to be acceptable. A few small dictatorial régimes would not perhaps matter much, but so long as major powers like the Soviet Union and China, and a majority of states generally, prefer not to conduct their affairs openly, a democratically-minded state can only disclose the substance of its diplomatic dialogue with authoritarian states at the cost of severely limiting its exchanges with them. This is not in its interest, or in the interest of international society as a whole.

The criticism that modern technology has made diplomacy *obsolete* is sometimes merely part of the wider charge that a society of independent states (or 'the nation state') is incapable of dealing with the problems of the contemporary world. But many critics who fully expect independent states to continue, and to conduct a dialogue, and to maintain departments of foreign affairs, use the expression 'diplomacy' loosely, to mean the institution of resident embassies and the special immunities and privileges which (with occasional exceptions) they are still accorded. We saw in the last chapter that the speed of modern communications is such that statesmen can learn certain aspects of the news faster from the ticker tape and the monitoring reports of foreign broadcasts than from their own agents abroad, and can bypass their ambassadors by talking to each other by telephone or flying to meet each other in a few hours. A variant of this argument, put forward by diplomats more often than by scholars and journalists, is that both the functions and the status of an ambassador have been devalued. Ambassadors have multiplied so much in the last fifty years that many capitals have over a hundred. The United Kingdom and several other states maintain three in Brussels alone: one accredited to the Belgian government (technically to the king), one to NATO and one to the E.E.C. Also the small élite society which alone made foreign political decisions in the European society of states and in which the many fewer ambassadors of the European system moved and exercised a real influence, has largely disappeared. An ambassador, so this complaint goes, has shrunk from being the representative of his sovereign, or at least of his government as a whole, to being merely the instrument of the ministry of foreign affairs, one department among many engaged in the extended diplomatic dialogue of the modern world.

The decline of the role of embassies in the diplomatic dialogue of today as compared with a century ago raises the question of the immunities and privileges accorded to them. The functions of a resident embassy today are still very considerable, and they *need* for their operation the basic immunities accorded to the persons of resident diplomats, their offices and residences, and their communication with their governments. The immunity of a herald from arrest has been regarded in all states systems as an obvious and necessary condition of his function, especially in hostile countries. No major state has proposed a curtailment now of these immunities, or of the courtesies which grow out of them. A striking reaffirmation of their universal acceptability and usefulness occurred when the revolutionary government in Iran recently endorsed violations of the immunity of the United States embassy buildings and personnel. These violations were condemned by virtually every other state, including those sympathetic to the Iranian revolutionaries, and the Iranians themselves carefully respected the immunities of other embassies and of the diplomatic emissaries who negotiated the eventual release of the hostages. The taking of diplomatic hostages, the burning of embassies and the assassination of ambassadors has made the diplomatic profession more dangerous everywhere, and the diplomatic dialogue less civilized at the fringes. But such acts are rarely committed by governments, and should not be seen as a collapse – or so far a modification – of the rules of immunity governing the institution of resident embassies in international society generally. Even where members of an embassy staff are deemed by a state to be guilty of espionage in violation of the accepted rules, the universal custom is still to expel them rather than to arrest them, and the occasional exceptions do not disprove the validity of the rule.

Whether these necessary immunities need extend to parking offences in crowded cities, or whether resident diplomats should be allowed to import goods for their consumption including alcoholic drinks free of customs duties, is more debatable. These minor privileges cause much resentment, and could be modified without impairing the essential functions of embassies. It is true that the cost to a state of maintaining embassies abroad is roughly equal to the expenditure of other powers who maintain embassies in its capital; but perhaps all embassies cost more than they should. Undoubtedly also the personal prestige of ambassadors has declined, now that there are so many and that such a considerable proportion of them are without influence or expertise. This is the result partly of the proliferation of small countries, and partly of the practice of calling all envoys ambassadors (or equivalent terms, like nuncio or high commissioner). But it is also due to the subtle change in the stature of most ambassadors, from being men of some personal importance in their own country and the envoys of a sovereign, to being what in Britain are called senior civil servants. This change of stature and the closer re-identification of embassies with trade brings ambassadors back to something more like their original position of agents when the Venetians and Louis XIV were developing the practices of resident diplomacy. It is noteworthy that the United States' practice of appointing wealthy contributors and political figures to ambassadorial posts, and the custom in some new states of appointing relatives of the head of state, ensures that such delegates have a certain personal standing, and direct communication with the president or ruler, even though they lack the professional training of their colleagues. As a result the rank of ambassador, retained as a title after the position has been vacated, is taken more seriously in the United States than in most European countries.

The argument that technology, especially speed of communications, has destroyed the need for the diplomatic mechanism is largely illusory. For centuries it has been possible to read newspapers, which were likely to be seen by principals before their ambassador's report was laid on their desk. But journalism is concerned with effect and with newsworthiness; it is written under pressure of time, and based on much less information than is usually available even to secondary embassies; and newspapers normally only cover important or momentarily newsworthy countries, so that the general presentation is unbalanced and patchy. I have been told that French embassies in important capitals liked to wait until they knew what had been written in *Le Monde* before making their own comments, so as to amplify and correct what the recipients of their report would have read already, but that in less important capitals they could be fairly sure most of the time that nothing at all would appear in the press. More broadly it may be stated that even in countries where press reporting is uninhibited, what governments say in public and what is gleaned and surmised by journalists are together no substitute for what governments are prepared to say to other governments in confidence. In countries that exercise a press censorship or other means of pressure, reporting by journalists will inevitably contain less than the whole picture as the journalist sees it, so that in certain capitals like Moscow in Stalin's time the copy publicly telegraphed was derisorily called the application for a re-entry visa, and many journalists also corresponded with their editors through the diplomatic bag. The real difficulty is that governments are expected to react with increasing speed to events and the actions of other governments, so that they are less and less able to wait for the reasoned comments distilled by their diplomatic organization in the field and at home. Embassies are reduced to sending immediate telegrams referring to an event which is presumed to be known, and beginning with a sentence like 'The following points should be borne in mind'. Wiretapping and similar devices often still make it imprudent to telephone such confidential comments, even from very liberal capitals, though this technological problem may some day be overcome. The problem of striking a balance between speed and perceptive judgement remains, both for governments and for diplomatic services.

Nevertheless, when we have set aside what is untrue and exaggerated in these criticisms, it is true that technology has played its part in making the resident embassy, as opposed to the foreign ministry, a less important institution than it was, even though it still performs many vital functions. Direct meetings and communications between the statesmen who decide a state's policy are now much more frequent than before. If they are frequent enough not to attract undue attention they seem to the statesmen concerned to offer real advantages over the previous immobility of principals except at congresses and at royal weddings and funerals. But senior statesmen have discovered – and those who have been many years in office readily assert – that though the closer contacts which modern technology makes possible are valuable and welcome, they are not by themselves enough. Senior statesmen find that diplomatic negotiations are almost always too intricate and specialized, and too time-consuming, to be conducted only at personal meetings. Eminent public figures therefore tend to use direct personal meetings for specific negotiation only in order to initiate courses of action, or when a definite stage in the negotiation requiring their decision has been reached. Such meetings require much careful preparation on both sides if they are to be successful; and this ancillary role falls inevitably to professional diplomats, including resident ambassadors accredited to other states and to multilateral organizations. The bulk of the negotiating must be left to them if only because no senior political figure can devote the time.

Awareness of the relative decline in the importance of the resident embassy, and a more general need to adapt the machinery of diplomacy to the opportunities offered by modern technology and also the extension of the dialogue into new fields discussed in Chapter XII, has led a number of Western states, and individual diplomats with long personal experience, to propose and implement reforms of their diplomatic machinery. The proposals can be grouped in three categories. Some advocate concentrating a state's embassies, and the work of the foreign ministry, on the other states with which it is most intimately involved, and enlarging its embassies there to make them more representative of all the government departments now affected by overseas policy. Others on the contrary favour concentrating traditional embassies in states with very different social structures and international aims, because they hold that embassies are less necessary the greater the degree of intimacy between two states and especially necessary in alien and hostile ones. The third group is concerned with the divergence in democracies between the policies recommended by professional foreign services and the views of the political parties and of the electorate.

One instructive example of the first view is the Duncan Report to the British Government on the changes required in the British service. (Its principal recommendations on the development and direction of British diplomatic activity overseas are set out in Chapters I and IV of the report.) The distinctive feature of that report was the thesis that as a consequence of decolonization and the decline of British power in the world, British foreign relations no longer required the maintenance of resident political embassies on a global scale in the capital of every member state of international society as those of a super-power presumably did. The United Kingdom, said Duncan, should deploy its diplomatic resources mainly in the 'advanced industrial countries with which we are likely to be increasingly involved to the point where none of us will be able to conduct our domestic policies efficiently without constant reference to each other'. These closely inter-dependent countries can conduct their relations 'in a style different from the traditional one': essentially within the European Community, and in the North Atlantic Alliance for collective discussions about and negotiations with the communist world. In the advanced industrial countries, the report argues, Britain will still need a comprehensive diplomatic network, bilateral and multilateral, so that governments can communicate with each other and 'bring political influence to bear'. Elsewhere the traditional diplomatic scale of representation can be much reduced. Duncan pointed out that both the French and German governments had already reached the same general conclusion.

Criticisms of the type of the Duncan Report implicitly foreshadow the end of 'foreign policy' conducted between the 'nation states' of Western Europe, as they gradually become members of the European Community. This association would, Duncan assumed, grow from its existing form into a confederacy concerned with the establishment of acceptable common internal policies and increasingly coordinated external ones.

An integrated Community of the size and widespread external connections of Western Europe would wish to exert political influence round the world. It is true that some collective machinery for foreign policy, some Community institutions for its formulation and execution, may very well be evolved; but this evolution is likely to be slow, and the new institutions are virtually certain to grow out of the existing diplomatic machinery of the member states. While this evolution is taking place, member states of the Community should not, according to the Duncan and similar proposals, continue to conduct their own diplomatic dialogue round the world, bilaterally and multilaterally, but should concentrate their diplomatic resources more than hitherto on the dialogue between themselves. This intra-Community dialogue would be mainly concerned with working out the bargains and compromises that determine how the Community functions, both internally and in its relations with the outside world. It would cover an extremely wide field, involving almost every aspect of life with which a modern state is concerned. Duncan and other such critics suppose that the main instruments and channels of communication between the member states will continue to be, on the one hand the resident bilateral embassies which each state maintains in the capitals of the others, enlarged to contain representatives of almost every government department; and on the other the diplomatic machinery of the Council of Ministers and their professional staffs, which is a complex piece of multilateral diplomatic machinery whose key members are drawn from ministries of foreign affairs. Negotiations inside the Community, and the somewhat wider ones on defence, monetary and other issues involving the United States and in some cases Japan, will require a real and increasing concentration of diplomatic capacity, which should for reasons of economy involve a corresponding reduction elsewhere.

The second set of criticisms of the existing bilateral diplomatic pattern is essentially the opposite of that in the Duncan Report. Though at first sight more radical, it is perhaps as pertinent. The nub of this criticism is that the closer the relations between two states are, and the more their affairs are interwoven, the greater the number of separate channels of communication there will be between various decision-makers; so that the dialogue between two very close and similar states can and does largely take place without the need for traditional resident embassies. This argument borders on the claim of the functionalists that independent states as such are largely being superseded by a multiplicity of separate international decision-making agencies (a view discussed in Chapter XII). But it is not necessary to suppose that the power of states, as the centralized institutions by which different groups of people deal with the outside world, is waning in order to maintain that the closer together two states grow, the less essential their resident embassies in each other's capitals are. Indeed, the critics most under discussion maintain that the converse of this thesis is also true, namely, that the less close, the more congenitally foreign and hostile two states are, the more the device of the resident embassy is needed to conduct an effective diplomatic dialogue.

One well-known exponent of this view is Zbigniew Brzezinski, who formulated it when after some years in the United States Department of State he became the Head of the Columbia University Research Unit on International Change. Professor Brzezinski argued that embassies as we know them have become superfluous between powers whose governments have and can expect to go on having close relations. In particular he suggested as an example that the very large U.S. Embassy in London could be substantially closed down, retaining only visa and other functions. The information about Britain which the U.S. Administration needs is almost all publicly available, and could, he claimed, be adequately analysed and submitted to it by experts working on it in Washington. The continuous and intimate exchange at many levels between the two governments about what is happening in almost every country in the world and how to deal with these developments could take place better directly by coded ticker between the experts in the two capitals and by direct discussion between members of the two administrations (where necessary, the Prime Minister and President) by telephone. Intermediaries would be cut out, and a direct working relationship between the governmental apparatus in the two capitals established. Brzezinski did not expect his proposal to be implemented literally, but rather wished to suggest more effective ways of deploying American diplomatic personnel.

At the other end of the diplomatic scale, according to this school of criticism, Western embassies are necessary in Moscow for two reasons. Relations between the Western and Soviet governments are not close enough to compare notes and work out policies that are in harmony if not the same: this means it is necessary to negotiate with the Soviet government (in areas where negotiation is practicable) as an opponent with which it is nevertheless possible to find areas of common interest or at least courses of action which avoid conflict. Secondly, the Soviet Union is a totalitarian state, in which most information is not published, non-diplomatic channels of communication are tenuous and journalists' copy is censored; therefore the instant and secret reporting of an embassy by diplomatic radio is necessary for the analysis in a Western foreign ministry. The professionals who negotiate with the Soviet authorities will know Soviet conditions, if not at first hand at the nearest practical range, by tours of duty in Moscow; but they will be briefed in their own capitals and negotiations conducted from there, either through the resident embassies, as was the European practice, or with meetings on neutral ground at the U.N. or for instance in Finland.

The principal effect in practice of this reform of diplomatic technique would be for a government to concentrate the observation and analysis of other countries and of the actions of other governments much more exclusively in the national capital, where some professional analysts believe it can be interpreted more effectively and linked up earlier with other sources of intelligence, including the conversations of the government's experts with their opposite numbers in other friendly capitals. This analysis, together with the country's defence, economic and other needs and commitments, and domestic attitudes and pressures, would then be examined by a committee (a National Security Council or a Foreign Policy Council), when necessary under the chairmanship of the Head of Government himself. Similarly, the personal contacts which already exist between, say, experts in various fields of defence and their home-based counterparts in other allied capitals could be developed to the point where embassies were not needed for this work.

Both the criticisms which I have discussed above incline towards functionalist ideas. The second alternative also inclines towards the theory that the conduct of a state's foreign policy has much to learn from the strategy of playing and winning formal games, from chess to football, and the belief that foreign policy can be much more a matter of calculation and less a matter of specialized political experience, understanding of foreign countries and judgement than the conventional diplomatic mechanism supposes. Its thesis that embassies are less necessary tools of diplomacy between a family of states with intimate relations than outside it, and scarcely necessary at all between countries like the United States, Britain and Canada, where a common language and a long tradition of cooperation can provide an adequate network of more effective direct contacts, is not unique. The Duncan report also proposes that 'members of Home Departments will deal regularly and directly with their opposite numbers on a visiting basis rather than through diplomatic intermediaries'. The question is whether such visits, which modern aviation makes easy and which are becoming a standard practice, lessen or, as Duncan argues, increase the need for large and comprehensive British Government Offices in other

Western capitals and as permanent delegations to the European Community and NATO.

To some extent direct contacts have already superseded diplomatic ones in the West. Thus Western embassies in, say, Amman or Kinshasa are usually overworked, while those in Western capitals like Oslo, Copenhagen and Lisbon often have too little to do. This is because contacts between, say, Britain and Denmark, governmental as well as other, operate without the need for 'diplomatic intermediaries' resident in each other's capitals. The channel is used because it is there; but it would not be difficult to use alternatives, even at the present stage of interdependence, and if the European Community and NATO become more integrated the tendency will increase. Ambassadors within the European Community could become like the envoys of German princes to each other after 1871: symbols of sovereignty and part of the ceremonial rather than the administrative side of 'international' life.

When we reach a point at which a Community or League conducts its own confederal foreign relations with the Soviet Union or the Congo, it will need, and organize, a diplomatic service of its own to perform the functions described above. This diplomatic instrument is likely to develop out of the professional services of the individual member states, as NATO armed forces are beginning to do. In this way we might perhaps find that embassies survive more vigorously outside the area of concentration than inside. That would be more than a change of style: it would be a significant innovation in the techniques of conducting the diplomatic dialogue.

Another criticism not only of embassies but of foreign ministries and of diplomatic and foreign services generally is that they are undemocratic and élitist. In so far as the criticism is directed against embassies as bastions of social snobbery, that is becoming more out of date every year. Embassies do entertain important people, not merely in politics but in every walk of life: this is one of their functions, and one that excites an understandable but disproportionate amount of envy. But today the social standing of a distinguished person, and of a professional diplomat, depends more on performance than on pedigree. A more serious charge, which needs to be considered, is that a foreign service tends to arrogate to itself the formulation of what it considers to be the basic national interest of the state, and resists any major deviation from it by elected political leaders, whether these leaders are supported by the public mood of the moment or not. By what right does a foreign service do this? Is it anti-democratic? If war, and even military planning, are too serious to leave to generals (as many besides Clemenceau have felt), is the diplomatic dialogue, on which so much hinges, too serious to leave to foreign service officers? These are somewhat rhetorical and emotionally loaded questions. More dispassionately, it is reasonable to ask whether a foreign service should be more like a firm of family solicitors in England, able on account of their learned expertise to advise the clients who employ their services about how a given policy can best be carried out, but not to advise what that policy should be.

This criticism takes us back into the past, to the days when the working agent of a prince abroad was entirely his creature and served his interests. The agents of the Medici family or of the Signoria in Venice reported the options open to their masters, and sometimes indicated which course of action would have the biggest local advantage; but they did not presume to formulate policy, and certainly did not think of the interests of the *stato* separately from those of its ruler. '*L'état c'est moi*', declared Louis XIV, and Callières and his colleagues did not distinguish between the two. So, similarly, the envoys of Cromwell, of James II, of William and Mary served a man and a régime, though as a result of the many dramatic changes of régime, statesmen were beginning to distinguish the concept of the welfare of England from that of those who held power there at a given moment. The ambassadors of George I and George II implemented and to some extent made foreign policy in the interests of the House of Hanover, rather than an abstract national interest, and none would have remained in office under a Jacobite restoration. But in the nineteenth century we begin to see statesmen like Talleyrand consciously serving what they conceived to be the long-term interests of the state. In Talleyrand's view, the welfare of France required the removal of his master Napoleon, and he remained in office to protect the same French interests after the Bourbon restoration. During that century and this, the establishment of professional diplomatic services, and the interchange of their personnel between embassies and legations abroad and foreign ministries at home, made possible a continuous discussion on foreign policy between a small group of experts in each state. Out of this discussion the professionals distilled a concept of their state's diplomatic interests and how to defend and advance them as opportunity offered, in much the same way as groups of officers developed their ideas of their state's military interests. This formulation of the national interest, and especially of the available ways of promoting it, is made by diplomats who in the exercise of their profession are brought into continual contact with the similar purposes of other states, and study in great detail how they converge or conflict, and what inducements could bring about greater convergence. So the national interest emerges in practice from these diplomatic deliberations as a many-faceted affair, tempered by the art of the internationally possible, the art of the negotiable, rather than as simply the determined assertion of the national will. Professional diplomats and those who agree with them consider that the people of a modern democratic state, who know well enough by direct experience how they want their own country governed, cannot have the expert knowledge necessary to know what is practicable outside the borders of their own state. Against this it is argued that diplomats are, and should act as, agents of the sovereign people in the same way as they were agents of a sovereign king – or if not of the sovereign people by direct instruction, at any rate of the temporarily ruling political party. The formulation of the national interest, and perhaps even of a hardly avowed *raison de système*, by a bureaucracy of permanent professionals who – it is said – can all too easily persuade or browbeat politicians in office, is stigmatized as undemocratic because it consciously distinguishes the national interest from the popular will and from the 'mandate' of the last election. Some critics have argued in particular that a foreign policy, or an attitude to the outside world, endorsed by a political party inevitably does and should have a considerable ideological content, and that a collegium of diplomats who arrive at their conclusions privately and who spend more than half their lives outside their country and insulated from its public opinion, should not stand in a victorious party's way about what is to be done, though their advice may be useful as to how to do it.

One remedy suggested by such critics is to appoint party political figures, or men who have the personal confidence of the head of government, to the key posts abroad. These might in Britain's case include the ambassadors to Washington and Moscow, to the United Nations (which in several countries carries ministerial or cabinet rank) and the European Community, and to certain other important capitals. The result might be rather less efficient, rather more dangerous, and marginally discouraging to the recruitment of able people into the foreign service, but these losses would, it is argued, be more than made up by the gain in the democratization of foreign policy and in the conduct of the government and party's policy abroad by men who believe in it. It would amount to a return to something more like the partisan diplomacy of the agents of James and William two hundred years ago. Some American critics go further, and maintain that the job of an ambassador, as personal representative of the president, is not to formulate an arcane national interest but to do what he can to execute the partisan policy of the president and to help re-elect him or his successor. One politically appointed U.S. ambassador, Laurence Silberman, proposes that any American foreign service officer appointed to be ambassador should resign from the foreign service and entrust his future to the political party that appoints him, in order to ensure a personal commitment.

This criticism overestimates the present importance of ambassadors as independent political figures. Statesmen in democratic countries are usually party politicians. They have much greater opportunities than their predecessors of a century ago to meet and negotiate directly with their opposite numbers in other states, and to ensure that the views and beliefs of the government in power are clearly understood. The criticism also lays too much stress on the issue of how far elected or politically nominated ministers of foreign affairs can and do control their bureaucracy, and how far they are influenced by the advice of their professionals. In a modern democracy a great number of pressures and influences go to shape the state's foreign policy and the content and aims of its diplomatic dialogue. The personal interests of members of the government, the commitments of the party and the pressures of public opinion all carry great weight – some would say too much weight for the welfare of the state. It is surely most desirable that the arguments in favour of long-term continuity of policy across party lines, in favour of prudence and expediency and compromise, and a sharp awareness of the interrelated complexity of international affairs and of what can be obtained by skillful and elastic negotiation, which are the considerations advanced by a professional diplomatic service, should also play some part in shaping a state's international conduct. Diplomatic expertise is inevitably adulterated in a democracy, as it often is with other forms of government, but the expertise itself is not anti-democratic, any more than are military, medical or other categories of expertise offered to governments. However, in practice the advice of professional diplomats tends to be anti-populist and anti-ideological.

These criticisms of the machinery of contemporary bilateral diplomacy are diverse and in some cases contradictory. Their general tenor is to recognize that bilateral and confidential diplomacy continues to have an indispensable part to play in international affairs in our technological age, but to demand an extension of public knowledge about and influence over the details of the dialogue and the course of negotiations, as well as the final results. The criticisms emphasize and usually welcome the increasing direct contacts between the statesmen who take the policy decisions and the good offices of shuttle diplomacy which rapid communication makes possible. They play down the role of resident embassies abroad, but not of foreign ministries at home. The more voluminous and more intimate the dialogue between two states is, so the channel of the resident embassies is increasingly supplemented and perhaps in some cases virtually eclipsed by other forms of contact and communication between the various branches of the two governments. These criticisms are not directed against the diplomatic dialogue as such: most of them are concerned to bring it into line with contemporary political and technical developments. Only if diplomacy is unduly identified with the embassies and 'diplomatists' of fifty or a hundred years ago, contrary to

the historical record and in my opinion to common sense, can such criticisms
be regarded as hostile to diplomacy, or diplomacy itself be regarded as in
decline.

The criticisms of multilateral diplomacy divide into two categories. There
are first of all general criticisms, concerned with the usefulness of all forms
of multilateral diplomacy which operate now or have operated in the past,
and secondly the criticisms of specific aspects of contemporary omnilateral
institutions, such as the United Nations.

We may begin with one very general criticism of multilateral institutions,
namely, that they are a babel of voices, a confusion of tongues and serve no
very useful purpose. According to this criticism an effective diplomatic
dialogue has to be between two or three parties talking in private. If the
parties cannot or will not talk to one another directly, then an intermediary
should go from one to another, gradually elaborating a formula which will
correspond with realities (such as the strength and influence of the parties)
rather than abstract dogmas or the opinions of states not directly concerned,
and which will satisfy both sides. At large international gatherings the formal
sessions are mainly for show, in this view, and the real business is either
prepared in detail beforehand by bilateral dialogue and bargaining, or else
it is done in private at the time of the conference, in the corridors or over
the meal table. In this view the formal sessions of such conferences, especially
when they are held in public, are little more than ceremonial ratifications or
occasions for oratory.

'Realist' criticism of this kind is directed more at omnilateral, quasi-
parliamentary conferences like the U.N. General Assembly than at technical
gatherings like the World Sugar Conference. It is made by those who consider that traditional bilateral diplomacy is the only effective kind. It is true
that multilateral diplomacy is not a substitute for the direct dialogue between individual states, but a complement to it. It is also certainly the case
that bilateral diplomacy is intensified in preparation for multilateral gatherings and is perhaps at its most active behind the scenes at such gatherings.
But that is not an argument against multilateral congresses, whether specially
convened to deal with a specific problem or in permanent or regular annual
sessions. Privacy is necessary for effective diplomatic bargaining: but
private discussions at multilateral gatherings are not all bilateral. Such
gatherings provide the occasions for intensive multilateral private discussions that would scarcely occur without them. Where decision-makers
attend such conferences in person, the private discussions they are able to
have with their opposite numbers from other countries can be most valuable.
Even where conferences are made up of envoys and delegates, the task of
diplomacy is speeded up and made more effective by private discussions at

which large numbers of delegates attend at once. Sometimes indeed the prospect of an important conference leads to informal meetings of the ambassadors concerned in a given capital to work out procedures and co-ordinate certain positions of substance in advance. The multilateral dialogue thus draws on the bilateral method and acts as a stimulus to it.

The steady growth of regular and systematized multilateral diplomacy since 1815, as opposed to the fitful multilateral meetings before then, is in itself good evidence of its usefulness. We can count it as an important development of diplomatic technique which has both practical and symbolic value. But it does not replace other forms of communication between states.

Realist criticism of multilateral gatherings as babels of discordant voices is directed mainly at universal gatherings with general political purposes, and less if at all at functional meetings of delegates from states with a specific common purpose in view, like NATO or OPEC (the Organization of Petroleum Exporting Countries). It is not really concerned with the usefulness of such institutions in furthering the dialogue between states, but is directed against the unwarranted implication of world government which some people have seen in the vaguely parliamentary procedures which the United Nations has acquired. The criticism is made partly by people who consider that the diplomatic dialogue is impeded by turning such meetings into pseudo-parliamentary debates, which diverts the attention of the delegates from negotiation to polemics. It partly also reflects the concern of the realist school at the widespread scepticism and disillusionment caused by the realization that the United Nations is not a supranational authority, because this public disillusionment detracts from the limited but real use-fulness of what is still an imperfect experiment in omnilateral diplomatic dialogue. The main volume of this criticism of the general performance and achievements of the United Nations (as opposed to criticisms of the attitude of the majority towards specific issues like the Palestine question) comes, however, from those who on the contrary want multilateral and especially omnilateral assemblies to function as parliaments and even to assume some sort of executive authority. Such critics object to the babel of voices for the opposite reason from the realists, namely that delegates to the United Nations are too much concerned with the interests of individual states instead of working to develop the organs of an embryo world government.

So many specific criticisms of the United Nations and proposals for its reform have been made that it is impossible to list them here. Some of these, designed to cope with the problems caused by the great increase in the size of the United Nations as a result of the admission of so many new and small states, and also designed to facilitate the conduct of diplomacy by these new states many of which have no previous diplomatic experience to draw on, are discussed in Chapter XI. Another set of criticisms, which has been voiced from the beginning and which has been given increased weight by the accession of small states, is concerned with the discrepancy between the principle of one state, one vote and the realities of power in the world, economic and political as well as military. These criticisms refer particularly to the General Assembly; for both the Security Council by its composition, and most of the specialized agencies by the nature of their work, give more weight to the powerful and developed states whose contributions largely determine what action can be taken, than to the smallest and weakest. Moreover the General Assembly has grown in importance relative to the other organs of the United Nations, and has become symbolic of the whole institution. Most foreign ministers and many heads of government attend its annual sessions for brief periods.

Since persuasion is related to power, and the weight that states carry in the diplomatic dialogue depends on their capacities, can anything be done to make this universal assembly more effective by weighting the votes of its member states in some way? Or is it better to see its usefulness as lying in its universality and formal equality, and also in its being a forum where the power of numbers of small states finds an expression? No formula for weighting votes in the General Assembly has been devised that even remotely approaches acceptance by the member states. Population is a very poor guide to power; and in any case it is scarcely serious to suggest giving India a thousand times the voting power of Gabon or Iceland, and Brazil and Pakistan twice the votes of Britain and France. Wealth and degree of development are difficult to measure as well as controversial. A single vote shared between several small states would be impracticable. Combinations of criteria compound the difficulties. Critics of the existing wide discrepancy between voting and power find themselves forced back to the second alternative; and emphasize that little weight can be attached to resolutions in the General Assembly, which are far from being the verdicts of international society.

The Security Council is less of a diplomatic innovation. Like the Council of the League of Nations from which it was derived, and the nineteenth-century Concert of Europe before that, it was designed as a permanent concert or directorate of the great powers, with the addition of a rotating number of smaller states. It was to be the effective body of the United Nations, as opposed to the universality and formal equality of the Assembly. At present this effectiveness depends largely on agreement between the two super-powers, usually established by prior bilateral diplomacy. The requirement that the five great powers must approve or abstain if a decision is to be valid, reflects the reality in the world at large, outside the organization in New York, that the United States or the Soviet Union can in effect block or 'veto' international decisions which it opposes. The realist critics of the veto power of Britain, France and China argue that those states are not at present powerful enough to block international decisions outside the Council, though a West European Community or China may be so one day.

The Concert of Europe functioned on much the same lines. It was effective when the great powers concerned concurred in a solution or abstained from opposing it; and effective also for so long as the rulers of the great powers, or at least the men who controlled their diplomacy, remained in close contact with each other to maintain order in Europe and met together at times of crisis to manage change by agreement. Why then is the U.N. Security Council less effective? One answer commonly given is that it is not a meeting of the statesmen who take important decisions in the world: it is a body of ambassadors who reside permanently together in New York, far from where the decisions are taken. The Council would gain in force and effectiveness, it is argued, if the foreign ministers of the states concerned, especially the major powers, met regularly at convenient places. This would be a return to the practice of the Concert of Europe. A major objection to this proposal arises from the fear that the Security Council would then become a kind of world directorate, in which the great powers settled matters in their own interests and perhaps at the expense of the smaller ones. Nor does the rotating but fixed composition of the Council always include the states most concerned with a given problem. Statesmen therefore find it easier to arrange *ad hoc* meetings when they are concerned with a given issue, as and when necessary, and then to register their conclusions through their agents on the Security Council. Other suggestions include making the Security Council more representative, to reflect more accurately the real power situation in the world. One way of doing this would be to bring in more permanent members, like Japan, West Germany and India. It has proved extremely difficult to establish any substantial measure of agreement on any reform of this kind, since any change seems to many states to discriminate against their interests, and in favour of a directorate of powerful states. Another proposal is to invite to the Council delegates from all states and quasi-states particularly concerned with an issue. This is becoming the standard practice; but such invited states do not vote.

All in all, it seems unlikely that any major change in the composition and operation of the Security Council will come about in the near future. But even as it is now constituted, the Security Council has introduced a new element into diplomatic practice. When the major governments of the world there represented are in agreement on an issue, it can formulate and endorse that agreement in the name of the world body. A Security Council decision is thus more representative of existing power in the world than a resolution of the Assembly, and more likely to be carried out. But it is not regarded as having the same authority as international law. A state which refuses to comply with a Security Council resolution (for instance Israel since 1968) is not said to be in breach of international law. Much less does a Security Council resolution have the authority of a law duly enacted according to established procedures within a state which also has law enforcement machinery to ensure compliance. Major powers can decide to enforce it, of course, either by their own armed forces and the other means of compelling obedience at their disposal, or else by arranging for certain countries to lend U.N. troops for the purpose. Whether the decisions which the major powers take in the Security Council have more force or moral authority than those they take outside, such as those concerning Vietnam or European Security, is doubtful. But they are the voice of institutionalized, as opposed to *ad hoc*, collective diplomacy, speaking with at least the acquiescence of the two super-powers and a majority of a representative selection of states.

It has also been suggested that the powers of the Secretary General of the United Nations should be increased. The Secretary would then become not merely the servant of the organization but something more like a World Executive, with powers over United Nations forces and in other matters. These suggestions are opposed by most of the more powerful states in the system. Moreover, the greater the powers entrusted to the Secretary General, the harder it would be for the member states to agree on an individual to wield them.

How effective an instrument of the diplomatic dialogue is a permanent omnilateral institution? The League was a great step forward in the organisation of collective diplomacy, but made little and quite inadequate provision for change. The United Nations is better in this respect; however inadequately and corruptly, the collective diplomacy that issues from it does reflect the changing conscience of mankind, and is not committed to the *status quo*. It is generally agreed that the specialized and technical agencies of the United Nations serve a useful but subsidiary purpose – especially for the newer and smaller states. Beyond this, how far can we entrust to the U.N. the safeguarding of peace and order, and the adjustment to change and new ideas of justice? Whatever states may declare in public, the answer of almost all of them in practice is: not very far. The United Nations is hailed as an instrument of collective diplomacy, and also as a means for focussing the attention of the diplomatic process on justice and the need for changes in the existing system; yet the process of negotiation and adjustment between states, and even the process of establishing a safer and fairer and more civilized world which seems to many people the real purpose of the U.N., are still carried on largely outside the organization. Collective diplomacy in its various forms is gaining in importance over bilateral diplomacy; but even collective diplomacy takes place largely outside the United Nations, especially on the very important issues where peace and order are concerned. No responsible government, no serious student of international affairs, considers that the conduct of international affairs can be left entirely to the particular part of the modern diplomatic process which is the United Nations as that body operates at present. Certainly no government would entrust the constantly altering needs of the country and people it governs simply to action in U.N. bodies. Even on issues which are not directly concerned with peace and security, every government tries to safeguard the needs and interests of its people by explaining them and proposals for meeting them to at least some other governments directly, through the channel of bilateral diplomacy; and almost every government today is also involved in multilateral negotiations outside the U.N.

The advantage of the United Nations, in the eyes of most of its supporters, is symbolic. Whereas bilateral diplomacy is concerned very largely with the needs and interests of individual states, and bilateral deals and bargains may benefit both the parties concerned, but at the expense of other states or international society, there is at the United Nations a presumption in favour of decisions and recommendations which reflect the interests of mankind as a whole. Compared with this great general advantage, many of the disadvantages of the U.N. can be portrayed as incidental, due to defects in the machinery. Collective negotiation can be seen as an especially civilized and civilizing form of diplomacy, because it encourages collective responsibility. This has been said, and is substantially true, of all collective diplomacy from the Concert of Europe to the present day. But symbolism is not enough. The essential difference between the European Concert and the omnilateral organizations of this century concerns their relation to the power of their member states. The Concert was designed by the great states of Europe to manage the distribution and operation of their power, and to maintain order through a cooperative balance. The United Nations, in its organization and its operations, is almost wholly divorced from the actual power of its member states. It functions more often as a counterpoint to the distribution of power than as an expression of it.

The criticisms of contemporary diplomacy, bilateral and multilateral, all have one feature in common. They are all concerned with improving the existing general techniques and institutions of the diplomatic dialogue. The public debate on this subject is surely educative and desirable, in spite of much special pleading and some silliness at the fringes. It helps to facilitate the continuous process of change and development that has characterized the dialogue between states in a diplomatic society, and it is also part of the wider tendency in democratic states to subject diplomacy to closer public scrutiny. We now need to consider the general adjustments discussed in this chapter alongside the innovations required to cope with the special needs of the many new and small states which have been accepted as members of international society but which find difficulty in conducting diplomacy (and other activities expected of states in the modern world). We must also consider the effects on the dialogue of its expansion to include the economic and other fields into which the activities of all states are extending.

CHAPTER XI

Diplomatic Needs of New and Less Developed States

In the last chapter we looked at some general criticisms of the present institutions and methods of diplomacy. We now need to consider the effect of the expansion of our states system on the workings of contemporary diplomacy. A large number of newly created non-European states have recently been incorporated into the diplomatic dialogue. The resulting great increase in numbers has come in addition to, and has compounded, the previous expansion of the European system into a global one. This phenomenon is sometimes called the proliferation of states in the system, which is a convenient shorthand term.

More than half of the states now members of the United Nations have either resumed or acquired independence since 1945. Of the eighty or so states in this category, a few, like Morocco, Egypt, Burma and Fiji, have brought a foreign protectorate to an end and resumed the independent control of diplomatic relations with other powers which they had exercised in the past. The great majority have acquired independence as wholly new states as a result of the dissolution of former empires. This was the case especially in Africa and with groups of islands like those in the Caribbean. Lastly, fully self-governing states such as New Zealand have taken to exercising in the external field the independence which was theirs *de jure* but largely exercised in conjunction with the United Kingdom before 1939.

These new members of the world system of states are of course not alike. They differ immensely from one another in their capacity to conduct foreign relations and, more specifically, to operate the web of diplomatic contacts used by more established and especially by the larger states. States like India, Egypt and Israel, which vary enormously in size and population, have shown themselves to be highly competent both at bilateral and collective diplomacy, much more so indeed than many older states at the other end of the scale. On the other hand, some of the newest, smallest and least experienced members of the states system have hardly yet achieved that degree of internal control which is usually considered a minimum for statehood, and their diplomatic contacts are still necessarily limited and embryonic. Indeed in such cases it is not only the practice of diplomacy and the need for negotiation with other states that the small new states have learnt from outside: the whole concept of a modern state and modern government has been imported, along with the whole range of modern technology. Most of these states have achieved political independence before acquiring the capacities and the skills to end their economic and administrative dependence on the outside world; and their governments are also confronted with the rapidly rising expectations of their people and often a population explosion. In their efforts to establish acceptable levels of functioning statehood such governments surely have a real claim to the understanding, the encouragement and the assistance of the former colonial powers and of the other advanced states which insisted on their political independence and received them into international society. It is scarcely surprising that these new states, which are not yet used to governing themselves, and especially the majority which are made up of a mixture of different peoples, find that they need a firmer and more authoritarian executive than is now usual or approved in the West. It is not surprising that there is usually an authoritarian control of foreign policy and a simplified procedure for arriving at decisions. Such states need help in conducting their diplomacy, along with other forms of aid outside the scope of this book.

The problems of our dramatically enlarged international society are those caused firstly by the *numbers* themselves, compounded by the speed with which the numbers grew; secondly by the *increased diversity* of cultural background and state of development; and thirdly in the case of new states, by the technical *inexperience* of government, especially in the international field. I propose in this chapter to look at these three problems, and then at ways in which the new states, and international society generally, are trying to deal with them.

The most obvious aspect of proliferation is the actual increase in the *number* of members in the system. This increase complicates all diplomacy, both bilateral and collective. On the bilateral plane, the more states there are conducting negotiations, putting their case to one another, arguing and bargaining, the more complex the diplomatic pattern is. Active diplomatic

centres, where over a hundred embassies discuss a wide range of issues with
a ministry of foreign affairs and ask to be kept informed of the government's
views, and then compare notes with one another, are far busier places
diplomatically than they were when the number of states was much less.
Similarly, a ministry of foreign affairs which receives and collates reports
from a hundred of its embassies abroad has a much harder task than it
had when there were only forty or fifty such missions. There is in fact a
geometrical increase of complexity with the increase of numbers. This is
difficult to quantify. One figure mentioned by professional diplomats when
discussing the problem is that the complexity of the bilateral web of contacts
increases by the square of the numbers; but this can be only an indicative
guess.

   The effect of the increase of numbers on collective diplomacy is more
serious than on the bilateral dialogue. Let us take first the United Nations.
A Security Council of a dozen or so members – as it was originally constituted
– five of which, or nearly half, were permanent and could thus give some
continuity and bring long experience to the Council's deliberations and
methods of doing business – can settle down fairly quickly after each change
in the nonpermanent states elected. A Council so composed can hope to function as an effective body on issues where the aims of the more important
members are not too diametrically in conflict. Ways of working out compromises expeditiously come to be accepted, and the individual delegates
soon regard themselves, for all the differences between their countries,
as something like a team. A Council of fifteen, with ten constantly changing
seats, as it is constituted at the time of writing, is in practice a much less
workable arrangement. Both these numbers are still manageable, especially
in so far as the Council is a public debating body as much as a committee of
decision-makers. But a General Assembly with more than 150 delegations,
each of which wishes to express its own separate point of view, is liable to
become a different sort of institution from an Assembly of sixty: a delegate
may only be able to make one or two set speeches in the course of a session,
and there is little prospect of debate. The same is true of other United
Nations bodies with universal representation. The Food and Agricultural
Organization, the World Health Organization, UNESCO and other similar
specialized agencies, as well as the Economic and Social Council, all have
their work complicated and their efficiency impaired by the complexities
arising from the weight of numbers, as well as from the increasing demand
for their services from the new states.

   Secondly, the phenomenon of proliferation has also brought complications of *diversity* in addition to those directly associated with the statistical
increase in numbers. The spreading out of the collective diplomacy of the

European society of states to the whole world has taken it outside the cultural framework which has in the past been the cradle of effective states systems and of their diplomacy. It has involved giving equal representation and largely equal responsibilities in world organizations, and thereby a substantial voice in shaping the diplomatic dialogue generally, to states with very different cultural backgrounds and very different assumptions about the nature of society.

In the period of European domination of the world, non-European countries, and especially their European-educated élites, acquired a great deal of European (in the wider sense, including American and Russian) culture, values and technology. Now that the European empires have disappeared and European domination is retreating, previously existing cultures, values and traditions will manifest themselves again to some extent, adapted and hybridized with European ones. The question is: to what extent? The answer is of obvious importance, but highly controversial. Nobody seriously disputes that there were, before the age of European expansion over the globe, very different cultures and cultural traditions, with different values; and that the diffusion of certain economic skills and techniques – such as those connected with wheat, iron, horses, writing – extended the capacities of the different civilizations but did not alter their basic character. European expansion, combined with the industrial revolution and especially the development of instant communication, has produced a more homogeneous world, as in its time the Roman Empire did round the Mediterranean. The collapse of the Roman Empire led to a great re-diversification of the Mediterranean lands. Will the ebb tide of the European empires and of Western dominance lead to a significantly diverse world again, even if the different cultures and values of Asia and Africa retain much that they were obliged to learn from the West? Or will the forces of modernization and industrialization, which are everywhere the same, combined with the shrinking of the world and the continuing imprint of the West and its values on the educated leaders of Asia and Africa, lead to a common global civilization and shared values? Or, as Marxists claim, are economic interests and the class struggle the real issues, so that cultural differences will dwindle to the level of local dialects, folk music and cookery? Thinkers like Toynbee, Spengler and Professor Bozeman have argued that the deep-seated traditions and thought patterns of cultures and civilizations are not easily modified at all, and remain substantially intact even when they adopt techniques and ideas from others. Their thesis covers not only cultures with a long history of highly developed civilization, like the Islamic, Indian, Chinese and Japanese, but also pre-literate cultures like those of black Africa which have not yet achieved the full development of their potential.

It is not necessary to accept this thesis entirely in order to recognize that the Europeanization of the rest of the world, as opposed to its technological homogenization, has not been complete and permanent, and that the effects on international society of the re-emergence of other cultures and values cannot be put at zero, but may well be considerable.

These problems can conveniently be illustrated by taking as an example an international organization much more closely knit than the United Nations, namely the European Community. If, say, Scotland and Catalonia were given separate representation in the organs of the Community, if Italy were to dissolve again into a dozen states each with its own government, delegates and officials, the task of the Community would be more complex by reason of the greater numbers and the different interests expressed. But if the Community were enlarged to include, let us say, the Arab states of North Africa just across the Mediterranean, there would in addition to the increase in numbers also be complications of a different kind arising from differences of culture and tradition and existing levels of education and development. Yet these disparities are far smaller than those which exist in the world as a whole.

Perhaps more difficult still at the present stage is the third problem, that of technical *inexperience*. The states which now make up international society are at very different stages of what in United Nations terms is called economic and social development. The least developed, indeed, are composed largely of pre-literate tribal peoples: states which have not a different tradition of international relations and the diplomatic dialogue, but no experience or tradition of dealing with other states at all. Over the medium term, this difficulty is likely to diminish as the new members of the system gain experience; whereas the cultural disparity seems likely to increase. In the transition period the problems of inexperience at a collective level are mitigated by the concentration of power, and especially of administrative responsibility, in less developed states in the hands of small Western-trained élites. Some observers have seen the position of these élites as corresponding to the position of the European settlers in many American countries with predominantly non-European populations in the nineteenth century.

The progressive involvement of North and South American states in the European diplomatic system at the beginning of its overseas expansion in the half-century following the organization of the United States as a member of international society in the 1770s, presented no real difficulties, since the states which mattered were substantially of European stock and heirs of the European tradition. Important Asian states like the Ottoman Empire and later Japan and China could be brought into the dialogue smoothly too, because they were few in number, accepted European diplomatic methods, and had highly developed civilizations and administrative experience of their own. The sudden introduction of a large number of states such as Chad and Papua New Guinea has more serious consequences. In the course of a thoughtful discussion of the changes made necessary by proliferation in his book, *The Inequality of Nations* Professor Robert Tucker says:

> The sudden transformation in status of so many peoples gave an initial momentum to a movement that still shows few signs of slowing down. Had decolonization taken place over a substantially longer period, the consequences in all likelihood would have been quite different. A few new states could have been gradually absorbed into the existing system with little perturbation. In time, inequalities of opportunity as well as of condition would surely have been challenged. Even so, such challenge would have been of a different magnitude and, it is not unreasonable to assume, would have taken a different form.

What then are the adjustments to the practice and the machinery of diplomacy required to deal with the difficulties caused by this unprecedented expansion of international society, and how far are they being adopted?

It is sometimes thought that no far-reaching adjustments are necessary. The new states appear outwardly to 'join' international society. Many of the multilingual tribal countries use English or French for administrative purposes at home, and those in senior government positions will therefore be familiar with a world language. Indeed the less developed a new state is, the more likely it is to be ruled by a small Western-educated élite. The envoys and experts of the new countries and their political leaders on visits abroad usually find it easy enough to adopt the conventions and behaviour of the international political world.

But the underlying reality is not as simple as that. The greater the disparity between the cultural assumptions, the political traditions and the level of economic and social development of countries working together in international bodies, the greater the complexity of the work. In the actual negotiations there are just that many more occasions for misunderstanding to be surmounted, each of which takes time and draws on the stock of patience and goodwill, itself a scarce and fragile political resource. Even where delegates come to understand one another, the governments they represent are less likely to do so. For these governments are working in widely different frames of reference from each other; and they govern, and therefore to some extent reflect the attitudes of, peoples with different and incompatible unspoken assumptions. It is a mistake to confuse the cultural homogeneity of the international fraternity of envoys and experts with the much less homogeneous society of states. Many observers of the international scene overestimate the power of the professional representatives of states – diplomats, lawyers and so on – who are much more like each other than are the states which employ them.

Let us begin with the remedies for the most obvious problem, that of the *increase of numbers*. Little can be done to cope with the effects on bilateral diplomacy in the larger capitals where almost every state wishes to maintain a diplomatic representative. No state wishes to discourage another from opening a resident embassy merely on the ground that there are too many others!

The only recourse open to the host government is to increase greatly the size of its ministry of foreign affairs: which is being increased also to deal with the extending range of subjects that states now wish to discuss with one another and which thus come into the diplomatic dialogue. In most of the developed states this increase has already taken place.

For states which still aspire to a comprehensive view of international society, a great additional burden is also imposed on other government departments concerned with aspects of each state's relations with other states and with the institutions of international society. Not only does the bureaucracy have to be larger. Senior officials, and especially members of a cabinet or its equivalent, find it increasingly difficult to be aware of each state and each problem in all its individuality and in sufficient detail to make valid judgements. Of course this difficulty existed even in the European and in previous states systems. But as the complexity grows so it becomes more necessary to group states and problems together so as to try to retain an overall view, which leads to inelasticity; and to accept the recommendations of experts on the region or the problem, and leave the day-to-day decisions in their hands, although the concentration of these experts' attention on local and limited issues makes it harder for them to see how those issues fit into the wider picture. (The desire to avoid this professional myopia is one of the reasons which continues to prompt governments to post their diplomatic personnel to a variety of assignments, so as to broaden the range of their awareness.)

However, the most serious impact of increased numbers is on multilateral and especially omnilateral diplomacy, where universality of representation is the determining criterion. As we have seen, there is in such cases a conflict between universality and effectiveness. One obvious and easy remedy, which is therefore frequently adopted, is to accept a ceiling of effectiveness for those international institutions where universality and formal equality are necessary, as they are for instance in most United Nations bodies; and to transfer serious discussion of important and tricky issues to *ad hoc* conferences where the problems of proliferation can be made less acute. Not every state needs to be asked to such informal exercises in collective diplomacy, and those represented do not all have an equal voice in the discussion. But while this may be an effective form of crisis management, it avoids rather than resolves the problems of proliferation.

The two main tendencies which contemporary collective diplomacy is developing to deal with its own complexities of scale and disparity are *regional devolution* and the *organization of blocs*.

Regional devolution within the framework of the United Nations has been a spontaneous development. The United Nations provides a place for regional organizations in Article 52 of its charter. But the universal organization did not itself act as a 'devolver', fostering regional sub-organizations. Regional organizations such as the Organization of African Unity have come into effective being, and their authority has increased, as a response by like-minded states who find the universal body too unwieldy for certain purposes they have in common. There is growing recognition that many regions, such as Latin America or Black Africa or Western Europe, have regional identities and interests. They have regional as opposed to universal problems which they need to tackle together, and also cultural and historical affinities; and the states of which each region is composed are at similar stages of development. They therefore find it convenient and effective to deal with many matters among themselves. Such regional organizations have the additional appeal that they exclude more powerful states from outside the area which have traditionally had an interest in it, and are therefore specially favoured by states which have recently emerged from colonialism. However, the wide acceptance of the 'continental formula' for such regional groupings, which brackets together all the states in a continent, has made it harder to exclude a big neighbour like the United States or the Soviet Union which can overshadow a regional organization. There is also the fear in some of the smaller countries that if all other influences are excluded they will be dominated by the most powerful state or states in the region. The relation of regional bodies to the United Nations, the degree of their devolution from the central and universal institutions of the world organization, and the demarcation of the various regions are therefore likely to remain matters of argument and subject to change.

Some practitioners and observers see bodies like the Organization of African Unity developing into regional U.N.s, taking over many of the functions of the unwieldy universal body, and at the same time developing techniques of conciliation and pressure which are the stock in trade of effective collective diplomacy and which are only practicable in a more limited and especially a more homogeneous grouping. There would doubtless still remain a ceiling of usefulness in such bodies, especially where matters of peace and security or financial aid are concerned. Some people, while recognising the trend, regard it as a retrograde one; others see it as a move towards efficiency and away from great power dominance.

The organization of blocs at the U.N., and at other bodies and conferences with wide representation, corresponds in one respect to the historic beginnings of political parties in democratic legislatures, where members who held broadly the same aims and views worked and voted together, usually under a leader, in order to operate more effectively. But it is important to remember that whereas the members of a legislature are dealing with a single executive government within a state, each diplomatic envoy at the U.N. and other conferences is the agent and spokesman of a different independent executive or government. The coordination of voting and policy at such collective diplomatic conferences is a matter of reaching agreement between the governments concerned. This is normally achieved through the channel of bilateral diplomacy. In the past the usual way has been to negotiate directly between the two capitals concerned; and instructions to coordinate tactics to an agreed extent are then sent to the envoys at the conference. More often the new tendency is for these bilateral negotiations to take place between the diplomats accredited to the U.N. or the *ad hoc* conference, who are most familiar with the issues involved and most aware of how a given joint policy will affect the many other issues also up for collective discussion. But this is merely a matter of diplomatic technique and the choice of channel: it does not dispense with the need for diplomatic agents to clear the policy of their bloc with their own government at home on each issue. The blocs which emerge in this way do in practice lead to greater simplicity and efficiency of negotiation: they reduce the number of variants to a manageable quantity. But the blocs are almost entirely determined by the affinities and policies of home governments, and the alliances and agreements which the states in question have already contracted, and in most cases scarcely at all by the personal views of the delegates as is the case in a legislature. In short, blocs reflect the realities of ideological alignment which prevail outside the conference, and perhaps increasingly also cultural ties such as those which bind the Islamic states. The formalization of existing informal patterns of bloc voting would thus provide a useful framework in many ways for the more effective organization of unwieldy omnilateral assemblies and conferences. But formalized bloc voting is less suited to a meeting of ambassadors than to a legislature. It would hamper and perhaps prevent diplomatic flexibility, both bilaterally and in collective negotiations. It would tend to push real diplomacy outside the omnilateral bodies, and lower still further their ceiling of usefulness. Many small and uncommitted states have shown their distrust of it.

The most famous example of the attempt to institutionalize a system of blocs at the U.N. was the proposal advocated by the Soviet Union during the 1960s to organize the member states into three general categories: the West, the communist states and associates and the Third World of non-aligned nations. There would be three deputy Secretaries General, and in other ways a balance between the three blocs would be preserved. The states which opposed this plan had valid reasons for doing so. It would have perpetuated the cold war. It would have given the Soviet representative undue control over the less docile members of the communist bloc, which would presumably have come to include communist China; whereas that degree of control would not be present in the Western and especially the Third World blocs. And it would have been unnecessarily rigid. But the Soviet proposal also had constructive aspects and might have helped to make the U.N. more effective. It should not simply be dismissed, but regarded as a biased proposal in a general direction which the U.N. appears to be taking. Special conferences outside the U.N., such as those dealing with European security (which are likely to re-convene at intervals and may become a regular diplomatic institution) have in practice fairly set patterns which reflect existing alliances and political blocs. The fact that a number of states round a table are able to coordinate the line they will take on various issues simplifies negotiations, which are still likely to remain extremely complex even with this major streamlining. It has for instance sharpened and clarified the issues in the bewildering intricacy of the United Nations Conference on Trade and Development.

These two tendencies towards regionalism and blocs have much in common. Many of the blocs of collective diplomacy are in practice regional groupings. The proliferation of states, many of them very small, has led to the practice of transacting business and organizing diplomatic negotiations among groups of states rather than between a large number of individual ones, in order to keep large-scale negotiations manageable. Sometimes these groups may come together in a confederacy or under the domination of one large state; but not necessarily. It is significant that the separate states in these groupings, unless they have ceased to be genuinely independent at all, almost always continue to supplement their collective diplomacy on a group basis by individual bilateral diplomacy, first with other members of the group in order to arrive at a favourable common position, and then with the more important and the more wavering states in other groupings too.

The problems raised by the *diversity* of cultural backgrounds and degrees of development of the states composing the modern world system are more complex. That the forms of diplomacy in use today were largely evolved in

Western Europe, and have now expanded far beyond the cultural frame-work which gave them birth, is historically true. Cultural and historical traditions and social patterns need more adaptation when transposed from one civilization to another than does technical knowhow. It is therefore significant, and has certainly eased the transition, that so little change has in practice been found necessary until now in order to accommodate non-European and non-developed countries in the diplomatic dialogue.

This continuity of diplomatic practice is not due to any obstinate refusal on the part of the established states of European origin, either Western or communist, to meet the formulated demands of non-European new states. There are several reasons for this willingness of the established states to amend the rules and practices of international society. To begin with, since World War Two there have been a number of changes in diplomatic prac-tice, and especially of emphasis, for reasons other than the demands of the new states; and some of these have incidentally helped to meet the needs of newer and smaller states. Secondly, the particular changes which these states have asked for are not momentous, or unduly difficult to accommodate within the existing framework. Thirdly, this framework, once modified to suit the needs of the new states, is advantageous to them, in particular because it affirms and strengthens their political independence. On balance they regard the benefits of maintaining this framework as out-weighing the inconveniences it may still have for them. Fourthly, in the European system there has traditionally been no significant opposition in principle to changing forms of dialogue between states, in the directions proposed by the new states. The established states are well enough aware that the nature and purpose of diplomacy is accommodation and adjustment, and that diplomacy is more effective the more diplomats and statesmen put them-selves mentally in the place of their negotiating partners and understand the requirements and the patterns of thought of those with whom they are dealing. In the period of the cold war the competition between the two rival blocs of developed states for the allegiance or at least the benevolent neutrality of the new and non-aligned states of the Third World was in-tense; and this competition would have ensured a greater adaptation of the rules to the needs of the non-aligned states if such states had put forward proposals or themselves adopted innovations to meet their special require-ments. But this they did not do to any significant extent. The difficulties which small and new states experience when trying to take part in the established diplomatic dialogue were also obscured during the period of the cold war by the tendency of both of the contending groups of developed states to treat the largest and culturally most highly developed non-aligned countries, like India and China, as spokesmen for the whole Third World.

The states of the West continued among themselves to practise and modify the diplomatic mechanisms with which they were familiar. The Soviet Union and other communist governments associated with it have been particularly insistent on using the diplomatic machinery which they found to hand, and on being accepted as equal partners in the operation of its practices. Consequently, the Indian, Chinese and other highly organized non-European governments also found it to their interest to take part in world diplomacy according to the rules which they found in operation; and they have not suggested or worked for any very radical changes.

On a more fundamental plane, new and non-European states have demanded so little change in diplomatic practice for the additional reason that the inhabitants of once-colonial countries rebelled against the domination of the Europeans in the exact idiom which they acquired from the colonizers. The frame in which the politically conscious leaders conceived of independence before obtaining it was nation, state and frequently socialism. Having committed themselves and their followers to these concepts, they have found that the fullest implementations of them can be realized only by participation in the existing international society of states. If to be rid of European rule comes to mean the political independence of newly postulated 'nations' in reconstituted ex-colonial states, then it also means participation on a basis of formal equality in the currently presiding features of international life. To will the state is to will the states system. So the leaders of the new states, whatever their domestic form of government, consider the diplomatic dialogue with other states as now conducted to be a condition or corollary of their own statehood. This is the case however unpalatable the configuration of influences on the international political stage may be. And the international order is the setting in which, through interdependence, new states are schooled in the – sometimes disappointing and painful – limits of independence, and come to accept the seeming paradox that the interdependence which provides them with a means of bringing pressure to bear on other states equally restricts their own freedom of action.

Thus the leaders of new states want to be accepted as full members of international society as the expression and, one might almost say, proof of their statehood and nationhood. They do not want to do away with the system, but rather to improve their own position within it. They want the protocol and the conventions which they associate with diplomacy to be fully observed in the case of themselves and their envoys. To Westerners, in whose cultural context the outward forms of diplomatic intercourse grew up, these forms have something of the quality of conventions and fashions, which can and should be modified as the pattern of society changes. To those who come to the diplomatic dialogue from outside, so to speak, these forms have the value of status symbols, which they are determined not to have skipped or omitted in their case. In the diplomatic life of Moscow, for instance, Soviet diplomats find that the insistence on such observances as black-tie dinners, ritual toasts, meetings at airports, comes especially from the representatives of new states, whereas the embassies of established Western powers are more inclined to informality and to cut down on ceremony in order to concentrate on exploratory dialogue. This is what one might expect. The more secure the social position of an individual is, the more casual and informal he is prepared to be.

This rigidity is likely to be a temporary phenomenon. As time passes, diplomatic practice changes. Though it is not possible to say what directions such changes will take as they emerge from the long process of diplomatic bargaining and unilaterally modified codes of conduct, it seems likely that certain European values and assumptions underlying the diplomatic dialogue will change more than the outward forms in the next phase of adjustment to a global international society.

More significant changes are already resulting from the third aspect of proliferation, the governmental *inexperience* and the *lack of capacity* of most of the new and small states. The lack of experience is particularly conspicuous in the international field, for in most new states there was some familiarity with internal administration through limited self-government before formal independence.

Small, new states cannot normally be expected to possess the experience of government, the resources of skilled manpower, the money, or the understanding of problems other than their own, which would enable them to operate successfully from the beginning the intricate web of modern diplomacy, which the addition of each new and different state makes more complex still. Much thought has therefore been given to ways and means of adapting diplomatic practice to the limited capacity of small states with underdeveloped societies. Political leaders of new states, colonial powers preparing to hand over power, aid agencies, the staff of international organizations like the United Nations, the International Bank for Reconstruction and Development and the Commonwealth Secretariat and academic authorities have all made important contributions to the discussion, based on their varying experience.

A diplomatic establishment like that of the United States or the Soviet Union, or Britain and France, is obviously quite beyond the resources of a small new state with an even smaller educated élite. A state with limited resources quickly runs into the problem of priorities. Where the number of

people with enough experience and training to perform usefully in a diplomatic mission is very strictly limited, their rare skills will also be needed for
many other essential tasks, and only a handful of them will be able to devote
all or most of their time to the diplomatic dialogue. In these circumstances
the élite few who run the small new states are naturally especially concerned
to make international society aware of the new 'nation', to manifest its
presence. Their aim, in the expressive French phrase, is '*se faire valoir*',
to be taken seriously. They value state and ceremonial visits by rulers and
heads of government, both for their symbolic value and also, because the
power of decision in these states is concentrated in the hands of the usually
authoritarian ruler who finds that acting through intermediaries in the style
of European diplomacy is less effective than direct contact face to face. By
state visits the new state manifests its presence while conducting or at
least clinching important business. The élites also incline to establishing
resident embassies to manifest the new state's presence in foreign capitals,
and visiting delegations to international bodies and conferences which give
the new state needed visibility, rather than to building up an effective
foreign ministry which collates evidence and formulates alternative policies.
As a result of this, the ratio of two professional diplomats abroad to one at
home, which is the rough proportion found most effective by large and experienced states, is reached in the new small states only gradually if at all.
Their ambassadors do not send back a stream of information and receive
in return a continuous flow of instructions and guidance. They often receive
detailed instructions and briefing only for conferences of key importance to
their state: in the case of Mauritius, for instance, a conference on sugar
quotas and prices. On other matters, such as debates on issues of principle at
the General Assembly of the United Nations, the representatives of new
states, who are usually associates or perhaps relatives of the ruling group,
have a wide latitude, and what they say on such occasions may not correspond to the policy finally adopted by their government. However, the
example and the advice of more developed states leads to a certain awareness
of the need for functional collation of policy and the formulation of instructions, as opposed to the ceremonial and representational sides of present-
day diplomacy. Many small states begin their independent relations with
other states and international bodies by the president, or prime minister,
sending envoys abroad and receiving envoys from foreign powers, and
keeping simple records in his own office, without setting up a separate
foreign ministry. But the new governments soon learn the advantage of
having a small collating ministry to supervise and coordinate relations with
the rest of international society.

Fortunately, many ex-colonies have a few ministers, professional diplomats and other civil servants who were trained in the service of the imperial power in the period of transition (or received a similar training period in Moscow). These men know the diplomatic ropes, so to speak. They often aspire to larger diplomatic establishments than the new state really requires; but on the other hand they are able to draw on their past experience in the diplomatic or governmental machine of an imperial power or an international organization to work out ways of obtaining the necessary information and briefing from international bodies, the former colonial power and other sources on matters of real concern to their new state. They do so while reserving their own judgement and exercising their own decisions about the new state's interests, which is the decisive difference between colonial and independent status. In my experience the most successful examples of this type of imperially trained diplomat representing a new state are to be found in the formerly French countries of black Africa. Those from some states of the New Commonwealth have also made impressive use of their imperial training.

The question of how many resident embassies and missions a small state should maintain abroad deserves special notice. It brings the problems of scale and need clearly into focus. The minimum with which small new states begin, except in the case of a few mini-states which hardly aspire to the international dialogue at all, is usually three diplomatic missions: one to the United Nations (which we will look at in a moment); one at the capital of the former imperial power; and one in some other important, often neighbouring, state. The bilateral embassies will almost certainly be multiple ones, accredited to several other states in addition to the one they reside in, and will conduct business with them by periodic brief visits. The other states concerned will make use of the same practice. For ex-colonial states a resident embassy in the capital of the former colonial power is the most obvious need. Formal political independence is the decisive step towards full separate statehood; but it is rarely the last step in the process of disengagement, especially for small and weak states; and whatever their political alignment in world affairs, close ties with the former imperial power, especially in the economic field, are likely to remain for several years. Moreover, most new states had quasi-diplomatic representation of one kind or another in the imperial capital before reaching the stage of a negotiated independence; and the continuing flow of aid, trade, communications, education and various technical facilities makes a channel of diplomatic communication, in the form of an exchange of resident missions, necessary to cope with the active post-independence dialogue.

The establishment of resident embassies in other capitals, and of a diplomatic dialogue with other states by means of occasional visits, opens separate bilateral windows on the world of international affairs. Through this channel the government of the new state can check and balance what it learns in the former imperial capital and at the United Nations. Many new states soon find it useful to have more than one such window, especially to rich developed states that offer aid. States with territorial neighbours also find it convenient to open permanent diplomatic contact with them. Diplomatic ties are often useful with countries of origin of the population, and with other states that have the same economic or other interests. (Mauritius, to take our example, is remote from neighbours, but has a large population of Indian origin and is also concerned with sugar prices.)

The multilateral diplomacy of small new states is broadly of three kinds. Politically and symbolically, and in other ways too, the most important is through participation in the activities of the United Nations, including its subordinate, regional and technical bodies. Secondly, multilateral organizations like the Commonwealth Secretariat and the corresponding 'francophone' institutions, and association with the European Economic Community, can be very useful technically and economically. Taken together they constitute a diplomatic innovation called into being by the needs of new states. And thirdly, participation in multilateral commodity negotiations is economically indispensable for most such states; and sometimes, as in the case of OPEC, highly profitable, but by its nature limited in scope.

Many small states, and international experts in larger ones, have advocated a modification of present diplomatic practice which would enable these states to use their missions to the United Nations not only for their present functions, but increasingly as a substitute for extensive bilateral diplomacy. 'Diplomacy through the United Nations' when used by spokesmen for the underdeveloped world means a number of things at the same time. It is partly a symbolic insistence on the formal equality of all independent states in the states system great and small, developed and backward. It also means the use of United Nations organs, and especially votes in the General Assembly, as a means of pressure on powerful and developed states. The underdeveloped states have developed this diplomatic technique considerably as their numbers and experience have grown; and they are concerned to make their pressure more effective still. But thirdly and less conspicuously, many governments of small states want to concentrate through one effective delegation in New York their more conventional and largely bilateral forms of dialogue with the other members of the international community with which they do not exchange competent and permanent diplomatic missions. The effectiveness of this adaptation of the diplomatic machinery is still alarmingly limited for many countries that practise it, when judged by advanced standards, although it is already a real convenience for some to be

able to transact bilateral business in this way. If the practice is extended
and becomes generally accepted, as seems likely, the U.N. delegations of
larger states will have to equip themselves to deal with a multiplicity of
bilateral issues which are not on the U.N. agenda, and the smaller states
will have to provide a more regular and sensitive link between the government at home and its U.N. delegation. In this way the U.N. may grow as a
centre for private diplomatic negotiation, as opposed to public pressure and
polemics. Bilateral diplomacy through U.N. delegations thus helps small
states, both because it enables them to make full use of one competent
diplomatic mission whereas they cannot manage a large number, and also
because the political climate and assumptions of the United Nations favour
the equality of all states. However, negotiation between United Nations
delegations has one obvious defect. Negotiation between two envoys, neither
perhaps an expert on the point at issue, is remoter and more indirect than
the traditional bilateral arrangement of one government negotiating in its
own capital with the envoy of another who is at least familiar with the range
of bilateral problems between the two states. Negotiation between delegates
to the United Nations needs to be supplemented by the inclusion of experts
sent out by the two governments, a practice which has been made much
quicker and easier by air travel.

Small new states often look to omnilateral organizations like the United
Nations, and also to more limited international groupings and individual
developed states, for technical help in diplomacy. The main fields in which
such help is given are: information; political analysis; the calling of attention
to negotiations and activities which can affect the new state's interests;
administrative and technical help with communications, security, translation, provision of a secretariat at conferences and similar operations; and
taking diplomatic action on behalf of the small state in countries and negotiations where it is not directly represented. Where such help is provided
by organs of the United Nations to small member states or associated mini-
states, there is normally no suspicion that the help and information will
contain a political slant, or have economic or political strings attached in
order to make it serve the interests of a donor power rather than of the
recipient. But the United Nations does not provide bag or pouch services, or
coding systems, or the confidential analyses of the policies and intentions of
other states on which a small new state may be badly informed; nor does
it act on behalf of a state to protect its nationals and interests where that state
is not represented. New states therefore also look, openly or discreetly, to the
former colonial power and to certain other large states for help. They realize
that this help is given because it benefits the donor, especially by maintaining
good relations with the new state in question; but it is also likely to benefit

the recipient, since the donor knows that otherwise it would not be accepted. The large established states which provide these services to small states on the largest scale are Britain, France, the Soviet Union and the United States. In the case of former British territories, help is usually also available from other members of the Commonwealth besides Britain. Since 1963 this provision of advice and technical diplomatic help among Commonwealth countries has been organised in the Commonwealth Secretariat, which now operates for the benefit of all its members and is no longer under the paternalistic or neocolonial control of one or two large states. The diplomatic services provided to small new states through this channel, and the general exchange of ideas through the dialogue 'within a family of nations', constitute a significant addition designed to strengthen the participation of these states in world diplomacy. Similar services are provided by France to the new states formed from its colonial empire. The French services operate on a broader and generally more effective basis than those provided by the Commonwealth Secretariat at present. But they still suffer from the accusation of neocolonialism, from which the Commonwealth Secretariat is now more free because it is not under British control.

A newer formula is provided by the association of many new states with the European Economic Community, in which former imperial powers play a major part. Associated status with the E.E.C. offers the new states many important economic and other advantages, as well as certain technical services, in a less directly dependent context than association with the former imperial power. Association with the E.E.C. is an important diplomatic innovation, which is supported by functioning machinery for a multiple dialogue, and which contributes materially to the establishment of new states in international society.

The modifications of diplomatic techniques to accommodate small and new states into the diplomatic system do not of course alter the fundamental nature and purposes of the dialogue. They are designed to make diplomacy more effective in the changed circumstances of today, rather than to supersede it. Many of them are temporary, designed as part of the transition from dependence to full participating statehood. Among the larger states, the task of innovation in devising new methods and perceptiveness in applying them has so far fallen inevitably on the former colonial powers which have been responsible for organizing the transition. But some of the changes are likely to last. It is certainly true that the traditional forms of diplomacy have already been considerably modified by the emergence of large numbers of small states. This process of adaptation is likely to continue.

CHAPTER XII

The Growth of State Power
and Interdependence

We must now consider the effect on diplomacy of two long-term trends: the increase in the domestic power of states and the growing interdependence of the world. One of the major transformations in the nature of state power taking place in our time is that states are visibly and steadily expanding their administration into areas of human activity, like industrial production and human health, that were previously not their direct concern. At the same time the world continues to 'shrink' and to grow more interdependent, so that what happens inside one state increasingly crosses state frontiers and influences what happens elsewhere. These tendencies might at first glance seem contradictory. But the effect of the two taken together is to enlarge the list of subjects on which governments feel the need to talk to one another, and to increase considerably both the scope and the intensity of the diplomatic dialogue.

The increase in the power of states within their own 'exclusive' jurisdiction, or what is often called the domestic force of sovereignty, is one of the most familiar historical developments associated with the state. But there is much confusion about the implications of this increase in state power, both domestically and internationally. It will therefore pay us to consider briefly its relevance to our theme.

It is sometimes supposed that because in the eighteenth century the power of the Crown gradually gave way to more popular forms of government in the English-speaking world, and in the twentieth century the semi–absolute monarchies of Europe and most of Asia have also been replaced by democracies or 'socialist' régimes acting in the name of the people, the power of the government over the citizens of a state has diminished and that 'freedom' has increased. But a moment's reflection will show that in so far as 'freedom' means freedom of the citizens from governmental control, this is not so. On the contrary, almost every community in the world is moving towards greater state control.

The 'socialist' states with communist governments have advanced furthest along that road. There the power of the state has so greatly expanded that it normally extends to public ownership and state management of almost all the means of production, distribution and exchange: that is, to almost all economic life. In particular, in such countries all commercial transactions involving the rest of the world become the direct responsibility of the state. Communists have been the pace-setters in enlarging the power of the state, but the underlying trend seems to be due to deeper causes than communist advocacy and practice. In the Third World the small élites who govern the new states want especially to establish economic independence by 'nationalizing' economic life, which in colonial times was largely in the hands of alien private companies. This is the most dramatic but not the only area in which state authority generally has expanded since independence. The ruling élites often have Marxist convictions. But even if not, their personal experience has usually been in the service of the state, in government or the armed forces, rather than in the private sector, and their attitude towards the role of government is coloured by their familiarity with it. (This aspect of 'Africanization' was first pointed out to me by President Senghor of Senegal shortly after that country's independence.) Even in developed Western countries where people are traditionally suspicious of the claims of governments to direct affairs, one can see the same process at work. Most states have long since taken over responsibility for education and health, not to mention the now unquestioned presumption that in wartime men and women will be drafted for national service. Even the more conservative Western governments now also recognize their general responsibility for the functioning of the economy. State activity in this field is not merely regulatory, concerned with economic 'guidelines' and the fixing of wages, prices and interest rates. The authority of the state usually now, except in North America, extends to state ownership or management of transport, power and at least some industrial production.

A source of confusion about the growing power of the state is the Leninist doctrine that the bourgeois state will wither away. According to current Soviet theory, when a communist party takes over power, the bourgeois state, in the special Marxist sense of the governmental instrument of the bourgeois and capitalist class, is replaced by the socialist state. (In Marxist theory the enormous extension of state authority which results is provisional,

pending the introduction of true communism, and some communists hold
that it is not necessary even in the present transitional phase for state
authority to extend so far as the Soviet 'dictatorship of the proletariat'. But
the state remains necessary until a fully communist society has been attained.)
In the sense in which the term 'state' is used in this book, communist states
have a greater range of authority than any others; and, what concerns us
especially, their diplomatic activity is as formalized and at least as comprehensive as that of any other member of international society. More generally,
it is a maxim of modern political life, and observable from experience, that
though the other effects of revolutions may differ, all social revolutions, as
opposed to secessions, in practice increase the domestic power of the
leviathan state over the lives of its citizens.

All over the world, therefore, the domestic authority of states is expanding.
And as states become directly involved in ever more aspects of the life of
their communities, these aspects come into the dialogue between states.
So the increase of state authority enlarges the scope of diplomacy.

The growing interdependence of the countries of the world is an equally
familiar phenomenon. The dependence of a state on outside resources is not
in itself new. Even in ancient times one state might be dependent on another
for essential supplies of food or raw materials. Both Athens and Rome had
to import grain from overseas, and Phoenician cities like Tyre and Carthage
depended for their livelihood on trade with countries which they did not
control. But the spectacular development of a common technology, particularly in the fields of communications and transport, has in this century
brought the countries of the world much closer together. It took Napoleon
as long as Hannibal to move an army across the Alps from France to Italy:
now aircraft can cover the same distance in minutes. Today economic
interdependence, the growing complexity of industry and technology, and
also rising standards of living, have created inflexible demands for the import
of raw materials and foodstuffs of every kind into developed countries, as
well as an active trade in industrial products. Less developed countries need
to negotiate for the import not only of virtually the whole range of industrial
goods and many other commodities, but usually the means to pay for them
too. So the decisions taken within one economy increasingly affect others,
whether or not those who make such decisions take account of the consequences beyond the borders of their own economy.

Until recently such matters as interest rates or price supports for agriculture were regarded by governments and private institutions alike as essentially
matters for domestic decision, although decisions about them were of course
influenced by the money and commodity markets elsewhere. Moreover, it
was generally believed in the eighteenth and nineteenth centuries that the

wise policy for governments was 'non-intervention' in the free flow between states of goods, services and money. But today the mixed – that is, partly state-managed and partly private enterprise capitalist – economies of Western states are so interpenetrated, and so sensitive to each other, that the repercussions of economic decisions taken by a state's economic partners and competitors are too great for any government to ignore. In addition, the social policies of Western democracies are now so finely tuned, and deter-mined after so much difficult domestic bargaining and balancing of the claims of competing pressure groups that, once reached, they tend to become rigid, unlike the ruthless but flexible play of a free market. As a result, Western governments find it difficult to reopen the issues and adjust their policies again in response to the requests of their trading partners. Yet the disruptive impact on their policies of economic decisions taken elsewhere can be very serious for the electoral popularity of Western politicians, who depend for favour largely on their record of economic and social policy. The same is broadly true, even if to a lesser extent, of the popularity of all governments in the contemporary world.

Thus the extension of a state's domestic control of and interference in the economic field makes it difficult for that state to maintain a *laissez-faire* attitude to economic activities in the world outside. In many cases a state will ask for, and perhaps obtain, a commitment from its trading partners to prior consultation before these partners take firm decisions in matters which are domestically crucial to it. For all governments know that they are in the same boat: each is increasingly affected by the economic decisions of the others, and all are in Karl Kaiser's formula 'trying to come to terms with processes working simultaneously within and without their own society and to which their society contributes'. This extension of the dialogue puts a new and great burden on diplomacy. Interdependence limits the domestic freedom of action of states; and the diplomacy of interdependence seeks to limit that freedom of action still further by mutual and agreed restraints.

These economic factors, together with the world population explosion, the food and energy crises, the spreading effects of pollution and the new perils of nuclear war, have so increased the general awareness of inter-dependence that the word has become a catch-phrase. Some scholars reject it altogether as too loose for their more precise purposes. More emotionally evocative concepts like 'spaceship earth' have come into being to emphasize the new reality. So significant has interdependence in the general sense of the term become that governments with widely differing international purposes are now driven to try to limit its random and destabilizing effects. States do this in two ways. On the one hand they will try to lessen their dependence on the outside world, to insulate the society they administer to

some degree from external economic pressures, to make the hide of their
leviathan-state more pachydermatous. On the other hand they will try to
regulate the pressures by acting in concert with other states to bring interdependence under joint state control.

The reaction of economically advanced states against the socially disruptive effects of external economic pressures is now fairly general. They do not
aim at the autarchy which the Soviet Union and Germany strove for between
the world wars; but oil, food and exchange rates are at the top of a long list
of sensitive areas of a modern economy where dependence is considered
socially and politically dangerous and should be reduced even at some
economic cost. The European Common Market and other associations of
neighbouring states owe much of their motive force to the need for immuniza-
tion against outside economic pressures. The industrially advanced states
also try more actively than ever before to coordinate their activities in these
fields. They use diplomacy both in order to mitigate each other's reciprocal
impact on their economies, and to tackle together those common economic
problems, and also quasi-economic problems like pollution and overfishing,
which can be solved only by cooperation between states that are prepared
to regulate the economic activities of their nationals.

In practice, therefore, these two tendencies towards greater state power
and greater interdependence do not operate separately, as we have been
partly considering them for clarity's sake, but together. The increasing
domestic power of states alters the forms which interdependence takes; and
at the same time the accelerating growth of interdependence affects the
nature of state power and internal jurisdiction as well as external independence. The areas in which the domestic jurisdiction of a state can operate
effectively without agreement with other states, and the extent of that
jurisdiction are changing rapidly in practice, regardless of the legal authority
of the state. The relations between states in the modern worldwide system,
and therefore the forms of the diplomatic dialogue, are modified by this
interaction.

A good example of this modification is the transformation in the nature
of international trade. Hitherto the actual organization of economic transactions across state frontiers has been very largely in private hands. From
its beginnings, European diplomacy has been especially concerned with
trade; and this is broadly true of earlier states systems too, back to the
earliest diplomatic records which still survive. But the concern of states was
until recently to provide opportunities for private traders: to allow merchants
to buy the products they needed in foreign countries, and to sell their wares
in return. Thus, for instance, the Asiento Treaty of 1713 between England
and Spain tried (unsuccessfully, as it proved) to regulate the quantities

and categories of goods that English merchants might ship to Spanish
territories in the New World. Similarly a principal motive behind the establishment by the imperial powers of Europe of colonies and protectorates in
areas unsuitable for white settlement – which includes almost all such
ventures in Asia and many in Africa – was to protect and further the interests
of their private traders. States did not themselves carry on the trade as
government corporations. The diplomatic dialogue was then concerned
with the promotion and regulation of private trade.

Furthermore the technology required to produce, and in the case of
minerals also to discover, essential raw materials became more sophisticated
and expensive, and so it became concentrated in fewer and more expert
hands. Powerful and wealthy 'multinational corporations' like the great oil,
mining and plantation companies acquired almost state-like characteristics
and became almost independent actors on the international scene: based in
more than one state, with huge bureaucracies, and conducting their own
quasi-diplomatic dialogue with many states great and small. Such companies
could until recently dominate the economy of small, undeveloped one-
product states like Liberia, Kuwait or Honduras; and in a few cases they
still can. This is an aspect of colonialism, even where the small state concerned is politically independent. But the day when a powerful imperial
state was able and willing to use force to protect the rights of its private
corporations, the era of 'gunboat diplomacy', is almost over. The restraints
imposed by international opinion, especially as expressed through omnilateral state organizations like the U.N., together with the increasing
domestic power of all states great and small, is gradually making even weak
states more than a match for multinational corporations. Today almost any
state can 'nationalize' or even expropriate the assets of the most powerful
foreign company without serious fear of intervention by another state or by
a world body, though not usually without some loss of wealth. It therefore
seems probable that the political heyday of multinational corporations is
drawing to a close. The agreements which govern their operations will be
more and more pushed into the diplomatic dialogue, and even negotiated
between states; and where they continue in business their effective bargaining counters will be limited to their powers of persuasion, their technical
knowhow which most states want to see used in their country, and their
ability to organize markets 'downstream' which is beyond the capacity of
smaller states.

At the same time powerful and highly developed industrial states are
becoming increasingly concerned, not merely to limit the disruptive effects
of interdependence but, more generally, need to assure the regular
supply of essential commodities like food, energy and the raw materials on

which their communities depend, and to pay for them by exports. Both sides of the operation are necessary if unemployment, under-utilization of industrial plant and falling standards of living in the developed world are to be avoided. The need to manage the external aspects of their economy is therefore becoming a major preoccupation of the governments of all industrialized states, whether communist or not. This need reinforces the tendency of states today to extend their domestic authority. Non-communist states are steadily bringing the private companies in their economy concerned with foreign trade under governmental control, and then taking them over. The smaller states will find themselves having to deal with state-run corporations in industrial countries in place of the private multinational giants. Even where these state-run corporations have a degree of autonomy within the governmental structure, and are not government departments in the narrow sense, the closer involvement of the state in foreign trade will bring the actual transactions more into direct government-to-government negotiations. There will be a further extension of the diplomatic dialogue.

The increasing preoccupation of governments with areas of society and human activities which previously were not regarded as a state's responsibility, and the steady extension of the state's authority to cover them, does not mean that governments are as successful in controlling and directing these new areas of state interest as they are when dealing with activities which by their nature can be more wholly determined by the state. For instance foreign policy, or the degree of military preparedness, are matters which within the limits set by the capacity of a state can largely be determined by its government. The governments of NATO can discuss with each other and with the government of Spain, for example, whether that state should join their alliance in much the same way as their predecessors in Europe did three centuries ago, and with about the same degree of certainty that in this area their decisions will determine what happens. But economic activity has shown itself a much more difficult thing for states to control successfully. Though the economy of a state is nowhere any longer left to the free play of the market, though in many states the 'commanding heights of the economy' have passed into state ownership, and in communist ones the government tries to plan and itself to implement all significant economic activity, yet so far economic activity has proved an elusive affair for the state to regulate: it runs through the fingers of governments like quicksilver. No government has yet learnt to achieve the economic results it aims at, in the same sense as governments can determine the terms of an alliance. Governments have a worried suspicion that the fundamental problems which beset developed societies and spill over into the less developed ones are beyond the power of any state to manage – or even, some statesmen fear, to affect more than marginally. But this suspicion does not make anxious governments hesitate to talk to one another about these new and seemingly unmanageable problems. On the contrary, the economic dialogue, both bilateral and multilateral, is ever more preoccupied with them. This is especially the case between states on close terms. Meetings of heads of friendly governments are now mainly taken up with the intractable areas in which state control is comparatively ineffective: it takes less time because it is easier to reach the decisions on issues which governments can determine. The less friendly states are with each other, the more their dialogue is concerned with those areas which have traditionally been the subjects of diplomacy.

The more incompetent and ill-suited as instruments for managing economic life that states at this stage of their development prove to be, the more they will feel the need to discuss with other states what they can jointly arrange to do in these intractable and awkward fields. The new and less developed states who now make up a half of our recently enlarged international society call for a new economic order and the organization of *collective economic security*. But the older and more established states are equally aware of their own need to match their increasing domestic responsibilities with more constructive and more predictable international arrangements. This attempt to manage economic interdependence by means of a co-operative but competitive partnership of states should not be seen as something new. It is the extension into the economic field of the effort which international societies make from their inception, the purpose for which they come into existence: namely the establishment by the member states of common rules and institutions, so as to bring some order and predictability into the chaos of their conflicting purposes. The desire of states to achieve an economic balance is basically the same as the desire to achieve a strategic balance, and the desire to regulate economic competition is the same as the desire to regulate war.

The intensive diplomatic effort that states have devoted since World War Two to managing international economic life has led to a great extension of the rules and institutions. It has produced a number of regulatory conventions, like the Bretton Woods agreement to determine the exchange rates of the world's leading national currencies and the General Agreement on Tariffs and Trade; new economic institutions like the Bank for International Reconstruction and Development (the World Bank), the International Monetary Fund and the Bank for International Settlements; and specialized omnilateral agencies for the dissemination of economically advantageous technology like the Food and Agriculture Organization of the

United Nations. Alongside these general and often universal agencies, several regional economic agreements have been negotiated such as the European Economic Community and the Latin American Free Trade Area, whose principal purpose is to channel international economic relations in certain politically desirable directions rather than leave them to the free play of the market, and in this and other ways to give the participating states, or wide economic communities of states, greater control over their economic life.

These agreements, treaties, institutions and codes of restraint have largely, though not entirely, been devised by the most developed and experienced states – the so-called First World. The United States, in contrast to the aloofness and isolationist sentiments which prevailed there after World War One, has taken the lead both in the diplomacy and in the financial costs of the omnilateral arrangements. It has done so in its own interests, and also in those of the international economic system generally as it understood them. The other great economic powers of the First World, notably the leaders of the European Economic Community and Japan, have also played constructive parts. In all the complex diplomacy involved, the degree of cooperation and of willingness to reconcile conflicting interests has been impressively high, and the level of confrontation and acrimony correspondingly low. By and large, these instruments of economic diplomacy, taken together, have served the interests of the First World states, and indeed the world economy as a whole, reasonably well, though naturally not as well as their promoters hoped. They have extended the control of states over the operations of the market, and the control of what we may call the Concert of Economic Powers over the actions of individual states. They have helped to mediate an orderly transition from American economic domination of a war-shattered world to the economic balance of power between competing yet cooperating states that we see in the First World today.

The Soviet Union has held itself aloof from most of these arrangements: partly because of the cold war, but more fundamentally because the Soviet state controls its economy and more particularly its foreign trade to a much greater degree than the democratic states of the First World, and is therefore better able to insulate Soviet economic life from external pressures. But the Soviet state has made elaborate and far-reaching economic agreements with the smaller communist states under its aegis. The Comecon structure includes joint economic plans for the whole area, which extends as far as Cuba.

The Third World no longer means those states that wanted to avoid entangling alignment in the political and strategic confrontation between the Soviet bloc and the West, and now usually means those states which are

economically underdeveloped. These states now make up a large numerical
majority of the present members of international society, though far short
of a preponderance of economic strength. They have been the beneficiaries
of the arrangements made by the First World's concert of economic powers:
partly because the arrangements were specifically devised to help them to
some extent through machinery like the World Bank and the Food
and Agriculture Organization; and partly because the economic plight of the
smaller and weaker states would have been considerably worse if the general
network of agreements and restraints had not existed. Nevertheless they feel
dissatisfied and resentful. Given the domestic pressures on these states, such
as their economic inadequacy, the rising expectations of their peoples, the
greater awareness of the gap between the standard of living and of technology
in the countries of the First World and in most of their own, and the
widespread dogmatic insistence that these difficulties are all the fault of the
First World, this dissatisfaction is understandable. In any case, their
numerical majority in the states system ensures that their interests figure
prominently in the diplomatic dialogue about how to manage economic interdependence for political ends.

One significant aspect of the North–South diplomatic dialogue concerns
foreign economic aid. Aid is of particular importance to the new and less
developed states whose general needs we looked at in the last chapter.
Whereas these states have had little to say in shaping the general agreements
and institutions devised by and for states with highly developed economies,
all the Third World states have an active interest in questions of aid. They
see aid as one way of taking greater account of their economic difficulties
than the operations of a free market can be expected to do.

Rich states have given subsidies and other forms of economic aid to allies
and clients for political and strategic reasons since the earliest recorded
histories. The archers on the gold darics paid out by the Persian Empire to
Greeks and others in classical times, and the 'cavalry of St George' on the
gold sovereigns paid by the British to their continental allies, are familiar
symbols of this politically motivated aid. Such aid is usually given as rent
for bases and material facilities, or to induce support for the foreign policy of
the donor power state, but sometimes also for the more general reason that
the donor considers that the economic well-being of an indigent ally will
strengthen both parties in their pursuit of agreed common objectives. The
advantages of such political subsidies to the donor are normally short-lived:
it is not possible to buy allegiance internationally, only to rent it short-term.
On the other side, while it is less blessed to receive than to give, the record
shows that recipients have been and are today at least as eager to obtain
subsidies as donors are to offer them. The political interests which subsidies

help to promote are usually genuinely common to giver and taker, and the subsidy itself is a tangible asset. Most of the aid disbursed today is given and taken for these time-honoured and legitimate reasons. A certain amount of aid is also given for humanitarian motives, for the relief of suffering as a result of natural disasters and war, or to alleviate starvation and epidemic disease. Such aid is dispensed directly from state to state or through such international agencies as the Red Cross.

What is new, and of great potential significance for the ordering of international society, is the extension of regular economic assistance by richer states to poorer ones, both bilaterally and through international agencies, in order to help poorer and less developed states to better their economic and social performance. Before World War Two no state received aid for these general reasons. The very concept of independence included the assumption that a state and its citizens wished to and would manage their own economic life as best they could. In the extensive aid pattern of today, when all allowance has been made for political, strategic and humanitarian motives, we find in addition a very widely accepted assumption (outside the communist world) that international society itself will provide aid on a regular basis to its poorest and most backward members. The richer members of the society contribute to collective assistance programmes and supplement these with bilateral aid, not just on reason of state or charitable grounds but for motives of *raison de système*, in order to make international society function more effectively to the benefit of all its members.

This extension of the requirements of *raison de système* on the part of the richer and more established states derived chiefly from practical expediency. The ebb tide of empires had resulted in the sudden addition of a large number of states which on the one hand could no longer in practice be governed by the former imperial power, because of the weakness of the maritime imperial states and because colonialism is no longer acceptable in the opinion of mankind, not least of the imperial states themselves. But on the other hand they cannot independently maintain a level of economic activity acceptable either to them or to the world society of which they make up half the member states.

The first fumbling steps to solve this major dilemma, by means of aid, have not been very successful. Bilateral aid in its various financial and technical forms usually has political strings; and where it does not, the donor usually makes conditions about the use of the aid that are unwelcome to the recipient. Aid through international agencies like the World Bank is not linked to the political and strategic demands of individual donors but usually carries stringent economic conditions which often cause hardship in recipient states. In any case there is, from the recipients' point of view, much too little of either kind of aid available. Many small states find that their economic plight is getting worse, not better. The donors for their part are coming increasingly to the conclusion that aid for development, as opposed to palliative aid for humanitarian purposes, has largely failed to achieve the results they hoped for. Aid programmes thus seem to be proving inadequate to ensure collective economic security, just as the provisions of the Covenant of the League of Nations proved inadequate to ensure collective military security after World War One.

The Covenant looked beyond sanctions against aggression to a new international political and strategic order, in which the League would establish independence, justice in the form of self-determination, and freedom from the fear of war. The new states of Asia, Africa and the Caribbean, joined now by most of the Latin American republics, demand in the same spirit that international society should first extend independence and justice to all colonial peoples, regardless of whether they are 'economically viable' or 'administratively unready for self-government' because these deficiencies are deemed to be caused wholly or mainly by colonial exploitation and oppression. Then, when the liberation is complete – as it now nearly is – aid of all kinds should be replaced by a New International Economic Order in which international economic life would be so managed and controlled by the society of states, and by institutions set up by and answerable to that society, that there would be a much more even distribution of purchasing power and of industrial and other types of 'development' between the member states than exists at present. This last demand, with its overtones of redistributive justice and of affirmative action to right past wrongs, corresponds to the demand within states for a more egalitarian distribution by the state of its citizens' wealth. One can reformulate the aspiration of the League Covenant at the beginning of this paragraph to say that the Third World demands the establishment of a new international economic order, with independence, redistributive justice and freedom from the fear of want.

The states which make this demand on international society act together diplomatically in the Group of 77 – now a larger number – in order to obtain from the First World a greater say in the management of the world economy, and, in order to achieve their objectives, a considerable extension of control over it by states. The Group of 77 are aware of their weakness at the diplomatic bargaining table, and that the New International Economic Order which they want to establish will depend on the consent of the highly developed donor states, and particularly the Concert of Economic Powers. However, they have been encouraged by the success of a small group of

Third World states, the oil exporting countries. OPEC has demonstrated what less developed states can do to increase their share of the world's wealth where they have economic power. But so far no other resource has conferred anything like the leverage provided by the First World's need for oil.

The North-South dialogue about managing the world economy in order to produce political and social rather than economic results is only just beginning. It will be a major diplomatic undertaking. The demands of the Third World have so far been couched almost entirely in terms of broad principles, and indefinable concepts like economic justice, rather than in terms of the complex and highly technical economic issues. There seem to be three reasons for this. The first is the familiar diplomatic tactic of trying to get the principles which they hold in common accepted on the other side as the basis for the dialogue. Secondly, on the economic issues as opposed to the political principles the interests of Third World states differ widely. Finally, most of them do not have the expertise needed to conduct discussions on the technical issues. It is arguable that nobody has. Though the more highly developed states of the First World have experts with enough experience to avoid some of the pitfalls of international economic management, the art of organizing a controlled economic world order is something that has yet to be learnt. Governmental efforts to manage even the domestic economies of states have not yet proved reliably successful. The North-South dialogue promises to be long and difficult. Even if the search for collective economic security achieves something, it seems likely to lead to the same sort of disappointment as the search for collective military security has in the recent past.

As diplomacy extends into these fields, it becomes not only wide-ranging but more technical. Governments have to draw for their external negotiations more and more on experts who understand the intricacies of the subjects which now come under discussion, even if they may not be able to expound effective remedies for the problems involved. Governments set these experts alongside the professional diplomats (whose expertise lies in dealing with other governments) both at home where policies and negotiating positions are worked out for the government's approval, and also at the negotiating table. These experts include officials from other 'non-diplomatic' branches of government, from the state-run corporations, and in Western countries increasingly also from the academic world and from the private sector of industry.

A team sent by a diplomatically developed state to negotiate in another capital or at an international conference today is likely to be made up of three elements. The delegation will, often but not always, be led by a political representative of the government of the day – in British terms a minister – whose job is to provide a general sense of direction and to exercise the authority entrusted to him by his governmental colleagues to conclude certain bargains, though he may not be there all the time. He will have with him a small personal staff. Then there will be professional diplomats, experts on the foreign countries involved and in negotiating with other governments, including the ambassador accredited to the state or international body in question, who is (or ought to be) the specialist on dealing with it. Thirdly there will be the technical experts on dealing with the various aspects of the subject in question. Their principal roles will be to serve on technical committees and to help to shape the negotiating position of the delegation; and in order to do this most of them will normally maintain close direct links with their own government department or other institution, as well as conform in their dealings with other delegations to the decisions of the minister in charge of the negotiation. How complex these technical aspects usually are can be seen from any practical example: for instance negotiations on fishing quotas in a given area of the sea. Any agreement will affect fish conservation, employment among fishermen, food supplies, the cost of living, international law and more generally the degree of tension or amity in the relations between the states concerned, which inevitably affects many other issues. Even a routine and specific subject like the measures required for international notification about and control of cholera in an age of long-distance air travel has many technical aspects. Much more complex are the great and lengthy multilateral bargaining negotiations between a number of states with varying interests, such as those leading up to the Lomé Convention on the preferential economic relations between the European Economic Community and over forty newly independent Third World states. These negotiations are basically economic, covering a large range of commodities and aid. But they have many political and emotional overtones, not least those arising from the fact that most of the newly independent states were formerly colonies of one or another member of the European Community. The negotiations themselves could not cover all these sensitive and confidential issues even if time permitted; but to leave them undiscussed would hamper the substantive negotiations. The plenary meetings which deal with the elaboration of the convention are therefore preceded and backed up by a continual series of bilateral dialogues: among individual states on either side of the table, and 'across the table' between individual European and Third World states. What results is truly an immense exercise in modern diplomacy, bilateral and multilateral, involving ministers, professional diplomats and technical experts at every stage. And the Lomé negotiations are only one example among many multilateral negotiations taking place at the same time.

So far we have treated the pressures inside the state, impelling it towards greater domestic authority, and those from outside caused by greater interdependence – Burke's empire of circumstances – as both pushing diplomacy in the same direction, towards an extension of its scope. But many people have seen the increase of interdependence as progressively limiting the freedom of action of states, and therefore as a tendency in contradiction to the growth in the domestic power of independent sovereignty. A few observers in the developed countries hold that the states are losing the battle to control interdependence, and consider that it is destroying the validity of such concepts as the national interest, and such cherished ideals as independence and freedom, or even undermining the state as we know it altogether.

Some political leaders and commentators especially in the newly independent countries see interdependence as a grave threat to their freshly acquired and still frail control over their own destinies, and regard advocacy of it in richer and stronger countries as attempts to reestablish at least the empire of circumstances, if not neo–colonial control by a former imperial power or its successor. Interdependence seems to them merely a diffused form of the dependence from which they have been struggling to escape. They want a brake not merely on the operations of the market but on the growth of interdependence altogether, at least until the establishment of a new economic order. These fears are reinforced when they encounter the demand increasingly heard in more prosperous countries that aid, both from the state and from private foundations, should be applied only to the specific purposes and individuals in less developed states for which it is given, and should not 'transfer wealth from the poor in rich countries to the rich in poor countries' – that is, to the ruling élites whose leaders conduct the diplomacy of their states. The free play of interdependence is also a politically sensitive issue in the First World. It is apt to lead to the transfer of jobs from the poor in rich countries, by taking advantage of cheaper labour costs in less developed states: or as others phrase it through a conspiracy between international capital and the ruling class in backward economies to exploit the natural resources and the labour of these states. These and other disturbing aspects of interdependence too numerous to list here impel states, especially new ones, to keep a critical watch on its manifestations and ensure a prominent place in the diplomatic dialogue for attempts by states to limit and control it, so as to maximize its benefits while limiting its impingements on their sovereignty.

Others on the contrary, especially in prosperous and securely established states, consider the increasingly tight and continuous network of contacts between experts to be not merely an expansion of the diplomatic dialogue, as we have treated it, but the embryo of a new collective administration of the world's affairs. For them this network is something which together with the United Nations and similar omnilateral agencies will become world government, not through a cataclysmic revolution or the conquest of the globe by one power, but gradually. They see world government as the logical answer, the collective response of mankind to the technical problems which confront us all alike. Especially in the periods of acute disillusion with the ability of sovereign independent states to protect their citizens which followed the First and Second World Wars, many people have believed that functional collaboration of this kind would pay rich and obvious economic dividends. By focussing attention on the advantages which men can share by working together, instead of the political controversies which divide them, it would gradually win the loyalties of the wider public which enjoyed these benefits away from the selfish and dangerous quest for power which states were thought to pursue. The theory of functionalism expounded by David Mitrany in his seminal book, *A Working Peace System*, supposes a kind of salami tactics whereby successive slices of loyalty are cut off from states and transferred to international agencies. This transfer of loyalty, first by the civil servants and experts directly involved in the international bureaucracy and then by the public in the states concerned, is pictured by functionalists as based on a real and irreversible vested interest, and therefore as leading to a world committed to peace and harmonious collaboration. How justified is the assumption of a fundamental contradiction between interdependence and domestic sovereignty? And more particularly, can we expect international negotiation to make the decisive transformation of its own nature from a dialogue between states to a world government superseding them?

Some who hold these views are partly influenced by wishful thinking. They look forward to world government, and consider individual states too parochial and too wilful to achieve global responses to global problems. By beginning with the less controversial issues, they hope to achieve their aim by stealth. Some also think, usually without explicitly saying so, that the valuable aspect of interdependence is private contacts between individuals, the free movement of men, ideas and goods across state frontiers. They see an inherent tendency in states to demand that their citizens should owe loyalty only to them, and renounce wider loyalties and wider ties. Such people believe that states therefore tend to use increases in their power to limit interdependence, to cut the private ties that bind people together across frontiers and to make each state more autarchic, more self-sufficient and more insulated from the rest of the world, not so much for the reasons given earlier in this chapter, but in order to defend what functionalists regard as the anachronistic institution of the state against the more beneficial global organizations of the future.

What substance is there in these changes? Certainly states, especially totalitarian ones, do sometimes adopt such restrictive practices. Communist governments, for instance, dislike their citizens having cultural or personal contacts with foreigners except under the auspices and with the blessing of the state. A case can certainly be made for saying that by its nature a state tends to increase its control over the people which it governs. But this is not the same thing as saying that states are by nature autarchic and opposed to interdependence. The extension of the power of the state brings it into new fields which, like many fields of traditional state activity, cut across state frontiers. A state rarely stops such activities as its power over them grows. It usually first regulates them and then administers them directly. To put it in other language, as the public sector takes over from the private, so it takes over the organization of those contacts with the outside world, economic, cultural and the rest, which were previously in private hands. The organization of outside contacts by the state means that fewer channels are used and that fewer individual citizens have contacts with foreigners, as is the case with communist countries compared with the West. The negotiations involved, whether they concern the sale of grain or the visit of a ballet, are conducted by the state and so enter more directly than before into the diplomatic dialogue. Also most statesmen, of whatever political colour, now recognize that the global problems that increasingly confront all mankind usually require action by states and cannot be left to private initiatives. States are not opposed to interdependence as such. But nowadays all of them like to manage and direct it through economic diplomacy to some extent; and many want to control it entirely and are opposed to private interdependence.

But will interdependence grow to the point where it becomes too overwhelming, and too technical, for states to control and conduct? Can international commissions and authorities, set up to deal with technical questions and composed of experts from a number of countries, gradually acquire an authority of their own which is independent of the states who delegate and pay for the experts, and become capable of imposing their collective decisions on the states?

Certainly experts who meet regularly to discuss the subject of their expertise soon become colleagues and personal friends, and gradually develop common attitudes and assumptions. This *esprit de corps* is similar to that which we have seen prevail among professional diplomats posted in a capital. They urge their joint conclusions and recommendations about policy on the governments which appoint them, whom they rightly regard as laymen in their particular diplomatic field. The natural scientists among them have by their training a sense of loyalty towards science itself and towards other scientists throughout the world. They have a propensity to look for formulae and solutions which have a general and universal validity, and to strive for accuracy and truth. They are also attracted by those aspects of a problem which can be measured and quantified. This approach is very different from that of diplomacy, which sees problems in terms of the conflict and congruence of independent wills, and which looks to intangible factors to help persuade these particular wills to accept compromises whose validity lies not in universal truth but in their individual adequacy. The natural scientists, in their search for universally valid solutions to what they see as technical problems, are apt to underestimate and to resent the obstacles to the implementation of these solutions in particular states by political authorities; whereas diplomats, with these political obstacles in the forefront of their minds, become impatient with technically desirable solutions which discriminate against the interests of certain states and are therefore unacceptable. In practice the scientists and the diplomats learn to understand and to live with each other's points of view. But the scientists are drawn to each other by their similar professional outlook, whatever their national allegiances and the interests of the states which employ them. Especially where the issues at stake are ones which confront all mankind alike, a sense of global responsibility develops. So the loyalties of international experts are, like those of professional diplomats – but more so – not exclusively to their own state and their own fellow countrymen, but to their colleagues and to humanity as well.

Even so, in present circumstances these experts have to convince their own governments, and collectively still depend on the states concerned to carry out the policies they recommend. When states find the conclusions of international technical authorities awkward, they will 'discuss them through diplomatic channels', that is, initiate another and more political dialogue about them. They will also tend to appoint experts next time who are more mindful of the particular and often very real interests of those who appoint them. For the deliberations of these experts are, in the present state of international society, extensions of the diplomatic dialogue. In the last instance every envoy is the representative of the state who appoints him. He may not be the advocate of that state's particular interests, a lawyer pleading his state's case, and he may reserve his eloquence rather for pleading with his own government to endorse the conclusions which he and his colleagues have scientifically reached; but he will at least be aware of the importance of carrying his government with him, and he will find that the majority of his colleagues have been chosen because they are prepared to bear the interests of their own states very much in mind. In most cases, when such scientific

or technical conclusions are reached by international authorities or commissions, it is then necessary to find a group of powerful states (the democracies among them need to be supported and guided by an informed public
opinion) with an interest in implementing the agreements and with enough
means of persuasion and pressure to bring other recalcitrant states into line,
if the implementation of these conclusions is to be assured.

Let us suppose that the prestige of such international bodies continues to
grow, so that individually and together they acquire an authority which even
the most obstinate states feel obliged to respect, while most states come to
see the implementation of these recommendations as a national interest. Even
so every state will want the recommendations, and especially the way they
are carried out in practice, to take account of the many other particular
interests of its citizens. The recommendations of international bodies will
remain subjects of the diplomatic dialogue, and are likely to make up an
increasing proportion of it. The choices available to individual states may
become steadily more limited by the collective conclusions which their
delegates reach in technical fields, and even more so by the pressures
exerted on them by other states which endorse these conclusions. But that is
still a very long way from the point where omnilateral bodies constitute an
area of world government, able to impose their decisions directly and exclude
them from the diplomatic dialogue. Pressure and coercion applied by a
group of states, even the great majority, to make other states comply is not
world government replacing the states system; it is a concert of the states
system operating through diplomacy and ultimately through force.

So we may say that the growth of domestic state power and the growth of
interdependence, different as they are, together increase the volume and
range of diplomacy. The more fields of human activity individual states
bring into their direct purview, and the more interdependent the world
becomes, the more subjects states will bring into their dialogue with one
another, bilaterally and collectively. Diplomacy evolves new procedures as
its subject matter expands and becomes more technical. In particular, it is
in the process of elaborating new rules and codes of conduct, and new
institutions, for the management of a collective economic order by the
society of states. The trend of the world's affairs shows little sign of diminishing the volume of the dialogue or of limiting its range.

CHAPTER XIII

Diplomacy and the Responsibilities of States

At various times in this book I have referred to the interest which member states in a system have in the effective functioning of the system itself, and of their responsibilities towards it. The conscious sense that all the states in an international society have an interest in preserving it and in making it work I have called *raison de système*.

One simple meaning of the word 'responsible' is '*mechanical cause*'. As when we say that a cold spell in winter is responsible for the deaths of birds, so we may note that larger states are more responsible for the way in which the diplomatic dialogue is conducted and the way in which the system operates than smaller ones are, without saying anything about the intentions of states or making any moral judgement.

Secondly, when we speak of 'international responsibilities' and of a state or a political leader acting responsibly or irresponsibly, we may wish to imply something about the intentions of policy makers, giving 'responsible' the meaning of sensitive to the well-being or the interests of a wider community. A responsible statesman, according to this meaning, pursues the interests of his state as best he can, for this is the function of a state in its relation with other states; but not uncompromisingly, regardless of the confrontations and clashes which such a policy may involve, like a bull in a china shop as the nineteenth-century saying went. He sees positive advantage in cooperating with other states and international bodies to make international society function smoothly, and is willing to pay a certain price in state interests, narrowly conceived, for the sake of the greater advantages which he sees that his state will obtain from the existence of an orderly society. The conventional usage of 'responsible' alludes to the fact that most states do, as a matter of observed practice, cooperate most of the time to sustain the system in which they operate, and pursue their interests within its framework and according to its rules, because they find that it pays them to do so. It is like saying that honesty is the best policy. We therefore need to examine how and why states find that as a rule it pays them to pursue their interests by acting cooperatively with other states, and where differences and clashes of interest exist (as they inevitably will) to try to resolve them through the give and take of a diplomatic dialogue. Further, we must look at the calculations which especially induce great powers with diverse and far-ranging interests to act in this way. All this we may call *prudential responsibility*.

Then thirdly we shall need to see whether we can go further than this, and identify a common interest of all the powers in a states system, and even more so in an international society whose member states and leaders are conscious of shared common cultural ties and moral assumptions: a common interest which goes beyond the expediency and individual self-interest which states obviously have in cooperating at least with their allies and friends. Do all members of a states system, great and small, have a *moral responsibility* towards this common interest, and towards the system itself, from which they benefit? For it remains true that in spite of all the arguments of Realpolitik and the varieties of systems analysis which try to reduce the relations between states to models borrowed from physics, the concept of international responsibility also contains a distinction between 'is' and 'ought': what Kantians call the *sein-sollen* dilemma. What moral, legal and contractual obligations do states in a system have to the world outside their own boundaries? To whom, and how, do these obligations apply? Does international responsibility mean something distinct from a far-sighted and sophisticated concept of a state's own self-interest? If a state does not carry out these wider obligations, if it behaves 'irresponsibly', to whom is it accountable? And in particular, what are the responsibilities of states in the field of diplomacy?

We can begin our descriptive analysis of how and why states act cooperatively by noting the effect on the diplomatic dialogue of that wide variation in the power of individual states which is characteristic of all states systems and determines their nature. Whenever a group of independent states exists, some will have more power than others. They may recognize each other as having a formal equality, and enjoying equal standing in international law, but that is not the same thing as having equality of power. The sources of power in different states are so many and so various that it would be beyond the capacity of international negotiation to arrive at a formula acceptable to them all. (It is even difficult to reach an agreed 'weighting' formula for votes at specialized international bodies concerned with only one form of power.)

In any case it would not be possible to divide the world up into a number of states all equal in power, whatever the formula. By the accepted standards of the time it is not only inevitable but also legitimate that some countries are larger, richer and stronger than others. The sense of nationhood is strong in the populations of many large countries like France, the United States and China. It may be possible, exceptionally, for the major powers, or for one super-power, to keep the Germans, for example, partitioned. But the smaller states do not have the power to partition all the larger ones against their will. Moreover, statesmen like Vattel and Burke have pointed out over the centuries that even if it were possible to redraw the map so that all states were equal in power at a given time, differences would quickly reappear: due to population growth, industriousness, good or bad government, inventions and discoveries of minerals such as oil. The job would have to be redone (but who could do it?) at frequent intervals. We must therefore accept that independent states do and will vary widely in power.

By and large, the greater the power of a state relative to that of other states in a system, the greater the effect which its outward policies and its attitudes towards attaining its ends by negotiation within the framework of the system will have on the diplomatic dialogue, and therefore on the extent to which the potential of diplomacy is achieved in the system. In other words, *the more powerful a state is, the more responsible in our first, or mechanical, sense it is for the workings of international diplomacy.* For effective diplomacy is related to power, in the sense which Frederick the Great saw as producing harmony. If states at the top end of the power scale refuse to limit themselves to what they can achieve through diplomacy and embark on a career of conquest, like France under Napoleon or Germany under Hitler, or if they find themselves unable to pursue a cooperative diplomatic dialogue, like the United States and the Soviet Union during the cold war, the creative possibilities of diplomacy are stultified. At the other end of the scale, if the weakest powers in the system do not play their small part the loss to the diplomatic dialogue as a whole is not serious.

This correlation is only general. The contribution which a state can make towards the effective working of diplomacy does not only depend on its power and wealth at a given moment. It also depends, to a lesser but significant extent, on tradition, on the experience and personality of its statesmen and diplomats, and on the confidence which other states place in its intentions and its capacities. I have cited in Chapter IX some of the services rendered by Switzerland to the diplomatic dialogue. The contribution of the Netherlands to the development of international law is also impressive. Some states are more acceptable than others when it comes to making up a peacekeeping force. A new state like the Ivory Coast or Kenya or Singapore may make a special contribution to the dialogue because of the exceptional personality of its leader, or a privileged link with a more powerful state. A state like Rumania may develop a special role (for instance in helping to bridge the gap between the United States and communist China) for other reasons. Moreover, smaller states do not act only singly but also in groups; and the impact of a group or bloc of smaller states, such as OPEC, may be considerable. Even so, these variations are minor. It is the larger powers that determine the effectiveness of diplomacy. This mechanical fact goes far to explain why in many systems of states special responsibilities for the functioning of international relations, the management of order and the leadership of the diplomatic dialogue have been entrusted by a general consensus to great powers, whether formally recognized as such or not. It will also be relevant when we come to consider the question of moral obligations.

We must now consider what the special responsibilities of these more powerful states are, and how they come to be recognized by other states – in other words the nature of *prudential responsibility*.

The greater the power of a state, the more manifold and far reaching its interests will be. Rousseau held that even a small state needs to take an interest in everything that goes on around it. This is certainly so, but except in matters that immediately concern it, its influence is likely to be limited, and in most matters a small state is not much more than a spectator. But a great power is likely to have active interests to defend and promote everywhere in the system. The German word *Weltmacht* connotes a power which in our century has interests and is in a position to further them not only in its area but all round the world.

It is of course true that a very strong state may emerge in a system with enough power to 'lay down the law' – that is, to dictate what is to happen in the world, or in Europe, or in the states system to which it belongs. It may be powerful enough to establish a hegemony in its system and restrained enough to achieve this even without the actual use of force, for instance by the use of money backed by an occasional threat. Or such a state may go further, and actually conquer most of the other states in the system and incorporate them formally or in practice into its empire, as Rome did to the Hellenistic world, and as Napoleon and Hitler almost succeeded in doing to Europe. These are historical examples of the general proposition that, when the power of one state in a system is greater than the sum of the power of the states prepared to oppose it, the system is unstable and apt to collapse. Some historians hold that a state which is in a position to establish a hegemony must be expected to do so, and that a state would be exceptionally virtuous or restrained if it did not take advantage of opportunities offered it in this way. However, we are not concerned here with the question of morality or of probability in the conduct of one dominant power. We are looking at the responsibilities which states, and more particularly large states with a penumbra of power stretching out beyond their own borders, have in balanced systems when none of them is in a position to dominate.

Where there are two or (preferably for the working of the system) more great powers, the range and complexity of their interests is normally such that, in so far as they rely on diplomacy rather than on the use of force to protect and promote their interests, they will be involved in diplomatic negotiation with most if not all the other powers in the system, on various different issues. On some of these issues the interests of a great power will line it up with certain states, on other issues with others. If it pushes its interests too actively on one issue or in one part of the world, it may pre-judice its interests elsewhere by alienating other powers. So the range and diversity of a great power's interests helps to check and restrain the pursuit of each of them. Smaller powers, with fewer interests and simpler demands on the system, are able to be more single-minded about pursuing them. A great power that relies on diplomacy – that is, on the persuasiveness which its power gives it – rather than on actual resort to force is aptly compared to a juggler trying to keep a large number of balls in the air at once. This simile is especially appropriate in periods where there are several great powers, and where at least some of them are in a position to conduct an effective diplomatic dialogue bilaterally and multilaterally with all their equals as well as with lesser powers. But even when great powers are locked into rival alliances or opposing ideological blocs whose relations are domi-nated by hostility and suspicion, even in the case of actual war between great powers when a meaningful diplomatic dialogue between the two opposing camps is altogether suspended, each great power continues, in its relations with its allies and also with neutrals, to have more varied and complex interests and more extensive diplomatic exchanges, and thus to be subject to more pressures and checks than smaller powers.

Where there are two or more great powers, all with their self-assertiveness limited by the fact that none of them is significantly stronger than the others and all entangled by the web of their far-reaching interests, as well as a number of other states with varying interests and capacities which the great powers cannot leave out of account, the minimum relation short of war is a mere co-existence, with the great powers in sullen opposition and diplomacy carried on only between allies and with lesser states. Where a great power stands alone with its clients in such conditions, rather than in alliance with other great powers, it is almost certain to exercise a hegemony or a domi-nance in the areas where it is preponderant. The first requirement of an effective diplomatic dialogue in a system of states is that all the great powers should be willing to talk to each other about their differences. If they cannot resolve them – for such conflicts of interest are often deep and persistent – they may be able to mitigate them and prevent their degenerating into war (if necessary by bringing an issue to a head or forcing a crisis in order to draw a new line or establish a new rule). From this low point the diplomatic dialogue can progress, through such agreed restraints as arms limitation and non-interference in areas of special sensitivity to an opposing great power, on to imaginative and constructive arrangements for joint action to manage international society, and to anticipate the longer-term problems that threaten to disrupt it in the future. For diplomacy to realize its full potential as a civilized and civilizing process, with a built-in bias towards cooperation and the search for the maximum of advantage to all the participants, the great powers must be willing to go beyond cooperation in the resolution of their direct differences and the pursuit of their individual interests. There must also be a general awareness among the great powers of the gains they can derive from an effective functioning of international society itself.

In their reasoning of state, that is in their search for a rational policy, great powers must consider the whole range of their interests and commitments, none of which they can pursue too far or too single-mindedly without damaging others. In making these calculations they must take into account their ability to induce other states to cooperate with them, or at least not oppose them. Since the web of interests of the great powers is system-wide, *raison d'état* leads them to think in terms of the system itself, with its basis of the balance of power, and of the rules and institutions of international society; and to consider to what extent they can further their interests, and limit the net cost of pursuing them, by preserving the system and making the society work effectively. Great powers, when estimating the value of the system and the society to themselves, start with the vivid (and sometimes exaggerated) awareness that the larger states are responsible, in our first sense of the term, for most of what happens in international affairs, and that the relations between them not merely set the tone of international society but provide its inescapable framework. This awareness leads to the realization that the great powers can, by agreement with each other, provide a certain direction to the course of international affairs, and manage the functioning of the system and the society so as to maximize their various interests, provided that each great power makes due allowance for those of the others. However, the balance of power also involves the other states in the system, and makes their independence and welfare a matter of interest, in almost all cases, to at least one of the great powers. In addition the interdependence of states, and the requirement that they should all, as members

of the international society, observe its rules and help to operate its institu
tions, enhances the importance of their actions to the great powers. So the
balance between the larger powers, and the rules and institutions which give
all members a status and a voice, seem to most other states also to promote
their interests better than either a hegemonic or a more anarchical pattern
of international relations. But if certain of them at certain times decide
otherwise, their disregard of *raison de système* will have less serious consequences in proportion to their weakness. The responsibility for the
functioning of the system and the society lies very largely with the great
powers.

What does the diplomacy of *raison de système* involve? To begin with,
there is the negative requirement that states with enough power to do serious
damage to the functioning of international society should accept the responsibility not to cause such damage, but to pursue their interests with
prudence and restraint. Secondly and positively, the great powers must
agree at least tacitly on a form of crisis management. In any system made up
of a number of states, conflicts of interest come to a head or suddenly find
themselves sharpened by circumstances. These crises will often find great
powers on opposing sides: either because their interests are directly involved,
or more usually because they have close relations – alliance, protection or
other affinity – with one of the smaller parties to the dispute. It is the great
powers, rather than the smaller and more immediate protagonists in the
dispute, on whom the responsibility falls to negotiate, and if necessary to
confront one another, only in such ways as to avoid a resort to force, or at
least to contain and localize the use of force by their clients so that it does not
drag them in. This disparity of responsibility is due to the difference in
power: *the danger to the system becomes serious above a certain threshold*,
usually the involvement of a great power. For the same reason the responsibility falls on the great powers concerned, even more than on the
protagonists, to devise a constructive formula or gradual evolution. Diplomacy reaches a higher level of achievement, and the great powers a higher
level of responsibility, when they not only devise the formula but also lend it
the weight of their support, and make a contribution to the settlement themselves. This support and contribution will cost them something in terms
of financial and other commitments, and perhaps also reproaches from their
disappointed minor allies; and they will need to reckon that their long-term
vested interest in maintaining and developing the system will more than
balance the immediate costs.

In such eras of constructive diplomacy it is usually recognized, and sometimes explicitly agreed – as it was in the heyday of the Concert of Europe –
that not all great powers in a system need be involved in the management of

every crisis, for not every issue directly concerns them all. Even where a
great power does see its own interests as directly involved, it will nevertheless sometimes resign itself to letting another great power with opposed
interests carry the ball at a certain stage in the negotiations with the protagonists, so long as it is satisfied that the other power is also interested in
managing the crisis and in seeking a solution that will not unduly prejudice
the passive power's interests and commitments. On several occasions in the
nineteenth century the other great powers allowed England to take the lead
in solving crises in Portugal and elsewhere, and on other occasions Austria
or Bismarck's Germany, though they did not all welcome the solutions
imposed or the resulting increase in another great power's influence. So
recently the other important powers concerned accepted Soviet mediation
between India and Pakistan at Tashkent, and even the Soviet Union has
acquiesced in the unilateral lead taken by the United States over Israel's
disputes with its neighbours.

But it is not only conflicts of interest which flare up into crises, and
unforeseen accidents of politics like a *coup d'état* in a strategically placed
country, that require managing.

As I have stressed throughout this book, the power and interests of states
are constantly changing. Order in a states system, as in the solar system or a
human body, is a complex and dynamic balance of moving factors; not
something static. The explosive growth of modern technology and changing
norms of justice both merely accelerate a process of change which has always
operated. Some of the most serious problems that confront an international
society are those which do not reach a sudden flashpoint but are built up
slowly by the glacial, inexorable pressures of change. Kimon the Athenian
told his countrymen that they and the Spartans were like oxen yoked together
by their position of leadership in Greece, and that they must pull with their
yoke-fellows. For diplomacy between independent states to rise to its full
potential, for it to play its part in avoiding catastrophes like World War One,
also requires the great powers to recognize that they carry a degree of
responsibility proportionate to their strength, and need to cooperate in
dealing with the longer term and more fundamental pressures of change that
have not flared up into a crisis.

Before World War One the gravest long-term problem was the development of military and economic power in the larger states of Europe, and
particularly the question of according a position to Germany commensurate
with her rapidly increasing strength and capacity but which would also be
acceptable to the other great powers which found themselves pushed into
closer association with each other to counterbalance her. Europeans of that
time did not realize that a major war would cripple their civilization. Between

the wars the problems that confronted international society became even graver, and the will and imagination to solve them constructively, or even to discern some of them, was less. Today the major powers are more conscious of the obliterating devastation which would be caused by a nuclear war between the super-powers, and they are becoming aware of the slowly increasing threats to the planet caused by other developments of technology. They are also conscious of the problems created by decolonization and economic interdependence. Many of these long-term and basic issues are not political in the sense in which more traditional problems like peace and war or the control of territory are said to be, but highly technical. Nonetheless they too can be managed only by active and conscious collaboration between the more important members of the states system. It is sometimes supposed that operations like the determination of exchange rates and the international monetary supply, or the control of pollution, can only be handled by experts, and are thus somehow outside the scope of diplomacy. But in fact all such arrangements to be effective have to be negotiated between authorized spokesmen of states and then implemented and enforced by the governments of those states. (For instance, central banks enjoy some degree of autonomy in the governmental structure of their countries, but they negotiate internationally in the name of the states concerned.) These are diplomatic negotiations; and agreements will be more effective and more easily reached if the negotiations are not conducted in isolation, as if they dealt with separate problems, but are coordinated by governments and treated as parts of a cooperative whole.

We can therefore say that in terms of prudential reasoning the final and most exacting requirement for diplomacy to reach its full potential in a states system is that the larger and more powerful states should cooperate to 'lay down the law' together in the interests of international society as a whole, and in consultation with its other member states. Alternatively, in order to avoid even a diffused and balanced hegemony, the potential of diplomacy can be realized when the great powers not merely observe prudent codes of conduct towards each other but also recognize, explicitly or tacitly, that the preservation and effective functioning of their system and of international society must be given priority whenever the point is reached where it appears to be seriously threatened. This attitude is something more than prudence and restraint. It is conscious *raison de système*, the use of diplomacy to achieve the ultimate purpose of an international society of independent states.

Contemporary international society, and the policies of the larger powers in it, falls well short of these ideal requirements of diplomacy. But it is encouraging to see that many of the conditions we have listed are present, and many of the practices observed. Today two very great states, the United States and the Soviet Union, are much more powerful than any others because of the extent of their territory, the size and technical skills of their population, and their industrial and military capacity. Moreover – and this is something new – their prodigious accumulation and development of strategic nuclear arms sets them in a category by themselves, and the nuclear balance between them, though precarious for reasons of technology and political determination, is now scarcely affected by any other power. The military gap in both nuclear and conventional weapons between them and the other states of the contemporary world has for some time been growing wider. But the suicidal destructiveness of the nuclear arsenals of the two super-powers makes a full-scale war between them increasingly remote from the rational pursuit of their state interests, from *raison d'état*. Each of the super-powers seems to recognize clearly enough the responsibility in our first descriptive sense conferred on it by its nuclear arsenals, and also the need for responsibility in the second sense, towards its own state and citizens in the first instance. As a result, willingness to use military force as the ultimate argument of states is inhibited at the centre; and is driven outward and downward into areas of action which will not provoke a direct military confrontation between the two nuclear giants. Both super-powers restrain client states and other actors from using force in ways which seriously risk making such a confrontation more likely. Moreover, the weapons themselves, and the awesome prospect of using them, loom larger in the diplomatic dialogue between the two states, and this dialogue about destruction reinforces the need for caution and restraint.

Meanwhile, aside from military power including the nuclear balance with its new inhibitions and responsibilities, other states are catching up with the super-powers or even surpassing them in such material and quantifiable respects as economic growth and living standards. Below the two giants in the hierarchy of power are several states which exercise a major influence on the international system, but in some fields more than others. Japan and West Germany have been described as economic and financial super-powers. Three other states, France, Britain and China, are recognized as secondary great powers, with their formal position symbolized by permanent membership in the Security Council with veto rights there, and are also minor nuclear powers. The non-communist great powers conduct an active diplomatic dialogue both about crises as they arise and about longer-term problems. Their cooperation, especially in economic matters, is impressive. The dialogue with the Soviet Union and China, and between these two powers, is still largely concerned with bilateral issues, the relaxation of tensions and mutual restraint.

In certain closely-knit international societies, such as Europe in the eighteenth and nineteenth centuries, certain of the stronger states were recognized as 'great powers' with special privileges and obligations in the system. A definition of a great power widely accepted in the last century, and formulated by the historian Ranke in his essay on the great powers, was a state able to maintain itself militarily – that is, avoid its own destruction – against a coalition of all the others. We must recognize that, whether or not this was possible in the past, no state is in a position to do so today, and is inhibited as well as protected to some indefinable extent by the general awareness that civilization, including the combatant states, might be destroyed in the process. No formal meaningful status of great power is now accorded to the strongest states in the system (though permanent membership of the United Nations Security Council is a relic of the concept). In the contemporary world it is difficult to draw a hard and fast line either of status or responsibility between great powers and others, which will be valid in all fields of inter-state relations. Statesmen find that, because of the military inhibitions of the two super-powers and the growing importance of economic power in the organization of international society, there is in fact an uneven gradation of power between the states in our system, with overlapping capacity in different fields. The lack of formal status and the fact that a state which is very powerful in one field may be weak in another complicate the contemporary picture, but they do not alter what is said above about the general nature of the responsibilities of great powers.

So far we have been discussing the reasons of enlightened self-interest which induce the states in a system, and particularly its great powers, to behave in a way which will give diplomacy its full scope, preserve the system and avoid catastrophes like a major war which would cripple or destroy civilization. We have also noted that while, alas, not all great powers act in this way all the time, yet most great powers have in fact usually – not always – acted responsibly in this pragmatic sense. But the matter does not end there. Men have principles as well as interests. The acts of statesmen are not normally governed by mere calculation, but also by a sense of moral and religious obligation. Richelieu, who did as much as any statesman to elaborate and put into practice the concept of *raison d'état* in the European system, was insistent that every aspect of foreign policy should be in accordance with the precepts of Christian morality and justice. Herbert Butterfield and Martin Wight in the preface to *Diplomatic Investigations* stated that their underlying aim was 'to clarify the principles of prudence and moral obligation which have held together the international society of states throughout its history, and still hold it together'. I now wish to look at the *moral dimension of inter-*

national responsibility and consider what moral obligations exist for states
and statesmen beyond the prudential assessment of advantage.

The first obligation of a statesman, beyond personal issues of integrity and
conduct, is to his state and to the people who compose it. He is responsible
for the long-term welfare of the citizens and their descendants. Almost every
statesman has recognized that he has a moral obligation to promote this
welfare as he understands it – which is not the same as gratifying the emotions
and desires of people less informed than he about the consequences for
them and for others of the policies they call for. A distinction is sometimes
made between the negative responsibility to avoid devastating damage to the
state and the positive obligation to further as actively as possible its welfare
and that of its citizens. The negative responsibility is generally recognized,
but the positive one is sometimes held to be too restrictive.

The obligation of the ruler or statesman to avoid devastating damage to his
realm or state through disastrous war, in however noble and just a cause, can
be traced back to the earliest records of statecraft, and has usually had a
moral as well as a prudential aspect. Medieval Christian theology, notably as
expounded by St Thomas Aquinas, emphasized that to wage war was not
just, even for a legitimate and righteous cause, if there was little prospect of
winning, because the loss of life and wealth would not be justified. Today it
is often said that all war, and the resort to force generally to obtain a political
objective, produces such ethically unacceptable loss and suffering that
states have a moral obligation, a duty, to rule out the use of force altogether
in their dealings with one another. This is certainly a moral attitude that
influences the conduct of many states, even if it does not determine their
policy; and especially in this nuclear age it reinforces the prudential restraint
that nuclear powers show about war with each other. But the renunciation of
the use of force weights negotiation heavily in favour of the *status quo*.
Consequently political leaders in many states, and leaders of political and
paramilitary movements which are not yet in control of states, feel today, and
have felt at various times in the past, that force, or the credible threat of
force, is necessary and legitimate, not only in self-defence but also in a
liberation struggle, or to recover lost territory, or to right some other injustice. In almost every case a state, or para-state, will try negotiation, the
way of diplomacy, first. But we cannot say that there is or has been a generally
recognized moral obligation to refrain from the use of force to right wrongs
if that seems to the states concerned the only way to do so. Most of the new
member states of contemporary international society support the principle
that some campaigns of violence short of war are just.

Moreover, the occasional and limited use of force does not of itself destroy
a states system or the fabric of an international society. The in-built bias of

diplomacy towards settling issues between states by negotiation presupposes that such negotiations and the settlements achieved will reflect the power of the parties and does not therefore exclude the possibility of the coercive use of power. The responsiveness of the states in a system to changing pressures and their willingness to adjust to them requires as a necessary ingredient the credibility of the alternative; and there is a strong case for the view that this alternative needs to include not merely economic and moral pressure, but also actual constraint or force. This view is held both by those who believe that such sanctions and constraint should be applied only by international society as a whole, acting through collective machinery free from the selfish pursuit by individual states of their own interests, and by those who hold the contrary view that in practice the pressure of individual states, and especially great powers, is more effective, easier to turn on and off and more easily combined with negotiation. Where international society is unwilling to take effective action on behalf of an aggrieved party – as is often the case – that party may, understandably, decide that only acts of violence, such as guerrilla warfare, will induce a change: either by compelling its opponents to make an adjustment, or by arousing the international community to act more vigorously. In this way the threat of force, or even a judicious introduction of force into a demand for an adjustment, may stimulate diplomacy. Thus it is possible to argue, as pacifists and many other people do, that the unilateral use of force by one state against another, and even that most rare phenomenon, genuinely collective military sanctions, are always morally unjustified (leaving aside the separate issue of the legitimacy of the use of force and constraint within a state); but in the face of the evidence one cannot claim that prudentially the limited use of force, well short of an Armageddon or cataclysm, necessarily inhibits diplomacy and negotiation or disrupts the states system.

This distinction gives us a clue to the question of the moral responsibility of states in a system. I said in my introductory chapter that the member states of an international society such as the present global one, and members of culturally homogeneous societies like eighteenth-century Europe to a greater degree, attain through their membership of that society a much higher level of civilization and well-being than they could hope to do alone. The individual citizens of a state, who enjoy the advantages and the protection which the state and society give them, are generally regarded as having something more than a prudential interest in preserving their state and society. They have a moral obligation in return for the benefits received, a responsibility not to disrupt and destroy it even though they may wish to change it and to right injustices within it. These obligations are partly codified within most states in the form of laws, which are enforceable, and which cover not only the obligations of individual citizens towards the state and society, but also the obligation to respect the rights of other citizens and to honour the contracts they make. Except perhaps in the most extreme dictatorships based on naked compulsion, citizens generally acknowledge a moral obligation to obey the law; and beyond the area of law and contract they recognize a general responsibility for the welfare and efficient working of the state and society in which they live. If the overriding claim of a society as a whole to the loyalty of the citizens who form its parts is no longer accepted – if the idea of the 'national interest' or the 'community' comes to be felt as a sham – then individuals or groups of them will go their own way and look out for their particular interests. But so long as the centre holds and things do not fall apart, the responsibilities of the citizens towards their society are more than a mere matter of prudential reasoning: living up to one's responsibilities to the community may require one to sacrifice one's individual interests to the greater interests of the whole, even to the point of laying down one's life to defend it. Thus men may have been born free, but as Rousseau observed, inside states they are now everywhere in chains – the outward chains of law enforcement and the inward ones of moral obligation.

Our present diverse international society, and even the most homogeneous societies of independent states that we know of in the past, are of course nothing like so tightly constituted or so obviously operative as a society formed of individuals within a single state. Nevertheless they are societies of a kind; and the looser relationship of an international society does provide certain less far-reaching but nonetheless real benefits to its members. These members may thereby reasonably be held to acquire what we may call moral responsibilities towards their international system. It follows that according to this line of reasoning the ultimate moral responsibility of states towards their system is an obligation, not to refrain from pressures for change (an obligation which states that feel disadvantaged and states whose citizens feel a moral responsibility to further international justice do not accept), but to ensure that the fabric of the system itself is preserved and its continuity maintained. Moreover, since the power of a state, in each particular field and overall, determines its effect on the functioning of the system, the moral responsibility of a state for the way the system functions and for attaining the full potential of its diplomatic dialogue also varies according to its power. Or to put it more mathematically, the differential obligation is a factor of the differential privilege. In the hierarchy of responsibility, the larger powers, and now particularly the two super-states, may be considered to have the greatest moral obligation, just as they have the greatest prudential one.

The moral responsibility of states, so defined, is not simply a theoretical proposition. It is widely recognized in practice. Smaller states constantly remind larger ones of the moral obligations that their power carries with it, and so does public comment and criticism. Statesmen of the larger powers are aware of a moral responsibility which impels them towards certain courses and restrains them from others, even if under the pressure of contending interests and other constraints they do not always heed it. This sense of moral responsibility plays a large part in moving statesmen to accept the less immediately obvious prudential arguments for *raison de système*; but it is distinct from even the most far-sighted calculations of a state's own self-interest, except in the teleological sense that all morality, and all obedience to the will of Heaven, can be regarded as unaware self-interest. The moral obligations of a state are usually perceived as limiting the means and the extent to which a state may pursue its other international objectives.

However, the moral responsibilities of states, and more particularly the moral obligations of statesmen, may conflict. The responsibility of the ruler for the welfare of his people, the obligation to be a good shepherd, has been emphasized by the procedures of democratic election. A democratic leader is influenced both by the political aim of getting himself, his successor and his party re-elected, and also by the moral sense that he is the representative and spokesman of those who elect him, and the defender and advocate of their welfare and interests in the face of the outside world. In discharging this trust on behalf of his wards (who have the power to dismiss him and to appoint another spokesman if they are not satisfied) a statesman will feel justified in limiting the individual interests of some of them in order to further the welfare of the whole community; and he can also justify a policy of *raison de système* on the ground that to forgo certain short-term advantages will bring his wards greater long-term benefits from the more effective working of international society. But when it comes to such issues as the redistribution of wealth from his state to poorer states for moral reasons as opposed to prudential ones, the ethical position of the statesman becomes more difficult. He may personally think that such a redistribution is justified for reasons of charity; or because the states of an international society are all richer by belonging to it, so that his wards do not have an exclusive claim to the extra wealth produced by membership; or for other good ethical reasons. But the wealth is not his to dispose of in this way: he is merely the trustee protecting the property of his wards, the lawyer defending the interests of his clients. He may well feel, as many statesmen in democracies do, that his responsibility is discharged only if his electors specifically endorse such redistribution of wealth, and that even then he has an obligation to them to secure a reasonable maximum of advantage in return, at least in terms of reputation and goodwill. For the reasons given in the previous two chapters, these dilemmas of conflicting responsibility are likely to increase for statesmen of the developed and democratic states.

I asked at the beginning of this chapter to whom a state that behaves irresponsibly is accountable. In a system that has no formally constituted international body such as the United Nations entrusted with the management of international order, an 'irresponsible' sovereign state is not formally accountable at all. But even then a state which shows itself indifferent to *raison de système* and the way in which the system functions, and spurns cooperative negotiation and diplomacy, will encounter the disapproval and opposition of other states, who in this sense may be said to hold it informally or *de facto* to account for its behaviour. If a formal body exists, it may call upon a recalcitrant member to behave more responsibly, or censure the uncooperative state, or institute sanctions against it. This disapproval can be a formidable deterrent, likely to make all but the most powerful states recalculate their balance of self-interest. A formal condemnation by an international body may seem to be a more effective deterrent than action by individual powerful states. But the rigidity of such international organizations and their commitment to ideologically loaded formulae and doctrines sometimes makes omnilateral public condemnation less effective and less likely to restrain the irresponsible power than traditional diplomatic pressure by a few other powerful states if this can be mobilized. The history of sanctions by the League of Nations against Italy in the 1930s is a useful object lesson in this respect. The Italian invasion of Ethiopia was certainly irresponsible by the standards of the time. But in spite of the provisions in the Covenant for sanctions against aggression and specific pledges by members of the League, many of the larger powers (Germany, Japan, the Soviets, the United States and France) were either sympathetic to Italian arguments against the *status quo*, or anxious to retain Italian support against Germany, or in two minds about whether the damage to the fabric and functioning of the system caused by sanctions would be greater than that caused by Italian actions in Africa. They wondered therefore whether the issue would be better handled by less formal diplomatic negotiations. All the great powers were aware that sanctions in the name of the League made bilateral negotiations more difficult without being likely to succeed, while bilateral diplomacy made sanctions less effective. Each approach got in the way of the other.

So far we have been looking at the problem of irresponsible behaviour by a state within a system. Beyond this lies the issue of moral obligation posed for other states by an already very powerful state which develops a dramatic increase of national power and will to dominate that lead it to demand something more than an adjustment within the system, or to a displacement which will give it an authority and perhaps territory corresponding to its new weight. What if such a state feels strong enough to try to overthrow the system of independent states altogether and substitute a hegemony or a new 'universal' empire? (This was the case with Napoleon; and it is how some people, including the leaders of great states, see the Soviet Union today.) Or what if other member states perceive that state as having grown so powerful that even if it does not deliberately overthrow the system it will exercise an unacceptable hegemony within it and jeopardize the independence of the others? Do they, and especially the great powers among them, have a moral responsibility to defend the system, even by a long and destructive war if necessary? In short, do states have a general anti-hegemonial moral obligation to their system which goes beyond prudent self-interest, and even their moral responsibility for the welfare of their own people? This, like the question of the moral obligation of the individual to resist tyranny within a state, admits of no easy answer. There have been times in the past when in practice most large states and their leaders have been aware of such an obligation, even though sometimes it has not prevailed against other arguments. The discovery and spread of nuclear weapons has added a further complication to the dilemma. The huge nuclear arsenals of the two super-powers complicate their ability to discharge their other obligations, especially resistance to hegemony. The prospect of a major war between them is so suicidal that many people consider the overriding moral as well as prudential responsibility of the super-powers is to avoid that catastrophe. Moreover, as proliferation puts nuclear weapons within reach of more and more states, and then terrorist movements, the predicament will grow.

Those who want a diplomatic solution emphasize the need for the states which value the system to bring the creative efforts of diplomacy, including the maintenance of an adequate balance of power, into play well before matters have reached such a pass, at a time when the growing energies of even a very powerful state can still be managed and constructively harnessed within an adjusted international framework. An acceptable adjustment between great powers must inevitably be complex, as the interests of those powers are. It will also depend on the imponderable clash and congruence of wills, on pride and resentment, on the random factor of chance. The problem may be beyond the ingenuity of diplomatic negotiation to solve. (This seems to have been the case, for example, with Germany before 1914.) The moral responsibility for restraint and patience falls mainly on the rising power in whose favour the adjustment is to be made. But the moral as well as the prudential responsibility to try to find an acceptable compromise, and to try in time, falls largely on the other powerful states in the system, and they are likely to recognize the obligation in varying degrees.

The Scope and Limits of Diplomacy

We are now in a position to determine the functions of the diplomatic dialogue in modern society, and to see what diplomacy can achieve when it is skillfully and imaginatively used.

We have seen that the need for the dialogue, and for the framework in which it operates, are likely to remain. We live in an interdependent but very diverse world, divided into a number of states – at present about 160 – whose governments regard themselves and each other as independent, in the sense that there is no higher authority having jurisdiction over them, *de jure* or *de facto*, and the only obligations they acknowledge are those which they have formally entered into by contracts and international agreements. Such systems of independent states have existed at certain times in the past – but not at others. It is impossible to see how long the present international society will endure. In the course of this book we have considered some alternatives to it which many people either fear or hope for and which some think may actually come about; but we also noted three factors which make the chances high that it will last for some time yet. Firstly, in periods like the present, when a large number of the states in international society have only recently acquired or regained their sovereignty, there is a fierce attachment to independence, especially on the part of governments and rulers, and a reluctance to surrender it or to pool it in a universal authority. Secondly, in periods of great ideological and cultural differences between states in a society, governments and peoples are especially unwilling to submit to any wider authority in which their deeply held convictions are likely to be in a permanent minority. And thirdly, in periods when the domestic authority of states is expanding to take over activities of their citizens which hitherto were left to private institutions and individuals – however incompetent and ill-suited governments may prove to be in these new fields – this expansion of state authority does not stop at the border, but seeks to control and influence the international aspects of its new activities. All things considered, we recognized the possibilities that a different form of political organization, such as another universal empire imposed by force, or a world government by consent, or creeping functionalism, could supersede the present system: but saw good reason to expect that in practice an international society of states will continue.

We have also seen that the affairs of a society of states are managed by the diplomatic dialogue between its members. So long as the present broad shape of international politics continues, diplomacy will be necessary and inevitable. Where there is a system of independent states – that is, where a group of states interact with one another to such an extent that each has to take into account the behaviour of the others – they will feel the need to communicate regularly with each other, and a continuous diplomatic dialogue will develop between them. When a system of independent states is so integrated that we may describe it as an international society – that is, when the member states, while acknowledging no common government over themselves, agree to regulate their relations according to a set of rules and operate a set of common institutions – the scope of diplomacy is greatly extended. In addition to the largely bilateral exchanges that are characteristic of any system, the diplomatic dialogue now becomes the medium through which, in the absence of a government, the society conducts its business.

The rules and institutions which we have defined as the requisites of an international society are established by diplomatic negotiation between the member states, and are continuously amended by the same means to meet the pressures of change. The institutions include the machinery of bilateral and collective exchanges which diplomacy creates for itself to operate. That is why it is legitimate to speak of diplomacy as shaping and organizing these rules and institutions, and of states so organized as forming a diplomatic society. States in a society use diplomatic channels not merely to communicate messages, but also to discuss, negotiate and assume mutual commitments; and the experience of taking part in a continuous dialogue of this kind itself influences the discussion and moulds the aims of the participants. Diplomacy makes states perpetually aware of the wishes and objections, and the power to insist on them, of other states whose consent is necessary in order to reach agreement; and this awareness of the intentions and capabilities of other states provides the opportunities and sets the limits to every state's foreign relations, developing them from random thrusting and yielding to a systematic policy. The dialogue induces states to realize the necessity for compromise and restraint, and indeed the positive advantages of such conduct. It elaborates new and constructive arrangements which diplomatic techniques make possible and which emerge only from the dialogue itself. Finally it fosters a sense of the value of international society in all its members – what is meant by *raison de système*.

It is remarkable that although there is no authority over a society of independent states capable of laying down or enforcing the law, yet the member states do, in most of their dealings with one another, in fact conform to the rules and operate the institutions which they have evolved through their diplomatic dialogue. The rules of an international society depend for their executive effectiveness not on consent, as is sometimes claimed, but on their active observance by the member states, especially the more powerful ones. This continual voluntary observance by independent states of rules drawn up by themselves is something quite different from the delegation of 'just powers' to enforce obedience to domestic law by the citizens to the government of a state, which the government is said to derive from the consent of the governed. In an international society there is no delegation, only the practice of rules made by the practitioners. Even less is the world managed by consensus. But the observance of the rules is none the less real. These are anarchical societies in the literal sense; but they may also be called diplomatic societies because they accept as legitimate – and therefore habitually to be obeyed – the arrangements which their diplomacy has established.

It may seem on first thought a truly marvellous thing that independent states, each composed of wilful men and each pursuing its interests in terms of power, should habitually conform to such patterns of predictability and order and peaceful intercourse – marvellous that they should cooperate to institute together, and continuously amend, the laws and organizations by which they agree to deal with each other; and that they should resolve the manifold conflicts of interest, which continually arise between them, either by diplomatic negotiation, or if a diplomatic resolution proves unattainable then by resorts to force that are themselves controlled and kept within limits by the rules which the diplomacy of the member states has devised and instituted. 'I easily grant,' said Locke in his *Second Treatise on Government*, 'that Civil Government is the proper remedy to restrain the partiality and violence of men.' For this purpose, he argued, men joined together to form a society by a social contract and to institute a binding civil government over that society. Whether or not we consider that it is a valid parable to say that men inside a single community or leviathan-state were once independent of one another and came together in a social contract to protect their lives, liberty and property, it is certainly legitimate and plausible to regard the states of contemporary international society not perhaps as born free but as having substantially freed themselves from the bonds of the European *res publica christiana*; and therefore to regard the institutions which now bind them – including the network of bilateral and multilateral agreements and also the machinery of diplomacy, international law, the United Nations and the other means of ordering the affairs between states which we have discussed in this book – as coming somewhere near the postulate of Locke. Even so, there is not a civil government in Locke's sense; and if we say that the sum total of international machinery, taken together, amounts to a 'government of international society', we must keep firmly in mind how little like the government of a state it really is. We may continue to wonder that such a system of governance ever works.

But work it usually does. And on further reflection the orderliness, the moderation, the cooperative nature of diplomatic societies at their best seems less surprising. Provided that the affairs of a system of states can, as the Florentines put it, hang in a certain balance, the *habit* of consultation and where necessary collaboration between the larger states can induce in their statesmen a sense of the very real advantages to be derived not only from resolving problems by diplomatic negotiation and therefore by compromise, but also from playing the game according to the rules they have devised for themselves, and from maintaining such governance as there is in the society and perhaps extending it. When these conditions are present, or can be brought about by the conscious resolve of the principal states in the system – that is, when at least the great powers have a conscious sense of *raison de système* as well as *raison d'état* – then at its best diplomacy is capable of great imaginative achievements, both in the settlement of disputes and in the realization of joint endeavours.

But if such achievements are to be realized, a number of other favourable factors are also necessary. In addition to the conscious will to use diplomacy in this way, skill and experience are required. These are not always available. The diplomatic dialogue is not an impersonal mechanism, but a multilateral exchange conducted by statesmen, by the rulers and leaders of states in the system, who are likely to owe their position to quite other reasons than their understanding of diplomacy and their ability to conduct it. It will therefore be no better, no more constructive and innovative, no more capable of rising to a difficult challenge, than they. Many influential rulers and leaders of opinion may not be interested in making international society work effectively, because of personal conviction or the pressure of circumstances. They may be driven by a desire to dominate, or by an uncompromising ideology, or by a preoccupation with their domestic situation which turns their eyes away from the wider issues, or simply by a reluctance or an inability to make the concessions and compromises which constructive diplomacy requires. Moreover, there are periods when the whole context of the diplomatic dialogue changes so radically that the states which conduct it find themselves faced with problems of a quite different order of magnitude from those which confront men in other less chaotic times.

The constructive task of diplomacy when the course of events flows fairly evenly is to negotiate adjustments between member states (perhaps as a result of a limited use of force) which if possible satisfy all the contending parties or at least obtain their resigned acquiescence, and which can also be accommodated within the system and its institutions. Such adjustments need to reflect the constantly changing balance of power and avoid temporary expedients that mortgage the future and lead to difficulties further down the line. This task requires imagination, and was achieved over long periods in the more homogeneous and limited European society of states. In periods of rapid change, where the flood of events flows turbulently, still more imagination is required, and still more willingness to regard international society itself as a joint interest, worth paying a price for and making some concessions to preserve and adapt. But it happens sometimes that statesmen who could have managed the affairs of an international society fairly adequately in a less exacting period are unable to rise to the exceptional occasion. The same over-demanding challenges occur in the internal affairs of states. Charles I of England and his ministers before the rebellion of Parliament, Russian statesmen before the Revolution, the United States federal government in the years before the Civil War, were no worse than those who came before and after them, and in some respects they were better: but events were too much for them. It is not surprising, therefore, that there are times when an international society is poorly managed, and when the diplomatic dialogue proves inadequate for the unfamiliar tasks which confront it. One of these bleak periods was the twenty-year interval between the two world wars.

When we consider the application of these general propositions about diplomacy and its potential to the particular problems of the contemporary world, we must be struck at the outset by the contrast between our global society and the European system, whose member states were very familiar with the inexorable pressures that states in a closely knit system exercise on each other, and the premium which these pressures put on negotiation and compromise. Such diplomatic experience is not merely a matter of familiarity with the dialogue between states as such. It induces an ingrained understanding of the opportunities and the missed opportunities which occur when the power and influence of many states with different aims operate in the same field, in such a way that no state can escape the pressures and no state is powerful enough to impose a solution. Neither the Americans nor the Soviets have been consistently subjected to this experience, although individual American and Soviet statesmen have shown great personal understanding of its lessons. The geographical separateness of the United States, combined with other circumstances, enabled that country to escape the severest pressures of the European system for a long time. Then its great wealth and power, which grew during the two world wars when the strength of other large states was declining or was virtually destroyed, enabled it to move from a position of relative isolation to one of informal but recognized hegemony outside the areas of Soviet dominance. Only recently has the United States found itself confronted with the problems of an undominated and therefore seemingly unmanageable world. It is addressing itself to these problems with characteristic vigour, resource and public argument. The Soviet Union has since World War Two become increasingly aware of previous Russian experience in helping to manage a Europe dominated by its great powers and a world dominated by Europe. But the relevance of this experience has been attenuated by the very different present context of international affairs; by the revolutionary purpose of the Soviets, though the extent to which this still animates the foreign policy of the Soviet state is disputed; and by the feud with China, which leaves the Soviet Union without partners, in a hegemonic if not imperial relationship to its clients and an adversary relationship to most other powerful states. For their part the new and newly re-established states, which now make up half the number taking part in the diplomatic dialogue, have little experience of it or of the workings of international society. Some have learnt fast where their interests lie and how to further them, and also how to operate within the rapidly evolving system so as not to lose the advantages of economic and political order. Others remain suspicious of the longer established states from whose toils they have been trying to escape, and indeed of the system itself. Therefore, in the present phase of our new global international society, in addition to the responsibilities which in any polycentric society devolve onto the shoulders of all the member states according to their power, and the additional responsibilities of the great powers in the sense described in the last chapter, an exceptional measure of responsibility also devolves on those states with a long tradition of diplomacy and experience of intimate involvement in and management of a states system. For historical reasons this means primarily the states of Western Europe, which are almost the only ones with a long and close enough involvement, and enough present authority, to make the voice of experience heard. This responsibility is a residual one, inherited from the European diplomatic society. It is gradually becoming less relevant as other states gain experience of the predicaments inherent in trying to manage a closely-knit international society, and as contemporary international society develops along different lines from its European predecessor. Also the record of European diplomacy in this century hardly justifies a claim to exceptional wisdom. Nevertheless the European responsibility exists; and both the Western European states themselves, and a number of others including former colonies show that in practice they are aware of the legacy of the European system.

For an international society to function effectively, the dialogue between its major powers must be *system-wide*. The record of the past shows that this is possible even when the interests of the great powers and the principles they wish to propagate are opposed, provided that they accept the overriding need to make the system work. In the period of the cold war the dialogue between the two super-powers fell short of the necessary minimum needed to make international society function effectively, though diplomacy was active enough within groups of like minded powers. Since then the dialogue has become more general and less ideological, and the two super-powers less dominant except in the new and special field of nuclear military power. As a result the way may become more open for a world concert of states. As one would expect, the second-rank states with experience of the European system seem more eager to travel this road than the Soviet Union and the United States; but what matters is that the two super-states, who bear the decisive responsibility because of their power, also appear to be feeling their way towards a meaningful dialogue.

It has been a principal theme of this book that the question of power, and ultimately the question of force, remains central for contemporary international society, as it has for all past states systems. All politics is concerned with power. Inside a leviathan state, force is normally concentrated in the hands of constituted authority, simple or complex – what Locke called civil government; and the exercise of power is through the control of the government. In any society where the capacity to resort to force is not the monopoly of a government but is diffused among its members, the question of power is open and inescapable. In a states system the diffusion of power is the price of independence. (Whether the price is too high, compared with the price of the alternatives, is of course another question.) An imbalance of power will lead to hegemony, in which other states are constrained by the dominant state. Where there is an equilibrium of power – a teetering dual balance between two camps, or a more stable multiple one – we must recognize that the resort to force, the ultimate argument of the sovereign member states, is an integral part of the system. It sets the limits beyond which one state or group of states cannot assert itself against another without also accepting the risks and costs of force to itself throughout the system, which in conditions of balance may be very great. The constant presence of this alternative to peaceful adjustment through diplomacy determines the relations of the member states. We can see it in its most typical form not where 'war-war' stands in naked opposition to 'jaw-jaw' – for the occasions where this simple formulation occurs are historically rarer than academic analysis often takes them to be – but wherever the haunting option of violence, in the form of threats open or implied, permeates and colours the voice of negotiation. Diplomacy between states does not and could not insulate itself from the influences which its purpose is to mitigate and civilize.

The problem which brings the issue of force into the sharpest focus at the present time is the dilemma of nuclear weapons. If the ever-present alternative of a resort to force is an integral part of a states system, and indeed the existence of this alternative is what gives diplomatic negotiation its reality and its ability to persuade, and yet a nuclear war between the two super-powers at the centre of our international society is impracticable because of its destructiveness, how does the system function at the centre?

The answer is more complex than the question. To begin with, the alternative of a thermonuclear war between the United States and the Soviet Union does exist, in the sense that the two super-states are independent of each other and have the capacity to wage such a war, however appalling the consequences might be and however utterly improbable it may seem that the two governments would actually resort to one. So the spectre of violence colours the dialogue between the super-powers with particular intensity, especially their negotiations about the strategic arms themselves but also about all other subjects. The preservation of the unstable strategic balance between the two powers is tacitly recognized as essential for both. The resort to force is thus banned at the centre, because its consequences are unacceptable, and finds itself limited to conflicts in which the two super-powers are not directly at war with each other.

The idea of the unacceptability of war between the great powers, because of the damage it does, is not so new. Statesmen before 1914, children of a long century without a major war in Europe, still considered war a legitimate last resort, and did not foresee the damage which a major conflict would cause. But the disastrous consequences of World War One to some extent taught us this lesson. Yet the lesson was learnt only imperfectly, and with deep awareness only in Europe and by those familiar with the achievements of European civilization. The second war in Europe was a delayed bout of the first catastrophe, which was largely responsible for the more immediate causes of the resumption of hostilities. These war-begotten disorders of

European society included fascist totalitarianism in Germany and Italy and the similar techniques and atmosphere of Stalinism, the failure to resolve the German problem, the inadequacy of the post-war states system, and the psychological and genetic damage to most of the peoples of Europe which helped to make adequate statesmanship and adequate public responses unattainable. But though the lesson of the intolerable destructiveness of major wars between great powers was taught by World War One only partially and locally, the two world wars helped to make statesmen familiar with the concept of the unacceptability of an Armageddon between two roughly equal groups of states on a scale capable of destroying civilization. The horror of a nuclear holocaust has dramatized and made rationally absolute something that was already widely understood. Since the 'equilibrium of terror' of the two super-powers, successive statesmen and the diplomatic dialogue itself have been imbued with the idea that nuclear war between them must be ruled out. It is excluded not for reasons of rational calculation, because the equation of rationality can become loaded with emotional factors that outweigh the sober estimation of interests; nor for moral reasons, because a moral verdict depends on one's ideology and one's hierarchy of values; but simply for the practical reason that it is the province of the Exterminating Angel.

This exclusion of force at the centre of the system has transformed ideas about the place and utility of force in the system itself and in diplomacy. The concept of collective military security, the idea that the supposed great majority of peace-loving states would take action together to deter and if necessary overwhelm a state that wished to bring about change by force – a will o' the wisp which bemused much of the diplomatic dialogue between the world wars – has shrunk from its previous prominence to a level of non-military sanctions against a nuclear power, and apparently down to that level against other states too. The persistence of two comparable blocs of military power, and the unacceptability of a full-scale conflict between them, has focussed the diplomatic dialogue on the grim realities, and on the need for restraint and responsibility on both sides, rather than on legalistic and sometimes polemical concepts like aggression, military sanctions and innocent parties to international disputes.

Resort to the ultimate argument in limited areas and for limited purposes, and with carefully limited means, has tended to become more frequent, and has turned out to be less dangerous to international society than most statesmen and observers expected, however monstrous any particular military action may seem to those who are directly affected by it or otherwise oppose it. The limited use of force is not confined to smaller, non-nuclear states and para-statal organizations. The two super-powers have come to regard their own limited and conventional use of force against third parties as more permissible and less risky than they might have done if escalation of such minor interventions into a nuclear holocaust between them did not seem to both of them so unlikely a consequence. Force thus remains a key element in the relations between states, and the link between power and persuasion remains a fundamental aspect of the diplomatic dialogue, both between the exterminatorily armed super-powers and elsewhere in the system. But the context has certainly changed. And among the significant changes since the beginning of this century is the heightened awareness by the largest powers of their overriding responsibility not to go to war with each other.

The problems arising from the use of force are not a special characteristic of our society. They are permanent features of every international society of independent states which retain for themselves the possession of force and the decision whether to use it. On the other hand the special problems caused by the expansion of international society, both geographically to include large numbers of new and diplomatically inexperienced states, and functionally into new fields such as collective economic security and the management of international economic life and interdependence, are of particular importance in our contemporary system, and were less acute in others, though both expansion to include new members and the regulation by states of international commerce were continuous problems in the European and earlier systems. This group of problems is even more complex than those raised by the rule of force and the relationship of power to persuasion in an international society. Their main features have been discussed in Chapters XI and XII. One aspect of the present unprecedented expansion raises a very general issue about the conditions in which international societies can function: namely, the extent of cultural diversity which societies of states can tolerate and still operate effectively. I have alluded to this question directly in Chapter XI and indirectly at various stages of the argument in this book, but I have not posed it categorically. One reason is because we do not have the historical experience to answer it. (So far as I can see, the most relevant evidence is contained in the course of Indian history from the irruption of Islam into Hindu society down to the European conquest: I have attempted to analyse some of this evidence in my *War of the Goldsmith's Daughter*, but without being able to reach any general conclusions for our own time.) The question is also difficult to pose because some serious observers of the contemporary world continue to doubt whether it even exists, or will continue to exist for much longer. It is an intangible spectre, like Milton's description of one of the guardians of the gates of hell:

The other shape,
If shape it might be call'd that shape had none . . .
What seem'd his head
The likeness of a kingly crown had on.

The societies of states about which we know have had a dominant culture, which the members either belonged to or accepted for international purposes. Will this be the case for the global society of the future? Or if a common post-industrial culture does not emerge, can we construct an effective society of states, with rules and institutions adequate for at least the regulatory tasks which will confront them, on the basis of increasingly diverse cultures and values? More specifically, so far as diplomacy is concerned, will cultural diversity, if it re-emerges, tend to limit the serious dialogue between states with very different cultural and social assumptions, confining it to the conduct of business and the mediation of interests, and excluding from it what Americans call the normative aspects of international law, of omnilateral organizations and other fields where ethical issues are now significant?

We cannot yet see clear answers to these important questions. My own impression, derived from some years of residence in non-Western countries and some interest in the subject, is that industrialization does not homogenize the cultural attitudes and values of whole peoples, as opposed to individual immigrants from one culture into another. It seems to me that below the élite veneer of Western and Soviet educated experts, diplomats, international lawyers and the like, a groundswell of cultural reassertion is mounting in Asia and Africa. This need not hinder the peaceful and even cooperative regulation of interests, but discussion of ethical issues could become increasingly at cross-purposes. However, it is best to keep an open mind on these questions, and to view with scepticism the facile certitudes that prejudge the answers.

In sum, many of the conditions needed for diplomacy to reach its full potential are at present lacking to a greater or less degree. This is not the fault of any one state. We can agree that at various times in the course of the century individual states, large and small, have behaved outrageously badly. But it is possible to focus too much attention on these individual sins of commission. If we look dispassionately at the period as a whole, we are also likely to be aware of what other powers failed to achieve or even to attempt, and to have the sense that the diplomatic dialogue taken as a whole has left undone many of the things which it ought to have done. In the last forty years or so, diplomacy seems to have become more aware of the problems which confront the society of states than was the case at the beginning of the century, and has certainly shown itself more clear headed and more resourceul than were its bemused and incoherent efforts in the period between the wars. Nevertheless, a number of factors limit the scope of contemporary diplomacy. The dual and unstable nature of the balance between the super-powers and the restricted range of their dialogue are sometimes singled out as the chief inhibiting influence on diplomatic achievement. But important as relations between the two largest powers in the system obviously are, many other aspects of the present diplomatic scene seem to me to have an equally limiting effect.

This book has been much concerned with continuity and change. That we live in a world of change, that all things flow, is a commonplace. I have been concerned to stress that this is particularly true of the relations between states. There are the changes that affect individual states, some of which grow stronger and richer, others relatively weaker and poorer every day. 'States rise and fall: empires wax and wane,' says the traditional Chinese formula. The number of states and their composition will continue to change, by smaller states coming together as well as by larger ones breaking up. There are also the changes in science and technology, which affect all mankind, but unevenly, creating new possibilities, new demands and new sources of wealth. Equally significant are the changes in the minds of men: new ideas of justice, of international organization, of human rights. What previously seemed right was hammered out with much controversy to replace older concepts still. As circumstances change and men's ideas change too, continual adjustment is needed. There can be no finality. It is not possible to make a settlement between a number of independent parties, however fair and acceptable it may seem at the time, which will simply stand fixed for the future. What is significant is not so much this change or that, or the pains which all change necessarily causes, but its relentlessness, its unpredictability and its moral ambiguity.

In these circumstances the central task of diplomacy is not just the management of order, but the management of change, and the maintenance by continual persuasion of order in the midst of change. If the diplomatic dialogue is to succeed in this task, it and the statesmen who conduct it must be flexible, ready for new compromises, willing to make constant adjustments. The most characteristic diplomatic concept is the balance – the multiple, constantly shifting mobile of pressures that no rigidity, no dogma, no institution, no canon of law can hold up for long, but that can be adequately maintained in balance by continual adjustment.

As the context of international relations changes, so the rules and institutions elaborated by the diplomatic dialogue to enable international society to function, also change. These institutions include the conventions and machinery for conducting the dialogue itself – diplomatic immunity, resident embassies, the United Nations and so on. We have seen how much diplomatic practices have varied from one states system to another, and in the course of evolution of an individual diplomatic society like that of Europe. The mechanics of diplomacy today are not those of yesterday; and those of tomorrow will be different from those of today. It would be a pity if the concept of diplomacy itself became identified in the public mind with any particular institution, such as the resident embassy or the United Nations, so that the decline or inadequacy of that piece of machinery appeared to indicate not the need for change to meet a new context but somehow the failure of diplomacy altogether. On the contrary there is a great need for adaptability in the dialogue between states. Most of the valuable innovations in diplomatic practice began as *ad hoc* arrangements and evolved experimentally, and were formalized only when their utility in practice had been amply demonstrated.

The continuities of diplomacy survive not in machinery and institutions but in the *accumulated experience of a dialogue between states* in conditions where negotiation and compromise are necessary because no state has the power to assert its will. The experience teaches states and statesmen that compromise is required in disputes about territory, economic advantage and other material issues where the interests of states may clash, but which are quantifiable and which are therefore divisible and for which substitutes can be found. But these are not the only issues.

States have principles as well as interests. Governments, and citizens in democratic states, have certain values and standards of behaviour which they regard as guides to their own conduct and also wish to see more generally accepted by other states and communities in the international society to which they belong. It is not realistic to expect every state in an integrated society to pursue its relations with other member states only in order to advance its material interests. The advocacy of codes of conduct between states, and beyond that the conduct of each state towards its citizens, forms an important part of the diplomatic dialogue today, as it has in the past on issues like the harbouring of conspirators and the practice of religion or slavery. The issues, and the states that raise them, change. But the experience of how to handle issues of principle, the awareness of the dangers which too great and too righteous an insistence on these issues can bring, the sense of where to draw a line between the advocacy of principles and an ideological crusade which threatens both the diplomatic dialogue and the maintenance of peace, have a continuity; and are in fact transmitted or else have to be re-learnt.

We can see continuity also in a statesman's awareness of how a diplomatic society works. It is present in his realization, or half-conscious assumption, that a state whose interests run counter to his own on one issue will share an interest with his state on another, and that the partner of today will be the opponent of tomorrow. Continuity is even more evident when the statesman accepts – as did those at the Congress of Vienna and those who operated the Concert of Europe – that every member has its appropriate place in the society, which can only be denied it at a heavy price in torque on the whole system; and that, leaving questions of morality aside, it simply does not pay to push any victory too far, to make any humiliation too absolute. It underlies what Butterfield and Wight called 'the principles of prudence and moral obligation which have held together the international society of states throughout its history'.

The most necessary lesson is that the diplomatic dialogue itself should be continuous. The need for the dialogue has never been put more clearly or with greater conviction than by Richelieu. In Chapter 6 of his *Political Testament*, addressed to Louis XIII, which he entitled 'The Need for Continuous Negotiation in Diplomacy', he says:

States receive so much benefit from uninterrupted foreign negotiations, if they are conducted with prudence, that it is unbelievable unless it is known from experience. I confess that I realized this truth only five or six years after I had been employed in the direction of Your affairs. But I am now so convinced of its validity that I dare say emphatically that it is absolutely necessary to the well-being of the state to negotiate ceaselessly, either openly or secretly, and in all places, even in those from which no present fruits are reaped and still more in those for which no future prospects as yet seem likely. I can truthfully say that I have seen in my time the nature of affairs change completely for both France and the rest of Christendom as a result of my having, under the authority of the King, put this principle into practice – something up to then completely neglected in this realm.

Some among these plantings produce their fruits more quickly than others. Indeed, there are those which are no sooner in the ground than they germinate and sprout forth, while others remain long dormant before producing any effect. He who negotiates continuously will finally find the right instant to attain his ends, and even if this does not come about, at least it can be said he has lost nothing while keeping abreast of events in the world, which is not of little consequence in the lives of states. . . . Important negotiations should never be interrupted for a moment.

For Richelieu the advantage of a continuous dialogue with every other state was something of a discovery. Today it is a piece of conventional wisdom which the heat of ideology or wounded pride may make a state forget.

These considerations bring us back to the question raised in the Preface to this book, of what should be the attitude towards diplomacy of private citizens in countries where they can expect to have some influence on the political process. The general question of course resolves itself in practice into a number of specific ones. I hope this book will help the reader to make more informed choices, in greater awareness of the consequences of those choices and of the scope and limits of the diplomatic dialogue. For instance, he may want to avoid the use of force by his government; and in so doing I hope that he will recognize how intimately all persuasion in a diplomatic society is related to power, even when a state is careful to limit itself in practice to what is obtainable by negotiation. I hope that in any case he will recognize the importance of *raison de système*, and will wish his government's policies to contribute to making our diplomatic society function adequately, as well as to pursue more directly his own state's national principles. In the coming decades the future of us all will depend to an exceptional degree on the policies adopted by the United States. In the formation of these policies of course the national interest, ethnic affinities and principles like democracy and human rights should carry their due and legitimate weight. But I urge Americans to look beyond their interests, their sympathies and even their cherished convictions to the compromises and the restraint needed to ensure a reasonably ordered international society and avoid catastrophe. This will require a high degree of American awareness and tolerance, and a willingness to understand and in some degree to satisfy other people's demands and prejudices even when this willingness is not reciprocated. In particular it will involve a patient readiness for the diplomatic dialogue with everybody all the time, privately and indirectly where it is not possible openly and face to face. This is a heavy burden, which America's allies and friends have an obligation to understand and assist. But it is a burden which American statesmen and the American public know they cannot escape.

Where I have expressed a hope or implied my own opinion, my aim has been not to provide answers to a reader's questions about foreign policy but to clarify the questions, so that he or she is more clearly aware of what they involve and what the implications of the different choices are. Diplomacy is an instrument of governments; and in states where the government is broadly answerable to the wills of the citizens, or at least subject to their periodic electoral vote, the aims for which diplomacy is used are matters that the citizen should decide for himself. An understanding of how the diplomatic dialogue works, of what it can and can not achieve, helps to make the choices more informed and to produce the results which the citizen wishes to accomplish.

Some suggestions for further reading

The following is a short list chosen from among the many books published since World War Two in the United Kingdom and the United States which deal with the subject matter of this book. I have omitted the standard works published before that date, some of which are mentioned and quoted in the text; and also the valuable works published in French and German.

United Kingdom

Harold Nicolson, *Diplomacy*, 3rd edn (Oxford University Press, 1963)
F. H. Hinsley, *Power and the Pursuit of Peace* (Cambridge University Press, 1963)
H. Butterfield and M. Wight (eds), *Diplomatic Investigations* (Allen & Unwin, London, 1966)
Douglas Busk, *The Craft of Diplomacy* (Pall Mall Press, London, 1967)
M. G. Forsyth, H. M. A. Keens-Soper and P. Savigear (eds), *Theory of International Relations* (Allen & Unwin, London, 1970)
Hedley Bull, *The Anarchical Society* (Macmillan, London, 1977)
Michael D. Donelan (ed.), *The Reason of States: Study in International Political Theory* (Allen & Unwin, London, 1978)

United States

George F. Kennan, *Realities of American Foreign Policy* (Princeton University Press, 1954)
Inis L. Claude, *Power and International Relations* (Random House, New York, 1962)
Henry A. Kissinger, *A World Restored* (Universal Library, New York, 1964)

Adda B. Bozeman, *The Future of Law in a Multicultural World* (Princeton University Press, 1971)

Robert W. Tucker, *The Inequality of Nations* (Basic Books, New York, 1977)

Hans J. Morgenthau, *Politics Among Nations*, revised edn (Knopf, New York, 1978)

Adam Watson, *Toleration in Religion and Politics* (CRIA, New York, 1980)

Index